P9-DGJ-544

History for Genealogists

Using Chronological Time Lines to Find and Understand Your Ancestors

By
Judy Jacobson

CLEARFIELD

Printed for Clearfield Company by
Genealogical Publishing Company
Baltimore, Maryland
2009

ISBN 978-0-8063-5439-2

Made in the United States of America

Table Of Contents

Preface

History and genealogy are entwined to such a degree that a researcher cannot consider one without the other. I have observed that some relate to genealogy as they would to a challenging crossword puzzle. The pleasure of adding generation to generation for the sake of itself, especially if one has good sources, appeals to many researchers.

When I do genealogy, I prefer to go one step further. In my research I try to understand why people made the choices they made, what type of people they were, and how they came to be that was. I like to see their world through the eyes of those ancestors. Acquiring birth, marriage and death records form what I think of as the skeleton of a genealogy that then can be fleshed out by history. This book is designed as a handy reference to provide researchers with what I consider to be a critical but often overlooked dimension to their genealogical research: an historical context.

The disciplines of genealogy and history can work together to the benefit of each other. Fortunately, genealogists are beginning to recognize the importance of history when researching their families and using it to interpret the past. Likewise, historians are beginning to explore genealogies for social data in their attempt to understand changes, explain traditions and provide insights into civilizations as a whole.

Genealogists often portray Great-grandma as growing up, getting married, bearing children and dying --- just another life no different than one lived today. When we think of our own lives, however, we realize that nothing could be further from the truth. In reality, our families faced extreme economic shifts during years of financial depressions; loss and separation at wartime; and clandestine gatherings and injustice when living under persecution. That is why it is important to see ancestors in the historical context in which they lived.

1

Seeing Ancestors in Historical Context

"There is a history in all men's lives."

-Shakespeare *King Henry IV*

The average person might define historical research as the study of <u>the</u> human past and genealogical research as the study of <u>a</u> human's past. History lays the foundation to understand a group of people. Genealogy lays the foundation to understand a person or family using tangible historic evidence. Yet history also lays the foundation to understand why individuals and societies behave the way they do. It provides the building materials needed to understand the human condition and provide an identity, be it for an individual or a group or an institution.

While history provides stories that entertain us, it also inspires us and speaks to our sense of our identity. Understanding the history of a people certainly sheds light on who they became and why. One such group is the "Scotch-Irish" / Scots-Irish. The history of the Scots-Irish explains a lot about why certain Americans turned out the way they did.

> Lowland Scots lived in disputed border lands and were constantly fighting off invasions by the Highlanders to the north and the English to the south, while working land owned by the gentry. Understandably, Lowlanders became a hostile, dour people who did what they had to do to survive. Scotland 's lack of leadership made the situation even more unpredictable when, between 1400 and 1625, five Scottish Kings were minors with regents who eroded royal control.
>
> At the same time, the English were also trying unsuccessfully to subdue the Irish, in particular those in the northern province of Ulster . All of Ireland shared a religion, a language, enormous poverty, and a hatred of the English. The Irish rebellion of 1595 gave the English an excuse for the settlement of Ulster by a friendlier people.
>
> Those presumed friends of the English were the Lowlander Scots who were promised a market for their wool and flax if they went to the Ulster Plantation. In reality, the English planned to use the Scots as a buffer against the Catholics, but with the land going to English and Scottish landlords who stayed at home and sent their tenants to the plantation. Pushed from Scotland by famine, epidemics, rebellions and grinding poverty; the Lowlanders had little choice but to agree to England's plan.
>
> Despite relocation to Ireland, Lowlanders took their customs and religion with them. They were called Ulstermen, but they didn't mix with the local inhabitants, and marriages between the Scots and Irish

were rare. Scots-Irish were not developed through the marriage of two groups. Instead, they were Scots through and through who managed to prosper and live peacefully with the Irish for the time being.

Eventually drought ruined flax crops and starving flocks of sheep hurt the woolen industry. Soon English merchants demanded Parliament take repressive measures against their competitors in the Irish linen and woolen industries. Religious persecution returned and Parliament passed a law requiring office holders to take the sacrament of the Church of England or the Church of Ireland

With little choice, the Scots -Irish left their homes again in groups of extended families, whole congregations and even entire villages. And, unlike others, the Scots-Irish arrived indentured to no one. They paid their own way, even if they had to sell everything they owned to do it.

When they found themselves unwelcome in Philadelphia, they took wagons west through the Great Valley of Pennsylvania, until they were blocked by mountains, then down the Shenandoah Valley into North Carolina. Unlike their Scottish cousins who settled along the populated eastern shore, Scots-Irish settled in the back hills of the Carolinas and Georgia where they found themselves well-matched to frontier life. Land was cheap and the cost of raising a large family affordable. Because they settled on the fringes of civilization, again they became a buffer colony -- this time between the colonies along the Atlantic and the Indians to the West. Their behavior toward the Indians was predictable: having already displaced the Irish , displacing the Indians seemed a natural step.

The Scots-Irish became self-reliant and protective of their freedoms. They went beyond the peripheries of civilization to establish themselves on the frontier where governments could not infringe on their lives. Although they were primarily Presbyterian, they were also the Dissenters Non-Conformists open to new religions. With their new found freedom, they did anything they liked, anytime and anywhere they liked.

They became the mountain men stereotyped as rough and uncouth people who loved their leisure and whiskey and who produced rugged, tenacious individualists like Andrew Jackson, Davy Crocket and Sam Houston.

The Long Range

The full effect of a single historical event is not always obvious. The Bubonic Plague changed the world forever. While thousands died, shortages of merchants led to economic instability, shortages in the labor force led to higher wages, shortages among ministers led to splinter groups.

Then consider the long range repercussions when Catholic Henry VII decided to divorce his wife and marry his mistress. A new religion was born which allowed Henry to remarry and produce Protestant and Catholic children, each of whom was destined to reign and encourage the persecution of the other's faith, which led to centuries of religious rankling and revolution which was followed by the departure of masses of English emigrants to the New World.

Andrew Jackson became a military hero at the Battle of New Orleans because word had not reached him that a treaty had already been signed. And partly due to that fluke, Jackson went on to become President of the United.

Had Hitler not been beaten regularly by his father or spoiled terribly by his mother, had he not become obsessed with the Franco Prussian War or loved to play war games, had his art work not been rejected or he not read anti-Semitic literature; would the holocaust have happened? Would Israel have become a country? Would the Palestinians have been forced from their land? Would US-Arab relations have been totally different?

Historians have long celebrated the dominant individual. Yet, it is hard to say how much credit should go to the individual and how much to the times. What would American history be without common men like Daniel Boone and Martin Luther King, Jr. who stepped forward to do great things when it would have been easier to live ordinary lives?

Just as history has heroes and villains, so do families. The lives our ancestors led made them who they were and influenced the choices they made.

And, just as our national history is taught "warts and all" including slavery, Trail of Tears, Japanese internment camps, segregation; our families are made up of humans who can only be understood within the context of their "warts." Each person has weathered storms that have changed them. Most of us have descended from foot soldiers rather than generals, from peasants rather than landed gentry. Those foot soldiers and peasants are the origin of our values, political views and beliefs.

2

Creating a Time Line

"Doing the history eliminates the mystery."
-Curt Witcher

Genealogists have charts for everything -- pedigree, family group, research calendars, and census extractions. They know the value of putting their material in quick to read formats. The time line is just one more chart -- this one to understand how an ancestor fits into history and to help the researcher better direct the research. It is the graphic representation that sews patches of people and places and events into a linear study with time being the thread that ties them together.

Why?

Granted, the people genealogists study usually had no affect on history, but, instead, they were affected by it. As a calendar of events in that ancestor's life, a researcher can use a time line to --

- demonstrate mathematical problems (such as a 5 year old giving birth),
- summarize a person's life,
- stay focused,
- keep chronology in mind,
- demonstrate how lives interconnected,
- divide an ancestor's life into workable parts (such as childhood, marriage, old age),
- discover discrepancies,
- aid in evaluating the quality of another researcher's work
- eliminate possibilities when two or more with the same name live in an area at the same time
- suggest cause and effect when compared to historical data.

How?

A time line can be as simple as a straight line with dates on one side and events of a person's life on the other. Or, it can be a complicated chart of floating bars. Identical, parallel time lines can be used to identify multiple people or themes. A time line can be very basic, handwritten one put together to keep the researcher on track or it can be very detailed, including even pictures. Time lines can run horizontally

Ancestry Data	Ancestry Data	Ancestry Data	Ancestry Data
1910	1920	1930	1940
Historic Events Events	Historic Events	Historic Events	Historic Events

or vertically.

Ancestry Data	1910	Historic Events
Ancestry Data	1920	Historic Events
Ancestry Data	1930	Historic Events
Ancestry Data	1940	Historic Events

Whichever type of time line chart is chosen, the steps for putting it together are basically the same -

1. Decide what the objective is and what sort of time line to use to reach that objective. Do you want to
   - compare members of a family,
   - look at the direct events of one person's life, or
   - compare an ancestor's life with what is going on around him?

2. Review records and decide which events to include. Begin with major events in the ancestor's life. In an attempt to determine what is important to include in a time line and what is superfluous, one technique is to write an obituary or a 1000 word biography of the ancestor. Limiting oneself makes the author more selective as to what elements to include.
3. List events to be included in chronological order.
4. Decide the units of time - months, years or decades - to be used.
5. Divide the line into an equal number of segments.
6. Label dates. Some events have definite dates, some have approximate dates and some have no time reference at all. John Fleetwood was married to Mary in the 1880 census. The 1890 census was destroyed. In the 1900 census, John's wife was Sarah. Mary died "after" 1880 or "by" 1900, or "between" 1880 and 1900.

Use history books to find out what was happening in the world at the same time. Frequently, encyclopedias and internet web sites already have historical time lines. Shgresources.com provides time lines for the history of each of the fifty states. Other internet sites report what happened on any given day in history.

Once the researcher has made a connection to a specific historical event, more study is needed. It is one thing to know you had a confederate soldier in as an ancestor. It is quite another thing to read details of the battle.

In addition to using a simple paper and pencil method, a time line can be created with any number of programs most people already have on their computers. A time line created with Power Point can be used time and again. A spreadsheet based time line is one of the easiest to use, while word processor documents allow the flexibility to include more information then spreadsheets do.

A tutorial on the internet for creating a time line with Microsoft Word even includes instructions for inserting images. For those who have Excel on their computers, the internet also provides instructions for making a time line with that program.

Some genealogy programs include time lines as part of their packages, while other genealogical computer programs can be downloaded or purchased that trace ancestors in the context of time. Certain historical events that surrounded the targeted person geographically, ethnically, religiously and occupationally are included while others can be added. Sources can also be included. The time line program then arranges people, places, events and time into a linear calendar of sorts.

ReadWriteThink.org provides free horizontal and vertical time lines on its website. At Ourtimelines.com, custom time lines are produced for free, although they do have a page asking for a donation. Just because the site is free, it is not free to the person who provides it.

Case Studies Using Time Line

Thomas Pound -- Tracking an Individual

Consider Thomas Pound, born just across the Thames from London circa 1655. Church, court and governmental records gave the official story of Thomas Pound -- those events listed on the right side of the time line.

On the left side are historical events which took place during Thomas' life which may have had some affect him. For instance, he grew up after the Cromwells had overthrown the King and while they ruled with their Puritan zeal. He lived during a terrible time of turmoil, a time when change of ruler meant a change of national religion; a time of splintered factions of Puritans, Anglicans and Catholics; and a time when two Lord Protectors and five monarchs ruled. It was a time when people hanged gypsies for being gypsies and people believed they could be bewitched.

We know that Thomas' mother had died by January 1670, because records show us at that time Thomas' father re-married. History shows that just beforehand, London had faced two major catastrophes. First, the Bubonic Plague raced through the cramped quarters of London, spread by the disease-carrying fleas in its filth. The Great Plague killed 60,000 Londoners in 1665. Was Thomas' mother one of them?

The next year, The Great Fire of London burned for three days as the fire raged in every direction through the closely-packed streets of the city. Although the Pound home across the Thames would not have been one of the 13,000 homes destroyed, was that when Thomas lost his mother?

Another facet of Thomas' life explained by history transpired during his first visit to America. Sir Edmund Andros was King-appointed governor of the Dominion of New England, working out of Boston. As a member of King James 's inner circle, New Englanders viewed Andros as the King's pompous and corrupt lackey, who brought a number of non-Boston lackeys of his own to rule the "Dominion" with a heavy hand. John George was seen as one of Andros' cronies in his role as captain of the royal frigate the *HMS Rose* and enforcer of the King's hated Navigation Acts.

By May 1687, Thomas Pound had arrived in Boston and was named by Sir Edmund Andros to serve as pilot of the *Rose*. Pound was on board the *Rose* when Andros ordered her crew to take part in the privateering of a French trading post. Then, on July 1688, Andros named him captain of his own vessel, the *Mary*.

The next record of Thomas Pound was the October 1689 deposition he gave after being captured as a pirate. Court records indicated he was found guilty and sentenced to hang in January 1690. Without looking at the history, it would be absolutely mystifying as to what caused his fall.

But Boston history tells us that the city's population rose up on April 18, 1689, and overthrew Andros' government in a bloodless rebellion. Andros was imprisoned, as were Capt. John George and others in the Andros government. Although Thomas Pound was not among those arrested, his ship, the *Mary*, was given to a colonial captain, leaving Pound, in addition to the Royal Naval men on board the *Rose*, unemployed with no salary coming in to feed themselves.

Should it be any surprise that it was just a few months later that Thomas Pound led a few desperate men who hijacked a local fishing vessel and began a series of piratical attacks? Court records also indicated that Pound and some of his fellow pirates were able to escape prison and managed to find refuge aboard the *Rose*, which had orders to return to England.

By 1691, Pound was again serving the British Navy and, in 1697, was assigned as the captain of the *Dover Prize* in Virginia waters. History books indicated that in 1692, Sir Edmund Andros had been sent to Virginia to serve as governor. It was not until 1698 that Andros was recalled from his post under a cloud of allegations of corruption. The next year, Thomas Pound was court-martialed out of the British Navy.

Thomas' petition to be reinstated in the navy interestingly coincided with England receiving a new ruler. Had he been forced out under the rule of William and Mary and hoped for reinstatement under the new ruler? If that was the case, it did not happen because he died the next year, leaving behind a wife.

Oliver Cromwell as Lord Protector of England	1649-1658			
Charles II attempted to recapture his throne	1651-			
			circa 1655	Thomas Pound born Southwark, across Thames from London
Richard Cromwell – Lord Protector	1659-1660			
King Charles II ruled	1660-1685			
Plague epidemic in London	1665			
Great Fire of London	1666		by 1670	Thomas Pound's mother had died and father remarried January 1670
King James II ruled	1685-1688		May 1687	Thomas Pound assigned as pilot of *Rose* in Boston by Gov. Andros
William and Mary ruled	1688-1702		July 1688	Andros named Pound captain of *Mary* in Boston
Bostonians toppled Andros	Apr 1689			
			Jan 1690	Pound sentenced to hang as pirate
			Mar 1690	Pound escaped from Boston jail
			Jul 1690	Pound wrote letter from London
			Aug 1691	Pound assigned to *HMS Salley Rose* in England
Andros named Governor of Virginia	1692			
			Feb 1695	Pound assigned to *HMS Dover Prize* off Ireland
			1697	Pound assigned as captain of *HMS Dover Prize* in Virginia
Andros recalled and relieved of duties in Virginia	1698			
			1699	Pound court-martialed out of British Navy
Queen Anne ruled			1702	Pound petitioned for reinstatement
			1703	Pound died in Isleworth, Middlesex, leaving a wife

Thomas Richey-- Designing to Find Mathematical Problems

Despite family tradition claims that an ancestor fought in the Revolutionary War and the War of 1812, time lines remind us that the Revolution began in 1775 and the War of 1812 was thirty-seven years later.

Consider if Thomas Richey actually did everything attributed to him by some Richey family researchers using a simple spreadsheet.

Historical Event	Year		Year	Thomas Richey's Life Event	Place	Age
Rowan Co. NC formed on VA border	1753					
Wm. Richey on Rowan Co. tax roll	1759					
			1761	Born	Unknown	0
Regulators active in NC	1763					
			1770	Witnessed deed	Rowan Co. NC	9
			1771	Witnessed deed	Rowan Co. NC	10
7th Regt. Continental Line raised in coastal VA	1776					
7th Virginia in Battle of Brandywine	1777		1777	Sgt. in 7th Virginia Continental Line	Virginia	16
7th Virginia in Battle of Germantown	1777		1777	Taxpayer	Washington Co. TN	16
7th Virginia in Battle of Manmouth	1778					
Earliest settlement of Greene Co. TN	1779					
7th Virginia in Siege of Charlestown and most were captured	1780					
Land set aside for NC Rev. War veterans	1782		1782	Constable	Washington Co. TN	21
7th Virginia disbanded & most E. TN counties formed from Washington Co.	1783		1783	On first tax list	Greene Co. TN	22

			1785	Wedding bondsman	Greene Co. TN	24
			1786	Witnessed deed for Wm. Richey	Washington Co., TN	25
Knox Co. formed from Greene Co. TN	1792					
			1793	Married Rosanna Fermault	Knox Co. TN	32
			1793	Received land grant	Hawkins Co. TN	32
			1794	On Grand Jury of Wm. Richey	Blount Co. TN	33
Blount Co. formed from Knox Co. TN	1795		1795	Thos. Richey heirs rec'd 1000 acres of Rev. War land	Blount Co. TN	34*
			1795	Owned surveyed land	Washington Co. TN	34
Tennessee became state	1796		1796	Jury duty	Blount Co., TN	35
300 from Blount evicted from homes over land dispute with Indians	1798		1798	Rec'd Cherokee county passport	Blount Co. TN	37
Blount Co. Population 5587 (incl. 345 slaves)	1800		1800	Married Jenny Greenaway	Blount Co. TN	39
"Fever" (prob. Yellow Fever) in Knox Co. TN	1800					
			1801	Personal property sold inventory	Blount Co. TN	46*
War of 1812	1812		1812	Enlisted under Andrew Jackson	Blount Co. TN	51
			1814	Died of wounds in Battle of Horseshoe Bend	Alabama	53*
Drought in TN	1819					
			1828	Collected pension	Virginia	67

Looking at it, does it make sense? Could there be more than one Thomas Richey? Were these the actions of just one man in four states? Did he die circa 1795, circa 1807, circa 1812, or after 1828? Could he have been both a 16-year-old sergeant in the Revolutionary War and a 53-year-old private in the War of 1812?

3

Why Did They Leave?

"Historians have a responsibility to make some sense of the past and not simply to chronicle it."

-Michael Howard. Review of Herbert Butterfield's "The Origin of History" *Times Literacy Supplement*, 07 August, 1981

Why did your ancestors leave their homes? The answer is so easily found in history.

They fled potato crops rotting on the ground and deadly outbreaks of typhoid fever and the mud flows and gaseous clouds of eruptions.

They fled from where soil had been exhausted, where swamp land had given in to malaria, where forests had been depleted for firewood, where drought had brought food shortages.

They fled when people were dying all around them and when their cities burned and there was nothing left.

The persecution of Quakers in Massachusetts led them to flee to Rhode Island in the late 1650's. The Dust Bowl of the 1930's plunged thousands of farming families into poverty and forced them to move elsewhere. Entire families were changed forever by the outbreak of smallpox in Pennsylvania in 1860, the theater fire in Chicago in 1903 that killed 602 people and the Great Smog of London in 1952 that killed 4000 and something as commonplace as the blizzard in Iran in 1972 that killed nearly 4000.

Military

American Military Actions

Some ancestors disappear for just one census or sometimes a young male suddenly appears to have died. When a person just disappears, ask why.

The British form of standing militia was transplanted to America as English settlers sought protection from the Indians, Dutch and

French. It became the only reliable means of defense in our country's earliest days. Although the time was full of wars with the French, Indians and Dutch, the militias were also involved in smaller skirmishes with Indians. These colonial militias were primarily made up of males aged 16-60. Since many had families to support with their farms and shops, they served for only short periods of time. But on training days, women and children were left unprotected by the men of their family and their fields were left unplowed. Local governments had to walk a fine line for fear that if serving in the militia became too much of a hardship, families might relocate.

Wars separated husbands from wives and parents from children. Below is a list of the military actions the United States has been directly involved in and the years of involvement.

1609-13	First Anglo-Powhatan War
1622	Second Anglo-Powhatan War
1636-37	Pequot War
1642-53	Iroquois War
1650s-1670s	Spanish invaded Pueblo Indian territory
1664	British took Amsterdam (NY) from Dutch
1675-76	King Philip's War
1680	Pueblo uprising against the Spanish
1689-97	King William's War
1702-13	Queen Anne's War
1704	French & Indians destroyed Deerfield, Massachusetts
1711-13	Tuscarora Indian War
1721-25	Drummers War
1740	King George's War
1754-63	French and Indian War
1759-63	Anglo-Cherokee War
1763-66	Pontiac's War in the Northwest Territory
1769	First Yankee-Pennamite War
1770	Boston Massacre
1774	Naval Battle against British off coast of Rhode Island
1775	Second Yankee-Pennamite War
1775-83	Revolutionary War
1778	Wyoming Valley, Pennsylvania Massacre
1783	Third Yankee-Pennamite War
1786-87	Shay's Rebellion
1789	US Army established
1794	Whiskey Rebellion in Pennsylvania
1794	General Anthony Wayne won Battle of Fallen Timbers, Northwest Territory
1797	XYZ Affair -- undeclared naval conflict begun with French interference of American shipping
1801-05	War with North Barbary pirates off Tripoli

1811	Harrison defeated Shawnee "Prophet" at Tippecanoe
1812-15	War of 1812
1813	Creek Indian War
1817-18	First Seminole War in Florida
1831	Nat Turner's slave uprising
1832	Black Hawk War
1835	Second Seminole War
1836	Battle of San Jacinto
1836	Siege at the Alamo
1837-42	Skirmishes along Canadian border
1838	Conflict over the New Brunswick and Maine border
1838-39	Aroostook County War over US / Canadian border
1846-48	Mexican-American War
1861	Apache declared war on US
1861-65	Civil War
1863	Draft riots of New York City
1864-65	Cheyenne-Arapaho Wars
1866	First Sioux War
1868-69	Southern Plains War
1869-78	Two hundred major battles between US Army and Indians
1871	Start of Apache Wars
1876	Custer's Last Stand at Battle of Little Big Horn
1878	Bannock War
1879	Sheepeater War
1879	Ute War
1890	Battle of Wounded Knee
1898	Spanish-American War
1898	Expedition against Ojibwa in Minnesota
1899-1902	Philippine Insurrection
1911	American troops sent to Mexican border
1914	Ludlow, Colorado mine massacre
1914	American occupation of Vera Cruz
1915	Marines sent to Haiti
1916-17	Mexican Border Campaign
1917-18	World War I
1919	US troops in Vladivostok Russia caught up in Russian Civil War
1941-45	World War II
1942	Germans began U-boat offensive along US east coast
1950-53	Korean War

Sometimes simply the arrival of the military could be a cause for alarm. In 1857, President Buchanan sent troops to the Utah Territory. Fearing a return of Mormon persecution, Brigham Young put the Territory in a state of readiness. Rumors started that a wagon train passing through Utah on its way from Arkansas to California carried some of those who had assassinated Mormon Prophet Joseph Smith thirteen years earlier. As a result, 120 men, women and children in the wagon train were butchered by Mormon militia and Piute Indians. Only the youngest were spared.

Major Revolutionary War Events and Battles

During the American Revolution the continental line covered all the colonies, but it was the local militias that fought from their homes and communities.

1774	October 26	Minute Men was established
1775	April 19	Revolutionary War began with the Battles of Concord & Lexington
	May 2	Virginia soldiers marched on Williamsburg
	May 10	Americans captured Ft. Ticonderoga in New York
	May 12	Green Mountain Boys captured Crown Point
	June 14	Continental Army was established
	June 17	Battle of Bunker Hill
	October 18	British ships destroyed Falmouth, Maine
	November 13	Americans took Montreal
	December 9	Americans were defeated at Battle of the Great Bridge, Virginia
1776	January 1	British Fleet bombarded Norfolk
	March 15	British evacuated Boston
	July 2	British captured Staten Island
	July 4	The United States declared independence
	July 8-9	Battle of Gwynn's Island in Virginia
	August 27	British won the Battle of Long Island
	December 13	General Lee captured by British at Morristown, New Jersey
	December 25	Washington & troops crossed the Delaware River to Trenton
1777	January 3	Washington won Battle of Princetown
	April 27	Benedict Arnold defeated British at Ridgefield, Connecticut
	August 16	Americans defeated British at Bennington, Vermont
	September 11	Battle of Brandywine
	September 26	British General Howe occupied Philadelphia
	October 17	Americans defeated British at Saratoga, New York
1778	May	Treaty of Alliance with France was ratified by The Continental Congress
	June 1	Mohawk Chief Joseph Brant burned & plundered Cobleskill, New York
	June 17	British began to evacuate Philadelphia
	June 28	Colonials won at Battle of Monmouth
	July 3	Combined forces of Indians & Tories massacred citizens of Cherry Valley, New York
1779	January 29	Battle of Augusta

	July 15	General Wayne drove British out of Stony Point New York
	August 29	General Sullivan trounced Indians& Loyalists at Newton, New York
	September 16	Siege of Savannah began
	October 9-10	Battle of Savannah
1780	May 12	British won at the Battle of Charleston
	July 11	French troops arrived in Rhode Island
	August 8	Battle of Camden, South Carolina
	October 7	Battle of Kin Mountain, North Carolina
	November 21	British lost at Newark, New Jersey
1781	January 17	Americans won at the Battle of Cowpens
	March 15	Americans lost at Guilford Courthouse
	July 4	British rebuffed Lafayette at Green Spring, Virginia
	September 8	Battle of Eutaw Springs, Georgia
	October 19	Americans & French defeated British in the Battle of Yorktown & Cornwallis surrendered

Major Civil War Events and Battle

Throughout the Mexican American and the beginning of the Civil War, the majority of the troops of the country's small regular army came from the militias.

1860	December 20	Southern states began to secede from Union
1861	February 4	Confederate States of America organized
	March 2	Lincoln sworn in as 16th President
	April 12	Confederates assaulted Ft. Sumter
	May 6	Confederates declared war on the Union
	July 21	Confederates won first Battle of Bull Run
1862	March 8	Capt. Nathaniel became America's last pirate hanged
	March 9	Battle of Monitor & Merrimack
	April 7	Union won Battle of Shiloh
	April 24-25	Naval battle at
	September 15	Confederates routed Union at Harper's Ferry
	September 17	Union won at Battle of Antietam
	December 13	Confederates took Fredericksburg
1863	January 1	Emancipation Proclamation
	July 3	Union victory at Gettysburg
	July 4	Union took Vicksburg
	July 11	New York Draft Riot
	November 23-25	Battle of Chattanooga
	November 26	Confederates won at Battle of Lookout Mountain
1864	February 16	Union won the Battle of Mobile
	May 5-7	Battle of the Wilderness
	September 1	Union took Atlanta
1865	April 9	Confederate States surrendered

	May 22	Three Virginians who refused to surrender attacked 500 Union troops in Floyd, Virginia & became the last soldiers killed in the Civil War

Major Spanish-American War Events and Battles

Although only approximately 400 died in battle, not including the 260 who died aboard the *Maine*, 3000 soldiers and sailors died of disease in this brief war which American troops fought in Cuba, Puerto Rico, Guam and the Philippines. Again, militias made up most of the manpower during the war.

1898	February 15	US Battleship Maine exploded in Havana Harbor
	April 20	US declared war on Spain
	May 1	Battle of Manila Bay
	July 1	Battle of Santiago
	July 1	Battle of San Juan Hill
	July 25	US invaded Puerto Rico
	August 12	Treaty of Paris signed ending the war

International Skirmishes Involving the United States

Throughout history, Americans have found themselves involved in minor incidences involving other nations. The first was given the odd name of War of Jenkins' Ear. Great Britain went to war when her merchant seamen were mistreated and Robert Jenkins lost his ear to Spaniards who suspected him of smuggling. The source of the problem was the commercial rivalry between two European countries in Central America, Florida and the Caribbean. Robert Jenkins' ear was just an excuse. Once war was declared, Georgia's governor James Oglethorpe decided it was a good time to invade Spanish Florida, whose boundary with Georgia was in dispute. Oglethorpe made some inroads and even laid siege to St. Augustine until the Spanish decided to invade Georgia. The Spanish were repelled and the American end of the War of Jenkins' Ear was over.

In an attempt to aid Canadians demanding a more democratic government, American citizens used a small vessel named the *Caroline* to transport supplies across the Niagara River in 1837. British and Canadian citizens seized the vessel, set it on fire and let it go over the falls at Niagara. Soldiers were sent on the American side primarily to prevent any violence.

Then, when a dispute between the US, Britain and Germany developed in 1889 over an eight year Samoan Civil War armed conflict seemed likely. An intense storm averted war when it destroyed all but one of the warships sent to the region by the three nations. Subsequently, German, British and American troops moved in after the King's death and Civil War erupted again in 1899. That time one American and two British warships opened fire on coastal villages and US Marines went ashore to help one faction. In all, six British and six Americans were killed.

In 1891, America encouraged the Chilean Civil War. Tensions increased when American sailors on shore leave in Valparaiso brawled with Chilean nationals and two Americans were killed. In 1919, the United States sent troops to where allied supplies had been stockpiled in , Russia, found them embroiled in the Russian Civil War.

Foreign Military and Armed Engagements

Generally the ending of a war increased the influx of immigrants to the United States. A revolt in Haiti brought French refugees. In the peace following the War of 1812, major ports, such as Boston, New York and Charleston, were flooded, frequently by sick or dying immigrants. Hungarians had little choice but to emigrate after being on the losing side of the Hungarian War of Independence. Although World Wars I and II brought the most immigrants, Hungarians fleeing a Russian invasion following their revolt in the 1950's and Vietnamese fleeing the aftermath of the war in their country in the 1970's also brought war zone immigrants to the United States

Many of these military actions may have eventually led to ancestors dying or emigrating from their homeland as refugees.

1337-1453	Hundred Years War (England & France)
1513	Flodden Field (Scotland & England)
1519-20	Spanish defeated Aztecs & seized Mexico
1526	Turks (Ottomans) took over Hungary
1546-66	Schmalkaldic War in Germany
1557-71	Livonian War involving Poland, Russia, Sweden
1562	Wars of Religion in France

1562-68	French Wars of Religion (Catholic League vs. Protestant Huguenots)
1572	Dutch revolted against Spanish rule
1585	Dutch used floating mines
1588	British defeated Spanish Armada
1605	Gunpowder Plot in England
1618	Thirty Years War began in Prague
1636-38	Pequot War
1638	Turks conquered Baghdad
1638-1746	Scottish Civil Wars
1639-51	Wars of the Three Kingdoms (England, Scotland & Ireland)
1642-49	English Civil War
1652-74	English-Dutch Wars
1655	Jamaica seized from Spain by the British
1661-62	Chinese Pirate Wars
1661-64	Turkey at war with Holy Roman Empire
1664	British defeated Dutch in New Amsterdam (New York)
1674	Dutch War of Louis XIV
1685	Monmouth Rebellion
1687	Venetians besieged Athens
1688	England's "Glorious Revolution" toppled James II
1688-97	Nine Years War (King William's War)
1689-91	First Jacobite Rebellion
1701	War of Spanish Succession
1702-13	War of Spanish Succession, also known as Queen Anne's War in America
1703-11	Hungarian revolt against Austria
1704	British captured Gibraltar
1709	Russia defeated Sweden
1709-1711	Afghan uprising against Persians
1715-16	Second Jacobite Rebellion
1718-20	War of Quadruple Alliance
1719	Third Jacobite Rebellion
1726	Persia defeated Turks
1727-29	Spanish wars with Britain & France
1733-35	War of Polish Succession
1736-39	Turkey at war with Russia & Austria
1740-48	War of Austrian Succession (France vs. Austria)
1744-48	King George's War
1745	Jacobite Rebellion (Scotland
1745-46	Fourth Jacobite Rebellion
1756-63	Seven Years War
1759	British defeated France at Quebec
1766-69	First Anglo-Mysore War
1775-82	First Anglo-Maratha War in India
1775-83	American Revolution
1779	Boer & Bantu War (South Africa)
1780-84	Second Anglo-Dutch War
1780-84	Fourth Anglo-Dutch War
1784-92	Third Anglo-Mysore War
1789	Paris mob stormed Bastille

1789-99	French Revolution
1791-1803	Haitian Revolution
1792	Franco-Prussian War
1793-1802	French Revolutionary Wars
1796	Beginning of Napoleonic Wars
1797-98	Irish Rebellion
1798-99	Fourth Anglo-Mysore War
1800-15	Napoleonic Wars
1803-04	First Kandian War
1803-05	Second Anglo-Maratha War
1804-13	Serbs revolted against Turks
1806	Vellore Mutiny in India
1808	Peninsular War against Napoleon (Spain)
1810-11	Anglo Dutch Java War
1812	Napoleon entered Moscow & found it burning & empty
1814-16	Anglo-Nepalese War
1815	Second Kandian War
1815	Napoleon defeated at Waterloo
1817-18	Third Anglo-MarathaWar
1818	Argentine forces defeated the Spanish, winning independence for Chile
1821	Greeks fought for independence
1821	Greek War of Independence from Turkey began
1823-26	First Anglo Burmese War
1824-27	First Ashanti War (Gold Coast)
1826	Turkish -Egyptian forces defeated Greeks
1827	Greece freed by Russian, French & British forces Defeated Turks & Egyptians
1830	Belgian Revolution
1830	French invaded Algeria
1831	The French established their Foreign Legion
1834	Carlist Wars in Spain
1837	Canadian revolted against British in an effort to unite Upper & Lower Canada
1839-42	First Anglo-Afghan War
1839-42	Chinese Opium War
1845-46	First Anglo-Sikh War
1845-72	New Zealand Wars
1846	US declared war on Mexico
1846-47	Bantu-British War in South Africa
1848	Revolution in Paris
1848	Revolution in Vienna
1848	Austrians captured Milan
1848-49	Second Anglo-Sikh War
1848-49	German Peasant Wars
1849	Italians& Hungarians unsuccessfully revolted
1850-64	T'ai Ping Rebellion in China
1851-64	Chinese Rebellion
1852-53	Second Anglo-Burmese War
1853	Turkey declared war on Russia
1853-56	Crimean War between France & Great Britain
1856	Persia captured Herat, Afghanistan

1856-57	Anglo-Persian War
1856-60	Second Opium War
1857	Indian Rebellion
1858	French occupied Saigon
1860	English & French occupied Peking, China
1863	French captured Mexico City
1863-64	Unsuccessful Polish insurrection
1864-80	Russia conquered Turkistan
1865	Anglo-Bhutanese War
1866	Prussia invaded Austria
1868-78	Ten Years War in which Cuba fought Spain for independence
1870	Franco-Prussian War
1870	British put down the Red River Rebellion in West Canada
1876	Execution of members of terrorist Molly Maguires
1876	Turks massacred thousands in Bulgaria
1877-78	Russo-Turkish War in Balkans
1878-80	Second Anglo-Afghan War
1879	Anglo-Zulu War
1880-81	Gun War
1880-81	First Boer War
1882	British occupied Cairo
1882	Sudan revolted against Egypt
1885-87	Third Anglo-Burmese War
1886	Haymarket Massacre
1894-95	Sino-Japanese War
1895	Turks attempted to exterminate Christian Armenians
1895-96	Italian -Ethiopian War
1895-98	Cuba revolted against Spain
1896	Ethiopia defeated of Italy's invasion
1896	Anglo-Zanzibar War
1897	Greece & Turkey fought over Cyprus
1899-1902	Second Britain & settlers in South Africa
1900	Boxer Rebellion in China
1901-02	Anglo-Aro War
1904	Russo-Japanese War
1910	Italo-Turkish War
1910-20	Mexican Revolution
1911	Sun Yat-sen overthrew the Manchu dynasty in China
1912	First Balkan War (Estonia, Latvia, Lithuania)
1913	Second Balkan War
1914-18	World War I
1915	German submarine sank the *Lusitania*
1916	Easter Uprising in Ireland
1917-21	Russian Revolution
1919	Third Anglo-Afghan War
1920	Irish Civil War
1920	Russians attempted to invade Poland
1925-26	Arab revolt in Morocco
1927	Civil war between Chinese Communists & Nationalists
1931	Japanese occupied Manchuria
1935-36	Italy invaded Ethiopia

1936-39	Spanish Civil War
1937	Japanese captured Shanghai
1938	Germany annexed Austria
1939	Russia & Germany invaded Poland
1939	Germany annexed Czechoslovakia
1939-40	Russo-Finnish War
1939-45	World War II
1941	Japanese attacked Pearl Harbor, Hawaii
1941	Anglo-Iraqi War
1941-49	Greek Civil War
1945-91	Cold War
1946-	Israel-Arab Conflicts
1946-54	Civil War in Indochina
1948-60	Malayan Emergency
1950-53	Korean War

Caution should be taken when generalizing lives in the face of huge events such as war or the Holocaust. To do so can distort an ancestor's situation. Not all who fought in the Civil War were generals or heroes. Actually many might be considered deserters by today's standards -- farmers who went home to plant their crops only to return to their units once planting was finished or others who hired replacements to go in their stead.

Racism, Injustices and Political Unrest

Although it is easier to think in terms of major military events, our history is filled with small events which have held great consequences for ancestors. The Regulators, for instance, began as a colonial vigilante movement organized to bring some law and order to the "backcountry" where none existed. Groups similar to the Regulators existed at various times from Vermont to California.

> Like most Americans in the 1760's the people of the Carolinas became increasingly distressed by excessive fees levied by a government they considered corrupt. Local officials were appointed cronies of the royal governor. Meanwhile armed bands of outlaws established themselves where no law and order existed. Wanting more control over their own lives, the locals organized themselves into an active group they named "The Regulators."
>
> In South Carolina, they organized with the approval of the governor. They established their own militia and courts, drove off vagrants, executed fugitives, set about ridding the area of outlaw bands and made themselves the government in the backcountry. The group was active in South Carolina for about

four years. After bringing law into the area, the group disbanded and most received pardons from the governor for any crimes they may have committed along the way.

But North Carolina was a different story. Regulators there were more violent. North Carolina 's northwestern Piedmont Region was the scene of rioting. In addition to outlaws, the governor and court officials at Hillsborough became prime targets. Regulators interrupted trials, drove away judges and assaulted citizens who did not support them. When officials at Hillsborough sold a Regulator's horse and saddle for taxes, other Regulators stole the horse back and shot up the town. When two Regulators were arrested, seven hundred men marched on Hillsborough and the jailed men were quickly released. With the goal of keeping courts out of their area, in 1770, the Regulators disrupted a Hillsborough District court session, attacked and whipped court officers, and broke into one official's home, destroying the contents and setting the house on fire.

Fearing more trouble, in May 1771, the governor called out the militia. Ironically, because the militia was made up of local men, as was the Regulators, families had participants on both sides of the ensuing Battle of Alamance. Between the thousand-man, trained militia and the two thousand unorganized, poorly-armed Regulators the battle ended with twenty Regulators killed, many wounded, and twelve captured -- six of who were eventually hanged -- and the rebellion crushed.

Many of the North Carolina Regulators retreated into the wilderness of North Carolina, Tennessee and Kentucky. The independent spirit of those old Regulators, however, was still alive when North Carolina at first rejected the US Constitution because it did not ensure enough freedom.

The Regulator Movement was not the last time that extralegal, vigilante or committee safety groups have formed on the American frontier because they considered the law as impotent or non-existent. Following the discovery of gold in California, there was such an outbreak of arson and general lawlessness that a citizen's committee of safety was proposed. In 1851 the First Committee of Vigilance was formed and by June 10th they had hung their first person -- a man caught stealing.

All sorts of political issues have resulted in people moving. Just as young American men moved to Canada to avoid the draft in the 1960's and early 1970's, Antoine and Louis Stoll (b. 1845) left Alsace for America to avoid conscription into the German military which had taken their land from France.

Uncivil Disobedience

Since the 1600's, defiance has been used in America to defend the public welfare from government, almost to the point of being acceptable. Yet, through the years, discontent, riots, uprisings and strikes have caused many Americans to rethink where they wanted to be.

1641	Liberty of Conscience Riot (Providence, Rhode Island)
1654	Battle of Severn (Severn River, Maryland)
1682	Tobacco Plant Cutter's Riot (Virginia)
1689	Massachusetts & New York colonial governors toppled
1699	Sailors' Riot (Portsmouth, New Hampshire)
1699-1700	Land Riots (New Jersey)
1704	Riot of Young Gentry (Philadelphia)
1705	Privateer's Riot (New York City)
1710	Food Riot (Boston)
1711	Dutch Church Riot (Flatbush, New York)
1713	Bread Riot (Boston)
1722	Jailbreak Riot (Hartford)
1724	Riot against ship seizure (Hartford)
1734	Mast Tree Riot (Exeter, New Hampshire)
1737	Anti-Markethouse Riot (Boston)
1737	Anti-Quick Rent Riot (North Carolina)
1737	Brothel Riot (Boston, Massachusetts)
1738	Fish-dam Riot (Schuykill River, Pennsylvania)
1742	Election Riot (Philadelphia)
1746	Tenement Riot (New Jersey)
1747	Anti-Impressment Riot (Boston)
1756	Knowles Riot (Boston)
1757	Riot against recruiting for royal troops (Brentwood, NH)
1764	Paxton Riots (Paxton, Pennsylvania)
1765	Anti-Stamp Act unrest (began Boston & spread to all colonies)
1770	Boston Anti-Loyalist Riot (Boston)
1770	Boston Massacre (Boston)
1772	Pine Tree Riot (Weare, New Hampshire)
1775	Philadelphia Anti-Loyalist Riot, (Philadelphia)
1775	Anti-Loyalist Riot (East Haddam, Connecticut)
1786-87	Shays Rebellion (western Massachusetts)
1788	Doctors Mob Riot, also know as Anti-Dissection Riot (New York)
1793	Brothel Riot, (New York City
1794	Whiskey Rebellion, (western Pennsylvania
1807	Doctors Riots (Baltimore, Maryland)
1825	Brothel Riots (Boston, Massachusetts & Portland, Maine)
1826-27	Fredonian Rebellion (Texas)
1829	Charlestown Anti-Catholic Riots, (Boston, Massachusetts)
1829	Brothel Riot (Lenox, Pennsylvania)

1831	Irish Riot (Philadelphia)
1831	Nat Turner's Slave Uprising (Southampton County, Virginia)
1832	Anti-Abolitionist Riot, (New York City)
1834	Anti-Abolitionist Riot, (New York City)
1835	Bank Riot (Baltimore, Maryland)
1835	Gentleman's Riot (Boston)
1837	Flour Riots (New York City)
1841	Whig Party Riot (Washington, D.C.)
1842	Dorr's Rebellion (Rhode Island
1844	Catholic Riots, (Philadelphia)
1845-46	Tenant Uprisings (New York)
1849	Astor Place Riots (New York City
1851	Militia killed & wounded railroad strikers (Portgage, (New York)
1855	Know-Nothing Riot of 1855 (Louisville, Kentucky)
1855	Wakarusa "War" (Lawrence, Kansas)
1855	Lager Beer Riot (Chicago)
1856	Know-Nothing Riot of 1856, (Baltimore)
1856	Slavery Riots (Lawrence, Kansas)
1857	Know-Nothing Riot of 1857 (Washington, D.C.)
1857	Police Riots (New York City)
1860	Shoemakers strike (Lynn, Massachusetts)
1861	Secessionist Riot (Baltimore)
1863	Draft Riots (New York City
1866	New Orleans Riot (New Orleans)
1866	Memphis Race Riot(Memphis)
1868	Pulaski Riot (Pulaski, Tennessee)
1873	Race & Political Riot (Colfax, Louisiana)
1874	Tompkins Square Riot of unemployed ()
1876	Race riots & terrorism aimed at African-Americans (South Carolina)
1877	Anti-Chinese Riots (California)
1882	Omaha Labor Riots (Nebraska)
1884	Vigilante Riot (Cincinnati, Ohio)
1885	Political coup & race riot (Danville, Virginia)
1886	Haymarket Riot (Chicago)
1894	Pullman Strike (Chicago
1894	Miners Strike (Connellsville, Pennsylvania)
1898	Race Riot (Wilmington, North Carolina)
1906	Black soldiers riot (Brownsville, Texas)
1906	Atlanta Riots, (Atlanta)
1907	Riots against East Indian Immigrants (Bellingham, Washington)
1908	Race Riot (Springfield, Illinois)
1909	"Uprising of the 20,000" female garment workers (New York)
1917	Race Riots, (St. Louis, , & East St. Louis)
1918	Race Riots (Philadelphia & Chester, Pennsylvania)
1919	Washington, D.C. Riot (District of Columbia)
1919	May Day Riots, (Cleveland, Ohio)

1919	Race Riot (Chicago, Illinois, Elaine, Arkansas, Longview, Texas)
1921	Race Riot (Tulsa, Oklahoma)
1937	Republic Steel Strike Riot (USA)
1940	Race riots (Harlem, Los Angeles, Detroit & Chicago)1943 Race Riot, (Detroit, Michigan)
1943	Zoot Suit Riots, (Los Angeles, California)
1946	Euclid Beach Park Riot (Cleveland, Ohio)
1949	Peekskill Riot (Peekskill, Rochester & New York City, New York; Paterson & Jersey City, New Jersey; & Philadelphia, Pennsylvania)

Political Motives

In an attempt to attract a new source of labor, in 1852, the governor of California encouraged the Chinese to come to his state. But in 1879, Presidential hopeful James Blaine wrote an odious letter to the *New York Tribune* which was reprinted by Andrew Gyory. Blaine called Chinese immigration"revolting" and suggested that America had

> "the right to exclude the criminal classes from coming to us, we surely have the right to exclude that immigration which reeks with impurity and which cannot come to us without plenteously sowing the seeds of moral and physical disease, distribution, and death."[1]

Blaine had found a political issue he expected would carry him into the White House. It did not.

Politics and laws led not just families, but larger groups of people to leave their homes. For instance, Acadians were descended from French settlers who went to Nova Scotia in the early 1600's. Nevertheless, in 1755, the British ousted them and they scattered. Large groups of them went to New England and Louisiana. The term "Cajuns" was a term for Acadian descendants in Louisiana.

The Basques were from the mountainous region of Spain and France, where the Bay of Biscay meets the Pyrenees. The French Basques were known as Navarrese and many settled in the San Francisco, California area. Spanish Basques, also known as Vizcayans, settled in Reno, Nevada. Most who arrived after the 1850's left their

1 Gyory, Andrew. Closing the Gate: Race Politics and the Chinese Exclusion Act. Chapel Hill: University of North Carolina Press. 1998.

homes because the French Revolution, Napoleonic Wars and Spanish uprisings.

Gypsies were descended from groups from India which fled from Alexander the Great. After settling in the Middle East they moved on to Europe in the 1400's where they suffered constant persecution. Since Gypsy slaves were legal in Europe until 1856, the earliest in the New World probably accompanied French settlers to Louisiana.

Frederick II of Hesse-Kassel (a principality in northern Hesse) supplied Germans to fight for the British during the American Revolution. Since more that half came from Hesse they became known as Hessians. After the revolution, many remained in the United States

Colonists who sided with the British during the American Revolution were known as Loyalists or Tories. Many were beaten for their loyalty to the crown and had their land confiscated. Scores immigrated to Canada, hiking along the St. Lawrence and the Niagara River into what would become Southern Ontario and along both sides of the Detroit River. Others trudged north to Canada's Maritime Provinces.

Both the French-speaking Walloons and the Dutch-speaking Flemish resided in Belgium. Their completely different socio-economic backgrounds also led to political divisions.

The Wends were descendants of Slavic tribes. After nearly being annihilated by the beginning of the 1800's, remaining Wends occupied a small area along the Spree River. Eventually, their Prussian conquerors ordered they join the state-regulated church, speak German, Germanize their names, and receive less pay for equal work. When laws that passed in 1832 seized their property, some Wends migrated to Australia. In 1854, over 500 went to Texas in search of religious freedom and the right to speak their own language. After associating themselves with the Missouri Synod of the Lutheran Church, they spread out across Texas.

Religion

The Thomas Jefferson Adair family from Lauren County, South Carolina had followed the Tennessee to Pickens County, Alabama, into

Itawamba County, Mississippi migration path by 1839. Part of Thomas' family just disappeared, only to show up many years later in Arizona and Utah. The key to the missing years lay with religion.

Thomas' son Samuel Adair became a registered "Christian Minister" at about the same time that much of his family joined the Mormon Church and Samuel began performing Mormon marriages. Thomas and other Adairs remained in Mississippi and did not convert, while still other family members made their way north to Mt. Pisgath, Union County, Iowa, one of the settlements constructed by Brigham Young along the route between Nauvoo, Illinois and the Great Salt Lake of Utah.

The Adairs remained at Mt. Pisgath for at least two years before joining other Mormons in Utah and fanning out through the West. Mangum and Richey families were among other Mississippi families who followed the same, but lesser known, path to Utah. And as with the Adairs, some of their family members remained in Mississippi following their old religion while others in the family turned to Mormonism and left for Utah.

Many have died for their religion. In 1641, Irish Catholics revolted and massacred 30 thousand Protestants -- while others escaped their homelands with little more than their lives.

1306	Jews expelled from France
1342	When Germany gave Jews the choice of accepting Christianity or death, Pope Clement VI intervened
1361-69	English Jews taxed to such a degree, many sold themselves into slavery.
1361-69	Black Death blamed on Jews in Catalonia, Aragon & Castile
1401	Lollards seeking Catholic reform were burned to death
1414	Parliament passed law against Lollards following John Wycliffe
1489	Five hundred "witches" burned to death in Geneva in 3 month time period
1492	Spain expelled Jews
1497	Portugal expelled Jews
1506	Thousands of Jews & Muslims who had converted to Christianity to save themselves were killed
1520	Pope Leo X declared Martin Luther a heretic
1528	Charles V of Spain decreed anyone baptized be killed
1529	Thousands of Anabaptists burned, beheaded or drowned in Tyrol & Gorts

1540	Reformation in Iceland
1550	Lutheranism became state church of Norway
1553	Queen Mary of England returned Catholicism to England forcing Protestants to begin migrating to Geneva & Zurich
1558	Queen Elizabeth I of England re-established Anglican Church in England encouraging many Protestants to return
1562	Massacre of 3 thousand French Protestants (Huguenots) at Toulouse
1562	French Protestants were slaughtered by Catholics in Burgundy
1567	Catholic uprising in Northern England
1570	Calvinists, Lutherans & Moravians of Poland united Against the Jesuits
1572	Catherine de Medici instigated massacre of 70 thousand Huguenots
1575	Elizabeth I authorized the burning of Anabaptists
1586	After a poor harvest, 118 women & 2 men were tortured & burned alive as witches along the Rhine
1602	Persecution of Protestants in Hungary & Bohemia
1606	Scotland reinstated Episcopacy & banned Presbyterianism
1613-48	Thirty-seven thousand Christians killed in Japan
1614	Jesuits expelled from Japan& many killed
1629	Bavaria restored to Catholicism
1629	Huguenots given religious freedom in France
1630-1650	Virginia Anglicans expelled Puritans
1630-50	Massachusetts Puritans hanged Quakers
1635	Pennsylvania banished Roger Williams for preaching separation of church & state
1641	Thousands of Protestants slaughtered at Ulster
1641	One hundred Protestants drowned by Catholics Ireland
1644	Massachusetts banished Baptists
1652	New Amsterdam banished Quakers to Rhode Island
1655	Protestants massacred in Savoy
1656	Massachusetts & Connecticut Quakers were banished or imprisoned
1660-85	More than thirteen thousand Quakers imprisoned or put to death in England
1670	Covenanters defeated at Bothwell Bridge
1673	Test Act enacted in England
1678	Persecution of Catholics in England
1685	Huguenots fled to Geneva, Holland, Brandenburg, England & America
1685	Catholic James II ascended to throne of England
1731	Salzburg's Catholic Archbishop expelled 20 thousand Lutherans
1733	Poland excluded non-Catholics from holding public office
1734	Two hundred Schwenkfelds Anabaptists immigrated to Philadelphia
1822	Turks massacred Catholics
1830	Mormon movement began in Fayette, New York

1898	Anti-Christian Boxer Movement founded in China
1899	Missionaries went to Japan
1900	Pogroms against Eastern European Jews escalated
1906	Eight hundred Jews died in pogrom in Odessa
1914-20	Violence increased against Russian Jews

Because of persecution, members of the French and Holland Protestant churches fled to England in the 1500s while English Catholics were fleeing their homeland. Elizabethan England supported the persecuted Protestants the English called "Strangers," who immigrated there from the Netherlands and France. But their support was not entirely charitable since the English primarily encouraged skilled artisans they expected would bolster English industries. However, the scale of the influx of the "Strangers" was almost overwhelming in some areas. While England took steps to support them, local governments worried about the reaction of English workers, as well they should. Many of the "Strangers" were involved in weaving and the cloth industries which led to rampant xenophobia among London artisans in the 1590s.

Xenophobia is a fear or hatred of strangers or foreigners. England is just one example that asylum and xenophobia can survive in the same place, at the same time. When Catholics regained power in England, it was the Protestants turn to flee. Along with the exile of English Catholics, and English, French, Walloon and Dutch Protestants came the beginnings of the settlement of America. Frequently exile began with the expulsion of priests and ministers, followed by the most highly educated and ending with the lay members.

Escape and Banishment

When British prisons became over-crowed and people living nearby began to complain, the idea of transportation pardons caught the fancy of British authorities. British convicts were sent to Jamaica, Maryland, Virginia and Georgia. These convicts should not be confused with religious or political prisoners. They were thieves and worse.

Be it political, social or religious, many have not chosen to leave, but were forced out through banishment or under the threat of death.

Mexican victims escaped a revolution. Armenians fled Turkish massacres. Jews escaped Russian pogroms.

Massachusetts proved it to be as religiously intolerant as the society its citizens had left behind in England. The same men who fled England to achieve religious freedom in America, exiled Anne Hutchinson and her believers. They also persecuted Quakers and Baptists and became famous for the Salem Witch Trials in the late 1600's.

Unfortunately, as Massachusetts went, so went most of the other colonies. By 1660, it was a fineable offence in New York to even socialize with a Quaker. Pennsylvania passed its first exclusion law in 1721.

Even when Native Americans had schools, roads and churches and tried to live peacefully with the whites who had invaded their land, the Southeastern American Indian tribes were forcibly expelled. With their homes burned and their property confiscated, thousands of Indians found themselves forced to face the food shortages, bad weather and even death along the long trek which became known as the Trail of Tears.

In 1941, Japanese-Americans were interned in guarded camps following the attack on Pearl Harbor. It did not matter that most were citizens of the United States or that many had been born in America.

The Chinese Exclusion Act of 1882 was probably a less expensive way to control a population. It just banned them from the country. It began with an 1879 bill which limited the number of Chinese a ship could carry to the US to fifteen. The 1882 Exclusion Act not only further limited the number of Chinese who could enter the United States it was also followed by the exclusion of Japanese, Koreans and, eventually, all Asians. The Chinese Exclusion Act was not repealed until 1943.

Genealogists tend to overlook incredible records from this time that have survived. All Chinese in the United States were required to register with the government. Professional genealogist Patricia Hackett

Nicola[2] found names, descriptions as to height, age and physical marks; port, vessel and date of arrival; occupation and residence; and other remarks of inspectors included in these documents. Later files added names of villages and provinces from which immigrants had come. Some even included birth, death or marriage certificates and photographs. Some of these records have been digitalized by the National Archives and placed online.

Followers of Judaism have probably become the best known of the banished. In 1290, they were expelled from France, England and Southern Italy: in 1492 from Spain.

Russia's treatment has been particularly harsh. After the 1881 assassination of Czar Alexander II, southern Russia erupted with rumors, followed by threats, beatings, and murders. Instead of aiding, the Russian government urged the Jews to emigrate and thousands fled.

Subsequent laws which made it illegal for Jews to hold land and expelled them from major cities, in conjunction with pogroms of violence, had the effect of banishment, if not the name. Even in early America, if a Jew could not become a freeman in one place, he moved his family to another.

Where does religion end and politics begin? The connection between the Holocaust and the establishment of Israel has long been accepted. After the Holocaust, the surviving Jews had no place to go. When the Americans and British restricted immigration and other countries denied entry, Israel became the refuge of religious Jews. Although the infrastructure and politics of modern Israel had been well in place before the Second World War and the Haganah Jewish terrorists were 25,000 strong by 1939, the reality of Israel as a political state still grew out of World War II.

The Ashkenazi Jews moved to America long before most Jewish immigrants. They had lived in western Germany and northern France in the Middle Ages, but later spread into Poland and beyond, while still

---

2 Nicola, Patricia Hackett. Chinese Exclusion Act Record: A Neglected Genealogical Source. Association of Professional Genealogists Quarterly. Vol XXI. No. 1. March 2006.

identifying with German Jews and maintained German customs. Constantly faced with persecution and massacres, many Ashkenazi Polish Jews fled into western Europe and, even to the New World, in the mid 1600's.

The Sephardic or Sephardin Jews of Spain and Portugal maintained their own language -- a mix of Hebrew and an archaic form of Castilian Spanish -- rather then Yiddish. The rituals they observed were more Babylonian then Palestinian Jewish rituals. When Spain and Portugal expelled them circa 1492, they fled to North Africa, Europe, the Middle East, and, eventually, the New World There they established the first Jewish congregation in North America 1654 New York City. When Portugal retook Brazil from the Dutch, the Jews, most of whom were Sephardic, fled to Barbados and Nevis. Others went into the southeastern colonies of the United States. However, Maryland, Virginia, the Carolinas and Georgia quickly passed legislation denying all Jews, not just the Sephardic, certain rights. Later Sephardic immigrants from southeastern Europe and Turkey discovered more discrimination in America when American Jewish organizations barely recognized them and began to refer to them as "Oriental Jews."

Throughout history, those of the Jewish religion have been persecuted, banished and exterminated solely because of their religion. Although the most famous, they have not been the only religious group forced to move because of persecution or banishment

The Covenanters were seventeenth century Scots committed to keeping the covenants of Presbyterianism as the exclusive religion of Scotland and to making Parliament supreme over the Scottish and English monarchs. Between 1557 and 1688, Covenanters were frequently persecuted: their revolts in 1666, 1679 and 1685 repressed.

Persecution of Czech Protestants began in 1624. Their clergy were banished and Catholic priests were the only ones allowed to perform marriages and christenings. The state-controlled Catholic Church even maintained Jewish records.

Members of the Society of Friends or Quakers belonged to a religious group that formed in England but went to the Americas as early as 1656. They opposed war and refused to swear in legal matters. Viewed as heretics in Boston, their books were burned and many were sent to Barbados. Later, Quakers were mutilated and, finally in 1658, four were hanged. Non-Quakers were ostracized for associating with them.

Beginning as members of a Swiss political movement of Protestants Huguenots fled religious persecution in France in the 16th and 17th centuries. Many went to Prussia, England, Ireland, the German Palatinate and/or the French West Indies before arriving in America.

Pietism began in the mid-1600's as a movement within Lutheranism which expanded into Scandinavia. It combined the Lutheran emphasis on Biblical doctrine with the Puritan distinctive dress and doctrine of individual piety. In the end, Pietism was attacked and its followers found themselves at odds with the state churches. Throughout the German states, they were forbidden to preach without a license or even meet in small groups. The term "pietist" was used as a pejorative. German Pietists arrived in America as early as 1683 and primarily settled in Pennsylvania. Scandinavian Pietists arrived later and moved into the Upper Midwest.

By 1703, the Irish Catholics had braved invasion by the Scots, the Rebellion of 1641, Cromwell, the Treaty of Limerick, the Penal Laws and the Test Act. Although Cromwell deported Irish Catholics to the colonies, others left on their own, driven by religious and economic conditions at home. The drought and potato famine emigration came later.

Despite the name, the Pennsylvania Dutch were Germans and a few Swiss, who were members of the Moravian, Mennonite, Amish or Dunkard sects. It has been hypothesized the "Dutch" part of their name originated with "Deutsch" which translates to "German" or because they emigrated from Dutch ports.

Other German Protestants were the Palatines who lived on the West Bank of the Rhine River. After the devastation of the Thirty Years War, local religious wars, the War of Spanish Succession and persecution by France; the Palatines were being hit with heavy taxes. Thousands fled to London in 1709. Nearly 800 families went to Ireland.

But the 3000 Palatinates who landed in New York in 1710 became the largest single group of immigrants to arrive in America during the colonial period. The majority ended up settling in Pennsylvania, others went to North Carolina and Virginia.

Followers of Casper Schwenfeld known as Schwenkfelders emphasized inner spirituality. They emigrated from Silesia to Pennsylvania beginning in the early 1730's, after facing persecution by Charles VI.

Members of the Society of Zoar (Zoarites) were German religious dissenters who immigrated in 1817 to Tuscarawas County, Ohio and formed a communal-type agrarian society of socialists, pietists and mystics.

Fearing a Mormon (Church of Jesus Christ of Latter Day Saints) voting block and economic competition, non-Mormons forced Mormons from their homes primarily in the North, to a swampy area they named Nauvoo outside Carthage, Illinois. However, suspicion still followed them. When leader Joseph Smith was imprisoned in Carthage, a mob took him forcibly from the jail and killed him. By 1846, the Mormons were forced west again, ending up in Utah.

The Hutterite Brethren or Bruderhofs of the Hutterite Brethren were a 16th century communal group organized by Jacob Hutter, who was burned at the stake during their persecution in Moravia. After their expulsion from Austria, the group migrated to Romania and Russia. In 1874, some joined Russian Mennonites immigrating to the United States and settled primarily in the South Dakota region. Because of their non-combat stance, many went to Canada during World War II.

The Russian Molokans of Transcaucasus began as Russian peasants who broke away from the Orthodox Church in the 1550's. They rejected the divine right of the Czar to rule, military service, baptism and the Holy Trinity. In the early 1900's, they migrated to California after persecution and prophecies of danger if they remained in Russia.

Christian Tasks came to America from southern Albania to escape starvation and unemployment aggravated by the Austro-Hungarian and Ottoman Empires. The first Tasks to arrive in America were single men or married men who intended to return to their families with their American earnings. However, most stayed and eventually brought their families from Albania to join them.

Genocide

Although escapes and banishments affected those who left their home country, for some, banishment or escape were not options. "Genocide" comes from Latin for "race" and "killing" and is the conscious attempt to destroy all or part of a national, ethnic, religious or racial group. Sometimes it begins with fear, sometimes hatred -- almost always with rumors. It has happened on nearly every continent and in societies thought to be civilized.

For nearly a thousand years, Jews have been accused of drinking the blood of murdered Christian children. The Nazis used a pattern of similarly absurd types of lies to justify their genocide of Jews. The Nazis also targeted Communists, Poles, Gypsies, Czechs and other Slavs for oppression and extermination.

Between 1895 and 1920, the Ottomans murdered an estimated million Armenians. Under the Khmer Rouge more than three million Cambodians were massacred. It happened again in Bosnia and East Timor and continues today.

Disease

Epidemics in America

Cases of ancestors disappearing from records can frequently be traced to dying during an epidemic or moving away from an affected area. Epidemics are outbreaks of disease occurring more often then expected. They can be spread from person to person, like the measles, or by a vector, like malaria and yellow fever.

Epidemics did not just kill: they also frightened people into leaving. Two such "epidemics" -- Yellow Fever (1898) and Influenza (1918) -- hit one university campus exactly twenty years apart. Although Yellow Fever was conveyed by mosquitoes; back in September, 1898, when a Yellow Fever panic hit Starkville, Mississippi, Dr. Walter Reed and his associates had yet to discover that.

It began in September with two suspected cases at Mississippi A&M in Starkville. Within two hours of requesting a specialist to confirm the diagnosis, the campus was completely surrounded by armed guards sent from town.

A special train was ordered to take residents to St. Louis, an area considered north enough to be safe from the epidemic. There were two coaches, one for residents of town and a second for people from A&M. Doors to the Starkville coach were kept locked so that those from the A&M car could not enter and "contaminate" them. Little thought was given that if someone on the train came down with the fever during the fifteen hour trip, the car and everyone on it would have been quarantined.

Those on campus who did not take the "Yellow Fever Special," found themselves in a precarious position. At the time, A&M was divided by the railroad. Campus was north of the tracks, while faculty housing and farmland were south. Those left on the south side of the tracks included General Stephen D. Lee, president of A&M, and other faculty members. Only one complete family remained. All were warned not to go within fifty yards of each other.

One servant who waited until after fences were put up before attempting to leave was shot by guards and lost an eye. Although the servant did escape, his injuries let those left behind understand the consequences of trying to leave campus.

Meanwhile, only one grocery remained open in Starkville. Supplies from town were delivered to the campus gate. Guards then carried the goods 150 yards inside. An A&M employee would gather the food and distribute it a safe distance from each occupied house.

General Lee even asked unmarried male instructors to select a site for a graveyard and mark off grave sites. Although Mississippi had 747 cases with 51 deaths during the outbreak, luckily none of the 9 confirmed cases at A&M proved fatal and the graveyard was never needed.

Starkville and A&M were not as lucky during influenza epidemic of 1918. With every doctor in Starkville either seriously sick or horribly over extended, one minister who had some medical training, and a doctor from the other side of the county were brought in to help.
When it hit campus, every healthy faculty member and student were called upon to help. There were over 1200 cases among the 1700 member student body. Forty students at A&M died and were carried away by trains. The college was forced to close down for the rest of the semester.

The first recorded case of the Influenza outbreak of 1918 was a soldier stationed in Kansas. Within nine months 700 thousand had died in the US alone. Worldwide, the number was more like 20 million.

Some major epidemics which affected the United States are listed below. However, keep in mind that just because an outbreak was listed as significant in a certain place did not mean other areas were free of the disease. Nor did it mean that the disease was absent in years before or after the "epidemic" year.

1657	Boston	Measles
1679	New England & New York	Smallpox
1687	Boston	Measles
1690	New York	Yellow Fever
1693	Boston	Yellow Fever
1699	Charleston & Philadelphia	Yellow Fever
1702	New York	Yellow Fever
1702	Boston	Smallpox
1712	Boston	Smallpox
1713	Boston	Measles
1721	Boston	Smallpox
1726	Philadelphia	Smallpox
1729	Boston	Measles
1730	Massachusetts	Smallpox
1732	Charleston, South Carolina	Yellow Fever
1732-33	Worldwide	Influenza
1735-40	New England	Scarlet Fever & Diphtheria
1736	Georgia	Malaria or Typhoid
1738	South Carolina	Smallpox
1739-40	Boston	Measles
1746	Albany, New York	Yellow Fever
1746	Philadelphia	Diphtheria
1747	Connecticut, New York, Pennsylvania & South Carolina	Measles
1753	Boston	Smallpox
1758	Chesapeake Bay Region	Malaria

1759	North America	Measles
1760	South Carolina	Smallpox
1761	North America & West Indies	Influenza
1764	Boston	Smallpox
1764	El Paso, Texas	Typhus
1768	Virginia	Smallpox
1769	Mobile, Alabama	Malaria
1772	North America	Measles
1775	North America (especially New England	Undetermined epidemic
1775-76	Worldwide	Influenza
1777	Virginia	Smallpox
1779	Texas to California	Measles & Smallpox
1781-82	Worldwide	Influenza
1783	Delaware	Bilious Disorder
1788	Philadelphia & New York	Measles
1791	Kentucky & Ohio	Diphtheria
1793	Vermont	Influenza & Diphtheria or Typhus
1793	Virginia	Influenza
1793	Philadelphia	Yellow Fever
1793	Harrisburg & Middletown, Pennsylvania	Unexplained deaths
1794	Philadelphia	Yellow Fever
1796	New Orleans	Yellow Fever
1796-97	Philadelphia	Yellow Fever
1797	Providence, Rhode Island	Yellow Fever
1798	Philadelphia	Yellow Fever
1802	Omaha, Nebraska	Smallpox
1803	New York	Yellow Fever
1814	Maine	Spotted Fever
1820-23	United States	"fever"
1821	Kentucky	Diphtheria
1830	Pacific Northwest	Malaria
1830's	Western Indians	Smallpox
1831-32	United States	Asiatic Cholera
1832	Major cities	Cholera
1833	Kentucky & Ohio	Cholera & Diphtheria
1834	New York	Cholera
1837	Philadelphia	Typhus
1837	Alaska	Smallpox
1837	Northern Plains	Smallpox
1839	Central Plains	Smallpox
1840	Kodiak Island, Alaska	Smallpox
1841	United States, particularly in the South	Yellow Fever
1845	St. Louis, Missouri	Diphtheria
1847	New Orleans	Yellow Fever
1847-48	Worldwide	Influenza
1848-49	North America	Cholera
1850	United States	Yellow Fever
1850-51	North America	Influenza

1851	Illinois, Great Plains & Missouri	Cholera
1852	United States	Yellow Fever
1853	Northeastern United States	Yellow Fever
1853	Hawaiian Islands	Smallpox
1855	United States	Yellow Fever
1857-59	Worldwide	Influenza
1860-61	Pennsylvania	Smallpox
1861	Colorado	Smallpox
1862	Vicksburg (Northern Troops)	Malaria
1862	Savannah, Georgia	Malaria
1865-73	Philadelphia New York, Boston, New Orleans, Baltimore, Memphis & Washington, D.C.	Recurring epidemics of Typhus/Typhoid, Scarlet Fever, Yellow Fever, Cholera & Smallpox
1866	Chicago	Cholera
1873-75	North America & Europe	Influenza
1878-79	Memphis & New Orleans	Yellow Fever
1885	Plymouth, Pennsylvania	Typhoid
1886	Jacksonville, Florida	Yellow Fever
1890's	Chicago, Illinois	Smallpox
1892	New York	Typhoid Fever
1897	Southern United States	Yellow Fever
1898	Dawson, Alaska	Typhoid Fever
1899	Honolulu, Hawaii	Plague
1900	Alaska	Influenza & Measles
1902	Reno, Nevada	Smallpox
1905	New Orleans	Yellow Fever
1907	New York City	Polio
1914	United States	Polio
1916	Eastern United States	Polio
1918*	Worldwide	Influenza
1922	Southern California	Tuberculosis
1931	New England	Infantile Paralysis

* More people were hospitalized during World War I with influenza than wounds.

These diseases were brought to America by our ancestors and attacked the Native American population with even harsher results. Entire villages were wiped out. French explorers and missionaries reported smallpox in the Massachusetts Bay Region before the arrival of the Pilgrims. Another outbreak in 1633 completed the elimination of any Indian resistance the Puritans faced.

Although smallpox made itself known in Europe long before Columbus, it did not become a major problem in Europe until after the first colonization of the Americas.[3] And its introduction to the Hawaiian Islands and Iceland were probably the most deadly. Curiously, by the Revolutionary War, the British had found an inoculation and were routinely using it on their troops. The Americans had no such protection.

It seems that the South had more than its share of diseases. In addition to smallpox, measles, yellow fever and diphtheria which were also seen in the North, the South had to deal with malaria, typhoid, hookworm and pellagra which also accompanied them in their westward movement.

The most fertile southern lands were river bottoms where mosquitoes thrived and malaria lay in wait. Twenty-seven percent of hospital admissions in Charlestown, South Carolina during the Civil War were for diseases with one of the many names for malaria.[4] Although cases of malaria could be found in the North, when the South became impoverished and her lands were left to stagnate during and after the war, the disease grew to epidemic proportions. That same impoverished condition also allowed other diseases to flourish.

Even the threat of disease could have a devastating effect on an area. In May 1890, city officials suspected Bubonic Plague had reached San Francisco 's Chinatown. Department of Public Health ordered that everyone had be inoculated. A court case determined the ruling was illegal. However, officials remained convinced and persuaded the Board of Supervisors to quarantine Chinatown. With the help of the police, Public Health managed to close all Chinese run businesses, fumigate mailmen and Christian missionaries, and barricade everyone else in Chinatown. It was even suggested to raze Chinatown.[5] Eventually independently hired doctors found no evidence of Plague and a ruling from the Federal Government lifted the quarantine.

---

3 Bollet, Alfred Jay. Plagues & Poxes: The Rise and Fall of Epidemic Disease. New York: Demos Publications, 1987.

4 Savitt, Todd L. and James Harvey Young (ed) Disease and Distinctiveness in the American South. Knoxville: University of Tennessee Press, 1988

5 Armentrout, L. Eve. "Conflict and Contact Between the Chinese and Indigenous Communities in San Francisco 1900-1911." The Life; Influence and the Role of the Chinese in the United States, 1776-1960: Proceedings / Papers of the National Conferences held at The University of San Francisco. July 10, 11, 12, 1975. San Francisco: The Chinese Historical Society of America, 1977.

Important International Medical Events Influencing Populations and Migrations

Just as diseases brought by Europeans to the New World devastated Native Americans, today new diseases such as AIDS and SARS are having an equally deadly and frightening effects on populations. Consequences are not limited to numbers of deaths. When large numbers of merchants died of the plague in the 1300's, the economy suffered, authority collapsed and cities succumbed. Many of those who did not die, fled. Many who fled carried the disease with them.

Infections from smallpox outbreaks in Western Europe could reach as high as 80%, mortalities as high as 40%. Of one thousand Polynesian men taken by Peruvian slavers in the 1860's, nine hundred died of smallpox in Peru. The remaining one hundred were quickly shipped back to Easter Island, but only fifteen survived the voyage. But those fifteen introduced the disease back to their island. In 1722 the island's population had been estimated at 103,000. After the smallpox epidemic of the 1860's had run its course, the population dropped to just 111.[6]

No one was immune. Although when epidemics hit, the royals usually fled to their summer palaces, smallpox killed Kings of Spain and France, a Tsar of Russia, Queens of Sweden and England and Emperors of Austria and China.

1333	Bubonic Plague (Central Asia)
1346-1451	Bubonic Plague spread through Europe: one-third of Portugal's population died.
1348-55	Plague (Egypt)
1361-69	Black Death (England)
1466-70	Plague (Ireland)
1517	"Sweating Sickness" (London & Oxford)
1522	Plague (Limerick, Ireland)
1556-58	Influenza (England)
1602	Plague (Latvia, Lithuania, Poland & Prussia)
1604-04	Plague (London)
1610	Scarlet Fever (Korea)
1623	Dysentery, Plague, Smallpox & Typhus (England)
1632	Plague (Lyon, France)

6 Bollet, Alfred Jay. Plagues & Poxes: The Rise and Fall of Epidemic Disease.

1639	Smallpox (New France)
1646	Yellow Fever (Caribbean & Yucatan Peninsula)
1647	Yellow Fever (Barbados)
1649	Yellow Fever (Cuba)
1656	Plague (from Sardinia to Naples, Italy)
1659	Measles (Mexico)
1660	Smallpox (Brazil)
1663	Plague (Mexico)
1665-66	Great Plague (London)
1671	Yellow Fever (Jamaica)
1673	Yellow Fever (Puerto Rico)
1680	Smallpox (Ecuador)
1680's-1700	Yellow Fever (Martinique & Barbados)
1688	Smallpox (Hispaniola)
1699-1700	Yellow Fever (West Indies)
1707	Smallpox (Iceland)
1709	Typhus (England)
1713	Smallpox (South Africa)
1720	Plague (Marseilles, France)
1732-33	Influenza outbreak (Worldwide)
1741	Typhus & Dysentery (Ireland)
1750's	Eight Year Typhus Epidemic (Netherlands)
1760	Plague (Syria)
1768	Measles (Mexico)
1773	Plague like disease (Persia)
1775-76	Influenza outbreak (Worldwide)
1776	Measles (Japan)
1781-82	Influenza outbreaks (Worldwide)
1789	Smallpox (New South Wales, Australia)
1790	Tuberculosis (Newfoundland)
1792	Plague (Egypt)
1800-21	Yellow Fever (Spain)
1801-03	Yellow Fever (Haiti)
1803	Measles (Japan)
1804-05	Plague-like pestilence (Spain & Portugal)
1816	Typhus (Europe, especially deadly in Ireland)
1820	Cholera (Philippines)
1823	Measles (Japan)
1826-37	Cholera Epidemic (Europe)
1828	Plague-like disease (Gibraltar)
1828	Smallpox (Newfoundland)
1830	Plague (Persia)
1831	Cholera (England)
1834	Plague (Egypt)
1844	Tuberculosis (Berlin)
1847	Typhus (England & Eastern Canada)
1848	Typhus, Cholera & Scurvy (Ireland)
1849-53	Cholera (Canada)
1856	Tuberculosis (Toronto, Canada)
1857	Yellow Fever (Lisbon, Portugal)
1857-59	Influenza outbreaks (Worldwide)
1862-63	Smallpox (British Columbia, Canada)

1870	Scarlet Fever (England & Wales)
1873-75	Influenza outbreaks (Europe & America)
1875	Measles (Fiji)
1894	Plague (Canton & Hong Kong, China)
1895	Sleeping Sickness ()
1900	Cholera (India)
1911	Typhoid (Ottawa, Canada)
1918-19	Influenza outbreaks (Worldwide)

Yet death did not have to come from an epidemic. Tuberculosis was a constant in 17th and 18th century England. During the colonial and frontier periods, deaths came in winter when dysentery was at its worse. A mother's death during childbirth was common place.

Human disease has not been the only way disease has affected families. After Rinderpest was introduced in cattle in East Africa in 1889, human starvation followed.

Because of the vulnerability of the human food supply, plant disease epidemics, such as wheat rust cause havoc. The Potato Famine of Ireland, drastically altered human history and helped shape modern Ireland and America. The first indication there was a problem was the stench of the fungus which killed the crop. Add one of Ireland's coldest winters, outbreaks of typhus, scurvy and dysentery to the mix and the effect was the same as if the Black Death had returned. Mix in England's bungling of the crisis which contributed to a lasting hatred for the English. Nikeforuk pointed out that the Irish had felt they had been "blighted by both the fungus and the English

Economics

Much of the world's exploration and migration was based on economics. Trade required geographical outreach and necessitated funding of exploration for new sources of merchandise and the discovery or settlement of new consumers. America's development was evidence of the power that merchants wielded in the monarchies of Europe. From America, it was a simple for Europeans to move on to Asia and Africa.

In the beginning, large English corporations were formed solely to settle the New World strictly for economic purposes. The Dorchester

Company was begun to advance commercial fishing off New England. The London Company, predecessor of the Massachusetts Bay Company, saw the New World as a supply house of sorts. So while the Pilgrims left England for purely religious reasons, the middleclass Puritans had more financial reasons in addition to religious.

Later, steamship lines, railroads, even moneylenders described America as a place of limitless opportunity in order to attract business. Young men left families behind in European homelands. In some cases, such as with many Greek emigrants, the plan was to find employment and then return home to their families after making their fortunes. Other young men, as with many Scandinavians, went ahead to find employment and housing before sending for their families to join them.

Chinese were the first non-European, non-slave immigrants to arrive in any numbers in the United States. They fled China's Opium Wars and natural disasters. They came enticed in by the discovery of gold in California, the promise of jobs and the opportunities they envisioned the country held. The governor of California perceived them as a new labor force. Then in the 1860's thousands of Chinese were brought to work on the transcontinental railroad. Other Chinese laborers were used to break strikes. But in 1879 and 1880, thugs marched on San Francisco factories demanding Chinese laborers be fired. Resolutions were passed to demolish Chinatown and its residents were given thirty days to vacate the area, leading to a mass exodus of Chinese east. When taxes and interest rates were raised in Greece and the demand for currants dropped drastically in the 1890's, thousands of Greeks emigrated. Many found their way to Boston, Chicago, Philadelphia, Savannah and San Francisco. The combination of economic and political issues on the heels of the Russo-Japanese War and the first Civil War drew Russians to the United States in the early 1900's.

In America between 1850 and the end of the Civil War, wages fell 20% in the North while the cost of living rose 70%.[7] As bad as that

7 Volo, Dorothy Denneen and James M. Volo. Daily Life in Civil War America. Westport, Connecticut: Greenwood1998.

was for the populace, it was even worse in the South where one federal dollar became the equivalent of 180 Confederate dollars.

Economics played a major role in the migration of blacks to America's northern urban areas between 1910 and 1930. These industrial cities held the promise of better wages, better treatment and more opportunities for their children while the South was a symbol of unreliability of crops, an impossible feudal system and lynchings.

In a boom, real estate prices rise, farmers purchase land and bank loans double. A crash leads to devaluation of money. Falling prices mean agricultural products bring in less, giving farmers little or no profit with which to pay their mortgages. The value of land drops sharply, giving farmers little or no chance to sell the land for anywhere near what they paid for it and is still owed on it. Unable to contend with the financial hardship, many farmers lose their land and some move away to find other ways to support their family.

This scene has been played again and again through the history of this country - with the most famous economically inspired migration coming during the Dust Bowl of the 1930's.

Events Having a Major Impact on Financial Stability in the United States

Many of America's rural Southern families made their way to Northern cities in hopes of earning a better living in the factories than they had on the farm.

Following the Dust Bowl came the Great Depression. A recession began in August 1929, and two months later turned into the crash of the stock market. In the intervening period, the production rate, whole sale prices and income dipped significantly. By 1932, the economic stability of the country was bleak. Since 1929, forty percent of all banks had failed, $2 million in deposits had been lost, stock had lost eighty percent of its value and more then thirteen million American workers had lost their jobs.

While the Great Depression touched everyone in the country, events occur every day that cause major financial instability in some area of the country. Consider, for example, the *Dallas Morning News* story which began --

> "The economic damage could not be worse if a tornado hit this North Texas town, a city official said last week"[8]

What was so devastating? K-mart was closing its superstore and regional distribution center in Corsicana, Texas, a city of about 25,000. Why was that so devastating for Corsicana? Approximately 8% of the county's workforce was employed by K-mart. Over 500 people were going to lose their jobs. Families could be financially ruined and the local government expected to lose millions of dollars in property and sales tax. If employees who had worked for decades at the distribution center could not find immediate employment, they would spend less or relocate, leading to local retail stores being forced to reduce their workforce.

For residents of single industry communities, the health of that industry is crucial for their survival. Boom or bust times can be critical turning points in a family's economic health and for good or bad, economic collapse brings about change to everything in its way.

1741	English began suppression of Colonial money
1764	Britain banned The American colonies from issuing paper money
1770	Inflation made Rhode Island 's paper money worthless
1789	US debt was $75 million
1799	Income Tax introduced by William Pitt
1819	Financial panic & serious recession
1837	Severe depression
1857	Financial panic
1857	Foreign coins were no longer legal currency in the US
1858	US stock market crashed
1859-60	US produced 66% of world's cotton which made up 58% of US exports
1861	Congress levied first income tax to pay for the Civil War
1862	John D. Rockefeller founded a company to refine oil (later Standard Oil)
1864	Wheat reached $4 a bushel
1865	Confederate money dropped to $1.76 per $100
1865	Nearly four million slaves freed
1866	Inflation reduced US dollar to 46 cents
1869	Wall Street 's first Black Friday

---

8 Parrott, Susan. Corsicana dealt economic blow. Dallas Morning News p. 48A January 19, 2003.

1873 Wall Street 's second Black Friday, led to a disastrous recession
1877 Cuts in railway worker pay set off violent strikes
1880 US had 100 millionaires
1883 Recession
1886 American Federation of Labor (AFL) organized excluding Blacks
1890 Average work week was 60 hours
1893 Financial panic erupted
1901 J. P. Morgan created US Steel
1901 Sixteen thousand patents were filed in one year
1901 Oil discovered in Texas
1906 Upton Sinclair's *The Jungle* detailed appalling living & ghastly working conditions in meat packing plants & led to government investigation of the food industry & new regulations.
1907 Financial panic & major recession
1908 Ford introduced the motor car
1908-9 Depression
1911 First minimum wage law in US passed in Massachusetts
1911 Standard Oil Company was broken up
1913 Personal insurance introduced in US
1913 Two percent of Americans controlled 60% of the national product. John Rockefeller & J.P. Morgan controlled 20% of it.
1916 US produced 1 ½ million cars
1917-18 World War I spurred the American economy
1919 US overtook Europe in total industrial output
1919-33 Prohibition
1920s An average of six hundred banks failed each year
1920s Value of farm land fell nearly 40%
1920s Federal spending was three times larger than tax collections
1921 Extreme inflation in Germany
1922 Supreme Court nullified child labor legislation
1923 Supreme Court invalidated minimum wage for women
1924 Stock market began to rise
1928 Construction boom ended
1928 United Mine Workers ' membership had tumbled to 75 thousand
1929 Just 200 companies controlled over half of US industry
1929 Wall Street Crash
1929 In excess of half of all American lived below poverty level
1930 First bank panic
1930 Gross National Product (GNP) fell 9% while unemployment rose to 8.7%
1930's Great Depression
1931 Second bank panic
1931 GNP fell another 8.5% while unemployment rose to 16%
1932 GNP fell another 13% while unemployment rose to 24%
1932 Congress passed Federal Home Loan Bank Act & created the Reconstruction Finance Corporation
1932 Twelve million Americans were unemployed

1932	Franklin Roosevelt was elected President & promised Americans a "New Deal" for economic relief
1933	Third bank panic led Roosevelt to declare a Bank Holiday, closing banks & stopping the run on them
1933	Congress passed Emergency Banking Bill, Farm Credit Act, National Industrial Recovery Act and created the Agricultural Adjustment Administration, Civilian Conservation Corps, Farm Credit Administration, Federal Deposit Insurance Corporation, Federal Emergency Relief Administration, National Recovery Administration, Public Works Administration & Tennessee Valley Authority
1933	GNP fell only 2% while unemployment rose to 25%
1934	Congress passed the Banking Act, Emergency Relief Appropriation Act, Social Security Administration & created Works Progress Administration & Rural Electrification Administration.
1935	GNP rose 8% while unemployment fell to 20%
1936	GNP rose 14% while unemployment fell to 17%
1937	Recession
1937	GNP grew 5% while unemployment fell to 14%
1937	General Motors was world's largest privately-owned manufacturing company
1938	Congress passed Fair Labor Standards Act & Agricultural Adjustment Act
1938	GNP rose 4.5 % while unemployment rose to 19%
1939	GNP rose 8 % while unemployment fell to 17%
1939-41	US manufacturing increased 50%
1941-45	Woman & minorities entered workforce in greater numbers
1945	US came out of World War II as the world's major economic power
1946	Industry began to use production techniques developed during World War II
1950	Introduction of first modern credit card

Property, or the lack of it, has caused the migration of millions. Economically it was the man on the lowest rung of the economic ladder who moved the most often, but he only traveled a short distance. The wealthiest stayed on their land, while the middle class - both upper and lower - were the ones who migrated the great distances.

In times of economic collapse, people from rural areas ended up leaving farming altogether and heading for the big cities. In boom times, they stayed where they were raised because they inherited land, while others were forced to leave because there was not enough land to go around. Eldest sons inherited, younger sons did not. Additional land was needed as the population grew.

The Ingebrigt Johansen family of Senja Island in northern Norway lived on a small rocky peninsula sticking out into the Arctic Ocean. The family made do as fishermen. Unable to survive on fish alone, what other foods they needed had to be grown in that barren ground. But Ingebrigt produced eighteen children who married and began having children of their own. His small piece of rock could never sustain so many. Eventually, only seven of the eighteen remained within twenty miles of Ingebrigt. Five migrated to America, four to other areas of Norway and two died young.

Loss of land does not necessarily signify economic turmoil. Though Landons fought on both sides of the American Revolution, many of those who chose to support the British had their land confiscated. Most of the Tory Landons who lost their land, headed for Canada.

Wars have always had financial consequences. After the Civil War, thousands of businessmen, political leaders and former soldiers from the North headed south -- most looking to invest in the South, others intending to get rich anyway they could. Southerners called them "Carpetbaggers."

When researching why a family left an area, look at the effect of the country's economy, of the frontier and agriculture, and of urbanization. People had to go where money could be made and families fed. Sometimes, possibilities for work prompted the move, leading to the transient or migrant worker. The term "migrant worker" brings up visions of farm workers following the crops, of the Jobe family during the Dust Bowl years in the *Grapes of Wrath* and of tramps doing odd jobs for a meal. But Nathaniel Smith of New York could also be called a migrant worker. Smith signed on to help build the Erie Canal and, as the canal progressed across New York, Smith's family moved along the route.

Natural and Unnatural Disasters

Mother Nature could be as bad as disease when she wanted to be. In 1875, a locust swarm wiped out field after field as it passed over crop land in Missouri. People worldwide have died from hepatitis from drinking contaminated water, just as Alaskans died in 1799 from eating contaminated shellfish.

As hard as it is to understand, not all disasters have been bad. The 1666 Great Fire of London came on the heels of the 1665 . Once the fire had burned through the city, the disease had been destroyed as well as the buildings.

International Disasters

1333-37	China	Famine	6 million died
1556	China	Earthquake	830 thousand
1623	England	Flood & Famine	
1642	China	Flood	300 thousand
1666	England	Great Fire of London	
1669-70	India	Famine	3 million
1703	Japan	Earthquake	200 thousand
1737	India	Earthquake	300 thousand
1738	Iceland	Volcanic Eruption	10 thousand
1769-70	India	Famine	3 million
1815	Indonesia	Volcanic Eruption	92 thousand
1822	India	Cyclone	50 thousand
1838	India	Famine	800 thousand
1845	China	Theater Fire	1 thousand
1845-48	Ireland	Famine	1 million
1857	Japan	Earthquake/Fire	107 thousand
1863	Chile	Church Fire	2 thousand
1864	India	Cyclone	50 thousand
1876	India	Tsunami	215 thousand
1876-78	India	Famine	6 million
1876-79	China	Famine	9.5-13 million
1881	Indochina	Typhoon	300 thousand
1883	Indonesia	Volcanic Eruption	36 thousand
1887	China	Flood	900 thousand
1896-97	India	Famine	6 million
1900	India	Drought	250 thousand
1902	Martinique	Volcanic Eruption	36 thousand
1906	France	Mine Explosion	1 thousand
1907	China	Drought/Famine	24 million
1914-24	Russia	Famine	25 million
1916	China	Ship Ramming	1 thousand
1917	Nova Scotia	Explosion	1.6 thousand
1918	Belgium	Train Explosion	1.75 thousand
1920	China	Earthquake	180 thousand
1921-23	USSR	Famine	1 million +
1923	Japan	Earthquake	140 thousand
1928-29	China	Famine	3 million
1931	China	Flood	3 million+

1932-34	USSR	Famine	5 million
1936	China	Famine	5 million
1939	China	Flood	3.7 million
1939	China	Flood/Famine	10 million
1942	Manchuria	Explosion	1.5 thousand

Although disasters in the above table account for deaths is in the thousands or even millions, other disasters with fewer deaths, like the 1836 theater fire in Saint Petersburg, Russia which killed 700, cannot considered inconsequential.

Hunger puts man on the move. Just as the number of vagabonds increased during the Great Depression, so many people wanted to leave Ireland during the potato famine that booking agents could not find space for all of them. Between the Irish Poor Law of 1838 and the Potato Famine of the 1840s, the only prosperous business in Ireland was coffin making.[9]

At the same time, the United States was in the midst of good economic times. Some of the Irish came directly to America while others traveled to Liverpool first. Many were in such poor condition when they left Ireland, they died aboard ship. In all 1.3 million Irish arrived in the US during that period.

Disasters in the United States

As with the more recent terrorist-type attacks on the Oklahoma Federal Building and the September 11, 2001 World Trade Center and Pentagon attacks and with natural disasters such as Hurricane Katrina, people disappear from records during a major disaster, either because they died during disaster or moved following it. The cost of a disaster cannot always be measured in human injury. Loss of herds, crops, homes can also bring about a change. Some disasters occurring in the United States which could have led to "disappearances" include --

1676	Fire	Boston
1805	Fire	Detroit, Michigan
1811	Earthquake	New Madrid, Missouri
1812	Earthquake	New Madrid, Missouri (quake was so strong it rang church bells in New York)

9 Hirschmann, Kris. Plagues. San Diego: Lucent Book, Inc., 2002.

1812	Earthquake/ Tsunami	Santa Barbara, California
1835	Fire	New York City (530 buildings involved)
1840	Tornado	Natchez, Mississippi (317 died)
1857	Earthquake	Fort Tejon, California
1864	Fire	Atlanta, Georgia
1865	Explosion	Mississippi River side-wheeler (1700 died)
1871	Forest Fire	Wisconsin (1182 died)
1871	Fire	Chicago, Illinois (250 died)
1872	Fire	Boston (800 buildings destroyed)
1872	Disappearance	Brigantine *Mary Celeste* out of New York
1875	Earthquake	Owens Valley, California
1875	Locust Swarm	Missouri
1876	Theater Fire	Brooklyn, New York (295 died)
1884	Flood	Ohio River
1888	Blizzard	Northeast US (500+ died)
1889	Flood	Johnstown, Pennsylvania (2209 died)
1899	Flood	Brazos River
1892	Earthquake	Imperial Valley, California
1894	Forest Fire	Hinkley, Minnesota (413 died)
1895	Cyclone	Sioux Center, Iowa
1899	Earthquake	Cape Yakataga, Alaska
1900	Hurricane	Galveston, Texas (6000+ died)
1900	Pier Fire	Hoboken, New Jersey (325+ died)
1900	Mine Explosion	Scofield, Utah (200 died)
1901	Fire	Jacksonville, Florida (1700 buildings destroyed)
1902	Church Fire	Birmingham, Alabama (100+ died)
1903	Theater Fire	Chicago, Illinois (602 died)
1906	Earthquake & Fire	San Francisco, California (500 died, 350 missing)
1906	Hurricane	Southeast Florida
1907	Mine Disaster	Monongah, West Virginia (361 died)
1907	Flood	Ohio River
1907	Mine Disaster	Jacob's Creek, Pennsylvania (230 died)
1908	Theater Fire	Boyertown, Pennsylvania (170 died)
1909	Mine Explosion	Cherry, Illinois (250+ died)
1909	Hurricane	Florida Keys and Texas
1911	Fire	Triangle Shirt Factory in New York City (147 died)
1912	Hurricane	Texas
1912	Shipwreck	*Titanic* (up to 1500 died)
1913	Flooding	Ohio, Kentucky & Indiana (450 died, 200,000 homeless)
1913	Flood	Brazos & Colorado River
1913	Mine Disaster	Dawson, New Mexico (263 died)
1915	Steamer Explosion	Chicago (800 died)
1915	Hurricane	Gulf Coast
1917	Munitions Explosion	Eddystone, Pennsylvania (135 died)
1918	Fire	Mobile, Alabama (40 blocks/200 homes burned)

1918	Forest Fire	Cloquet, Minnesota (400 died)
1919	Hurricane	Florida & Texas
1922	Flood	Mississippi and Ohio River Valleys
1925	Tornado	Indiana, Illinois, & Missouri (689 died)
1926	Hurricane	Miami & Ft. Lauderdale (200 died)
1926	Flood	Illinois River Valley
1927	Flood	Mississippi River
1928	Mine Disaster	Mather, Pennsylvania (195 died)
1928	Hurricane	Lake Okeechobee, Florida area (1836 died
1929	Clinic Fire	Cleveland, Ohio (125 died)
1930	Prison Fire	Columbus, Ohio (320 died)
1930s	Dust Bowl	Southwestern Great Plains
1935	Hurricane	Florida Keys (400 died)
1936	Flood	New England
1936	Tornadoes	Georgia & Mississippi (455 died)
1937	School Fire	New London, Texas (290+ died)
1937	Flood	Mississippi River Basin
1938	Hurricane	New England
1940	Dance Hall Fire	Natchez, Mississippi (198 died)
1942	Fire	Cocoanut Grove, Boston (491 died)
1943	Flood	Mississippi River Basin
1944	Ship Explosion	Port Chicago, California (300+ died)
1944	Hurricane	"Great Atlantic Hurricane"
1944	Fire	Hartford, Connecticut (160+ died)
1944	Explosion	Cleveland, Ohio (130 killed)
1946	Hotel Fire	Chicago, Illinois (100+ died)
1946	Tsunami	Aleutian Islands
1950	Blizzard	Twenty-two states (383 died)

While the fires in San Francisco (1906), Chicago (1871) and Atlanta (1864) took out enormous numbers of businesses and homes, disasters did not have to be on a massive scale to have dire consequences. It is all relative. Devastating fires occurred in smaller towns from Almont Michigan (1861) to Starkville, Mississippi.

It was a windy night in 1875, when the devastating fire swept through Starkville. The fire began in a doctor's office about 100 feet south of Main Street and spread, moving down the south side of Main Street, jumping Main and spreading along the north side. It took out homes, businesses and the courthouse in its wake. In all, fifty-two buildings in the central business district of Starkville were destroyed. Most merchants and homeowners either had no insurance or were insured by insolvent companies.

Disasters did not have to be designed by nature. While violence in schools seems to be a modern aberration, it actually began long ago.

Andrew Kehoe was a school board member for the Consolidated School of Bath, Michigan, when his farm faced foreclosure in May 1927. Irritated that his taxes were going to the school, one morning Kehoe planted dynamite in the school's basement. Back at home, he murdered his wife and set fire to his farmhouse and outbuildings. Shortly after school started that day, the north wing exploded, killing children and teachers. Fortunately, the dynamite under the south wing was discovered before it was able to detonate. Arriving back at the panicked school, Kehoe fired a shot into his dynamite and shrapnel-laden car, setting off yet another explosion. In all, forty students and teachers were killed and another fifty-eight injured.

4

How Did They Go?

"Men travel faster now, but I do not know if they go to better things."

-Willa Cather.
Death Comes for the Archbishop.

One of most noted means of moving from one place to another, the Underground Railroad, was not a railroad, or even a road or river or canal. Yet, the people taking the Underground Railroad might walk, ride, float or sail. And it did not appear on any published maps of the time. Even though it was not really a railroad, the routes the runaway slaves took to escape the south were called lines, the safe houses were called stations and those that helped the slaves were called conductors

Unfortunately, since secrecy was a necessity, records have not survived that make passage on the Underground Railroad easy to trace. Luckily information about other modes of travel is easier to locate. By using historic records, sometimes the routes and means our ancestors took on their migrations can be traced, or at least clues can be detect.

By Road

Animals followed trails for food, salt licks and water, and animal trails were adopted by the Native Americans. While some trails connected different Indian tribes for the purpose of trade, other trails were traveled to avoid enemies.

And just as the Native American had adopted animal trails, the white settlers became aware that these trails could be useful for them. The trails opened areas to settlement so colonists turned these trails into roads allowing them to get to markets. Roads were improved by necessity and for war. In 1803, two roads, the National Road in the Old Northwest Territory and the Federal Road across the south to New Orleans were authorized.

Even if researchers do not know from where their family came, understanding the routes used can lead back to where their journey began. For instance, paths ancestors who arrived in Parkersburg, West Virginia in 1830, could have taken were limited. Most likely they would have traveled via the Old Northwestern Turnpike. Ancestors of Spanish descent living in New Orleans in 1700 could have arrived there via El Camino Real.

Public coaches or stage coaches made their first appearance by 1640 in London. Soon the stage coach, which carried twelve people at best, became the primary form of mass transportation. By the 1800's, they had become the only means to travel long distances and deliver mail in the western United States. According to Browne and Kreiser,[10] one stage coach company offered a "reduced" fare of $300 for the uncomfortable tip from Omaha to Sacramento. Use of the overland stage coach dropped drastically once coast to coast rail service began.

For settlers migrating west, mules and horses were the primary mode of travel, be they ridden or driven. The Conestoga wagon, which had begun as a horse-drawn freight wagon in Pennsylvania in the 1700's adapted well to American roads and quickly became the mode of travel for Americans moving great distances. But they were slow and, unfortunately, wagon trains could only travel roughly fifteen miles per day.

However, unlike travelers on the Underground Railroad, ancestors on the wagon trains may be traceable. Lists of emigrant departures were published in the *New York Daily Times*, *St. Joseph Gazette*, *Frontier Guardian*, *San Francisco Ledger*, and the *Sacramento Union*. Meanwhile, other newspapers published arrivals.

By the 1860's, city roads were paved with cobblestone or brick while small towns had plank or loose gravel roads. But beyond town, roads remained rutted dirt lanes. This changed once Henry Ford began his automobile producing assembly line. Between 1909 and 1927, fifteen million Fords were sold.

---

10 Browne, Ray B. and Lawrence A. Kreiser, Jr. The Civil War and Reconstruction. Westport, Connecticut: Greenwood Press, 2003.

c1640	Stagecoaches were working in London
1663	First turnpike invented
1673	First mail carried via horse from New York to Boston
c1725	Conestoga wagons developed
1772	First Boston to New York stagecoach
1785	Macadam road surface developed
1793	First US turnpike
1821	Santa Fe Trail opened
1823	Horse drawn buses on a rail began in New York
1839	Bicycle invented (Scotland)
1840's	Oregon Trail scouted
1844	Charles Goodyear patented his vulcanization process, leading to rubber products, such as tires
1860	First Pony Express Rider delivered mail between St. Joseph Missouri to Sacramento, California in just ten days
1873	San Francisco began cable streetcar service
1880	First modern bicycle was built
1882	Electric cable car service began in Chicago
1878	Karl Benz began working on motorized tricycle (Germany)
1887	Daimler and Benz created first successful automobile (Germany)
1888	Pneumatic bicycle tire invented
1890	Electric street cars appeared (England)
1893	Federal Highway Administration created in US Department of Agriculture
1895	First automobile race organized (France)
1898	First automobile fatality occurred (England)
1903	Detroit, Michigan became center of auto industry
1908	First Model-T sold in United States
1908	First assembly line for manufacturing automobiles opened
1910	First self-starter installed in an automobile
1911	Truck made first Los Angeles to New York trip
1913	Ford created assembly line
1915	Tractor introduced
1916	First tanks used in warfare
1925	Nine thousand Ford Model-T's came off assembly line in one day
1931	Post Office purchased 1000 Ford Model AA's to deliver mail
1938	Volkswagen "Beetle" designed to Hitler's specifications (Germany)

By Rail

In the United States, the Baltimore and Ohio Railway began in 1827 and, by the late 1830s, railroads had become a popular mode of travel. However, according to Browne and Kreiser[11] in 1836 it still took twelve days and thirteen hours to make the trip from New Orleans to New York using a combination of rail and steamboat.

---

11 Browne and Kreiser. The Civil War and Reconstruction.

Between 1850 and 1870, the growth of railroads exploded and transformed everything. Trains first reached the Mississippi River in 1854. By 1853 a line connected New York and Chicago and by 1858 Philadelphia and Chicago. By the Civil War, railroads carrying mail and freight reached the farmers of the Great Plains.

The federal government routinely gave railroads tracts of land and, in 1863, even offered to pay Union Pacific and Central Pacific Railroads per mile of track laid. It had become evident that rail travel was better than stagecoach or steamboat travel. It was faster, safer, and passengers were protected from the elements.

In 1869, the Transcontinental Railroad linked the east and west coasts and changed the face of America. The American frontier was conquered. With railroads going into more remote areas, towns sprang up and new settler arrived.

Federal grants continued to give the railroads money and millions of acres of land. The money the railroads received from the government was helpful, although the land soon became a problem. Few people were interested in purchasing the millions of acres. Even fewer were interested in farming the land and shipping their crops via rail.

The idea came to someone that an untapped source of potential purchasers was sitting in Europe. Of course by then, most Americans were still of English descent. But beginning in 1854, the Illinois Central began an attempt to lure Scandinavians and Germans from their home countries. The Northern Pacific followed suit peddling the opportunities available in America's Midwest and Pacific Northwest.

In exchange, the railroad agreed to pay moving and transportation expenses and supply agents to guide the securing of passports and ocean transportation for any Russian, German, Irish, Polish, Italian, Greek, Scandinavian and Slavic emigrants who wanted cheap land and free transportation. At the American ports, more railroad agents would greet the newcomers and guide them to the train to take them west. The incentive for the railroads was the fares and the increased usage that settlement would bring. Many of those settlers would also provide cheap labor for the railroads. Rapid settlement of Kansas, Nebraska and the Dakotas followed.

1779	Earliest steam engine operated (England)
1789	First iron rail laid (England)
1789	Earliest public railway pulled by horses (England)
1803	First steam locomotive constructed (England)
1807	Railway passenger service began (Wales)
1815	First rail track laid in US
1825	Stephenson's first steam railway opened (England)
1827	Baltimore & Ohio, first US Railway, chartered
1829	Stephenson's *Rocket* locomotive set speed record of 35 mph
1830	World's first railroad passenger service established (England)
1830	Electric train ran in subway
1832	First mail carried by rail
1838	Congress affirmed railroads as Post Roads
1850	Rail connected Boston to New York
1850	Congress passed land grant for development of railroads
1853	New York -Chicago rail link completed)
1855	First train crossed Niagara Falls Bridge
1857	First steel rails laid (England)
1863	First underground train opened (London)
1865	George Pullman's sleeping car introduced in the US
1865	Union Pacific reached Kansas City
1865	World's first train robbery occurred
1869	Fresh meat 1st shipped from Chicago to Boston in refrigerated car
1869	Union Pacific and Central Pacific Railroad joined at Promontory Point near Ogden, Utah
1869	George Westinghouse patented the air brake, making high-speed train travel possible
1870	Boston, Massachusetts and Oakland, California railroad link finished
1870	First through Pacific coast to New York City service drastically reduced travel time from San Francisco to New York to eight days
1879	First electric railroad demonstrated (Germany)
1881	Southern Pacific opened New Orleans to San Francisco route
1883	First public electric railroad begins (England)
1883	Maiden trip of the Orient Express
1883	Dining cars were invented
1885	Canadian Pacific Railroad reached across continent (Canada)
1892	Diesel engine patented (Germany)
1895	Baltimore & Ohio Railroad introduced electric service (US)
1898	Boston opened first US subway
1904	Trans-Siberian Railway completed (Russia)
1917	United States federalized railroads during World War I
1920	Railroads returned to owners under new regulations
1920	Use of diesel locomotives began
1926	Congress passed US Railway Labor Act
1935	Diesel electric locomotives introduced for long distance use

By Water

In the beginning of the settlement of the New World, everything was water-centered. Most of our ancestors arrived by ship, be it the *Mayflower* or the QE 2. In those early days of Dutch New York and English Salem, Plymouth, Boston, and New Haven and all the other, smaller settlements that sprang up from Maine south, the only way to get from one place to another was by boat. The few trails through the dense forests were traveled by the French and Indians and deemed unsafe. Until safe roads were built, people depended upon rafts and other small vessels rather than wagons and early settlements sprang up along coast lines and rivers. But as the population moved west, strong currents and falls forced settlers to turn to roads.

Most of California's non-Spanish, non-Indian settlement also came by sea -- from Asia or around Cape Horn from North America's East Coast. It was a six-month long route that took the 49'ers to the California Gold Rush. Meanwhile, another group of 49ers took the "Panama Trail" which meant a sea voyage to Central America, a trek through the jungles of Panama and another sea voyage north to California.

After finding which ship an ancestor sailed on, records other then the usual passenger records can add so much more "history." The National Archives has ship log books which were kept detailing weather problems, day-to-day activities, accidents and deaths that occurred and even what provisions were brought on board. Local newspapers recorded arrivals and departures in port cities and described where they sailed from and what cargo they off loaded. Lloyds of London published detailed records about ships for which they were underwriters.

By its nature of being a major entry point for immigrants, New York became a migrant state with people leaving almost immediately after arriving. Many of those migrations were by rivers or canals. From the Northeast, settlers took the Connecticut and Hudson Rivers north and the St. Lawrence west. Because it was remote, most of Maine's settlers went inland up rivers such as the Penobscot and Kennebec Rivers inland from the coast. Farther south, it was the Delaware,

Susquehanna, Allegheny, Potomac and Mongehela west from the Atlantic. In the southeast, Cape Fear, James River and Roanoke River took them inland from the Atlantic. From the Gulf of Mexico they went up the Alabama, Tombigbee and Pearl Rivers. And of course, there was the Mississippi, which settlers took to the Illinois, Ohio, Wabash and other point east or the Missouri, Arkansas and Red Rivers to points west, or just north to Wisconsin and Minnesota.

Navigable rivers, like the Mississippi and Ohio Rivers, allowed flatboats, keel boats and river boats to travel long distances. One major trade route went through Pittsburgh, where the Allegheny met the Ohio which led to the Mississippi and south to the Gulf of Mexico or north to the Missouri River.

Once canals were built, they proved to be a preferred mode of traveling inland. If ancestors ended up in southern Michigan in the early 1830's, chances are they came through the Erie Canal. It was built in stages between 1819 and 1825 to connect the Hudson River to Lake Erie at Buffalo. In fact, much of the Great Lakes States were settled to a large extent by water through the Erie Canal-, Lake Erie, the Detroit River and on through the Great Lakes.

While the Erie Canal was the most widely known of the canals settlers used, in just New York State were the Delaware, Champlain, Genesee Valley, Chemung, Oswego, Black River, Hudson and Chenango Canals. Other states, such as Ohio, also built navigable canals connecting their rivers. In 1832 Ohio opened the Miami-Erie Canal connecting Cincinnati to Dayton. A year later the Ohio and Erie Canal connected Cleveland to Portsmouth on the Ohio River Then in 1845, the Miami-Erie Canal was extended to connect Cincinnati to Toledo, Ohio on Lake Erie.

Before the Civil War, Mississippi River steamboats, a popular way to travel, were manned by slaves and transitory labor. But once the Civil War began, traffic on the Mississippi fell off drastically and travel changed over to rail. At the same time, as rail travel increased, canals became obsolete.

1620 *Mayflower* set sail
1783 First paddle-driven steamboat built and sailed (France)

1789	Lighthouse Service created in Department of the Treasury
1790	First canal built in the United States
1807	Robert Fulton began world's first continuously, commercially-successful passenger steamboat service (US)
1811	First major US ferry service began from Hoboken, New Jersey to Manhattan, New York
1819	First steamship crossed the Atlantic
1825	Erie Canal completed
1836	Screw propeller patented (Sweden and US)
1838	Steamship made first transatlantic crossing
1845	First clipper ship launched
1845	Screw-driven ship made first transatlantic crossing
1848	St. Lawrence Seaway opened
1852	US clipper ships set transatlantic record with thirteen day trip
1853	Steamboat Act established US Steamboat Inspection Service
1860	More than 100 steamboats ran on the Mississippi River
1863	First mechanically-driven submarine used engine powered by compressed air (France)
1867	Mail service from San Francisco to Hong Kong via steamboat
1869	Suez Canal opened
1870	Steamships made up 16% of world shipping
1884	Bureau of Navigation created in US Department of the Treasury
1902	Congress authorized construction of Panama Canal
1908	Gyroscope compass produced (Germany)
1912	The unsinkable *Titanic* sank
1914	Panama Canal opened
1917-19	United States Coast Guard transferred to the Navy from Treasury Department
1941-46	Coast Guard transferred from Treasury to Navy Department

By Air

Although few of our ancestors arrived by air, some did -- by dirigibles from Germany in the 1930's to airliners from Vietnam in the 1970's.

1783	First passenger hot air balloon carried a rooster and a duck
1852	World's first airship took flight (France)
1852	First practical dirigible balloon powered by steam constructed
1900	First dirigible built by von Zeppelin (Germany)
1903	Wright brothers made first powered and sustained flight
1909	First airplane crossed the English Channel
1910	First aerial warfare was fought in Italo-Turkish War
1911	Italians dropped aerial bombs
1915	First metal aircraft built (Germany)
1919	First nonstop transatlantic crossing of an airplane achieved
1927	First solo transatlantic flight made
1930	Jet engine invented (Great Britain)
1936	Helicopter designed (Germany)

1936	Dirigible *Hindenburg* began airship service across the Atlantic (Germany)
1937	Dirigible *Hindenburg* burst into flames over New Jersey ending dirigible use for commercial transportation (36 killed)
1938	First flight of pressurized airliner in commercial service occurred
1939	First jet plane flown
1941	First jet powered aircraft flown in US
1944	Rocket propelled airplane broke sound barrier

5

Coming to America

The subject of history is the life of people and humanity.
-Leo Nikolayevich Tolstoy *War and Peace*

America has not become the melting pot most people think it is. But rather, it has become a patchwork quilt of many ethnicities, colors, shapes and sizes - a nation of black, red, yellow, white and brown; of Jew, Catholic, Protestant, Hindu, Muslim and Atheist. The great migration west began in Europe -- first from the European countryside to the cities; then from the cities of Europe to the Western Hemisphere. Sometimes entire villages or churches left together, sometimes on the same ship. They took these risks without knowing what the outcome would be.

Who Went Where?

Eventually, forty million people would eventually leave Europe to settle in the New World

1492	Spanish expelled from their home country fled to Portugal
c 1500	Portuguese settled in Holland &, then Brazil
1500-60	Emigrants from Holland, Belgium & Luxembourg traveled to England
1502	Portuguese arrived in North America
1528	The first Greek arrived in Florida with Spaniards
1540-1635	Portuguese settled in London & Holland
1555	Africans were taken to England
1559	Spanish settled colony at Pensacola, Florida that failed
1561	Dutch refugees settled in Norwich & Colchester, England
1562-1610	French migrated to England
1565	The Spanish founded St. Augustine, Florida
1600	Turks & Moors arrived in England
1607	English settled in the Tidewater area of Virginia
1608	Polish immigrants arrived in Jamestown
1609	Mexicans could be found in Santa Fe, New Mexico
1610	Dutch arrived in New York & settled along the Hudson River
1617	Dutch settled in New Jersey
1619	African slaves were brought to Virginia
1627-55	Swedish settled in Delaware
1630	Scandinavians arrived in New York
1634	Immigration to America increased greatly
1638	Swedes in Maryland
1641	Dutch colonized parts of Connecticut
1651	Dutch settled in Delaware

1654	First Portuguese established settlement in North America
1663	Settlers from Barbados migrated to the Carolinas
1664	English convicts were sent to Jamaica
1667	English convicts began to be sent to Virginia
1670-90	French arrived in the US
1682	Welsh arrived in Pennsylvania
1683	Rhinelanders & other Germans settled in Pennsylvania
1683	Scottish immigrants arrived in North Carolina
1687	French migrated to England
1688	French settled in New York
late 1600s	Swiss moved into Alsace France
late 1600s	Germans arrived in Pennsylvania
1700	French settled in Virginia
1700-10	Germans arrived in North Carolina
1709	Germans migrated to England
1710	Germans settled in New York
1714	Scots-Irish arrived in Pennsylvania
1716	French had moved into Mississippi
1717	More Germans began arriving in Pennsylvania
1718	Scots-Irish immigrated to New York
1719	Scots-Irish settled in North Carolina
1719	Irish arrived in New Hampshire
1727-75	Germans from Bern & Zurich arrived in large numbers
1730	Scots-Irish settled in western Virginia
1732	Germans & Scots migrated to Georgia
1732	Salzburgers moved to England
1736	More Scots reached Georgia
1745	Pennsylvania Germans showed up in North Carolina
1745	Scottish Highlanders arrived in North Carolina
1750	French-speaking Acadians arrived in Louisiana
1755	French made their way up the Mississippi River to Missouri
1767	Fourteen hundred Minorcans & Italians & five hundred Greeks settled a colony in Florida
1770	One-third of citizens of Pennsylvania were Ulster Scots-Irish
1781	Only 600 Spaniards lived in California
1791	French & French-speaking Haitians settled in New York, Charleston, Philadelphia & Baltimore
1800	The French had settled Louisiana
early 1800s	Basques could be found in California
1801	Russians appeared in Alaska
1814	French Canadians settled Winooski, Vermont
1815	French Canadians settled Madawaska & Burlington, Vermont
1815-60	First wave brought 5 million immigrants
1818	Liverpool became the center for British & Irish immigrants
1820	More than 150,000 immigrants arrived in that one year
1825	Overpopulation in England brought easing of emigration policy
1825	Norwegian began to arrive
1830	Major German migration to US
1830	Major Portuguese immigration to US began
1830s	French Canadians migrated to US & Germans to Missouri

1840s	Germans migrated to Texas & Dutch settled in Michigan, Iowa, Wisconsin, South Dakota
1841-50	More than 780,000+ Irish arrived in US
1845-60	English miners arrived in the Lake Superior mining areas
1846	Potato famine in Europe sent Irish to America
1846-47	Crop failures & mortgage foreclosures in Europe increased US immigration
1847	Dutch from Gelderland & Overijssel settled Holland, Michigan
1847	Dutch from Gelderland, Utrecht, Amsterdam & Frisian settled in Pella, Iowa
1848	After a failed revolution, German political refugees arrived
1849	Chinese arrived in California
1850	Many Portuguese mariners had settled in New Bedford, Massachusetts
1850	Only about three thousand Italian immigrants lived in US & they were primarily from Northern Italy
1850s	Hungarians traveled to the United States
1850s	Germans migrated to Wisconsin
1861	Roughly four thousand Hungarian immigrants lived in US
1861-70	Six hundred thousand English, Scottish & Welsh immigrants arrived in the United States
1864	Swedish miners migrated to Northern Michigan after US miners joined the Civil War
1866-73	One hundred eleven thousand Norwegians arrived in US
1865	Norwegian & Finnish miners worked in Northern Michigan
1865-1875	A larger influx of English & Scandinavian immigrants began
1870-1920	More than one million Hungarians (not including citizens of the Austro-Hungarian Empire) immigrated to the US
1879-93	Two hundred thousand Norwegians arrived in the US
1880	Canadians settled in Marquette, Michigan
1880-90	More than five million immigrant arrived
1880	Just over fifteen thousand Portuguese had settled in America
aft 1880	Arabs began to arrive in larger numbers
1881-90	More than 655 thousand Scandinavians & nearly 1.5 million Germans entered the US
1883	Dutch from provinces of Friesland & Overijssel settled in Charles Mix County South Dakota
by 1890	Eastern & southern Europeans arrived in Northern Michigan
1890	Germans from Hamburg settled in New York City
1890-1900	More than 3.5 million immigrants arrived
1890-1910	Basques arrived & settled in Nevada, eastern California, southeastern Oregon & southwestern Idaho
1890-1910	Cubans settled in Key West & Tampa, Florida
1891	Russians emigrated to US
1891	More than one thousand Greeks entered the US
1894	Provincetown, Massachusetts fleet was totally manned by Portuguese
1894-96	Armenian Christians fled to US to escape Muslim massacres
1898	More than 1000 Russian Doukhobors arrived in Cyprus

1899	Russian Doukhobors living in Cyprus migrated to Canada where other Doukhobors had already settled
1899-1931	Approximately1.5 million Polish immigrants arrived in US
1900	US had 8500 Greek immigrants -- half in Chicago, Boston, Philadelphia San Francisco, Savannah & Lowell
1900	The first Russian Molokans arrived in Los Angeles
c 1900	Koreans arrived in Hawaii
1900-10	Two hundred thousand Norwegians arrived in the US
aft 1900	Bahamians settled in Miami
1901	Molokans left Russia en masse to settle in East Los Angeles
1901-10	More than 500 thousand Scandinavians, 2 million Italians, 2 million Austro-Hungarians & 1.5 million Russians & others from the Baltic region arrived in the US
1901-20	Greek immigration to the US was at its peak
1903	Koreans settled in Hawaii
1905-20	Peak of Italian immigration to the US
1907	Theodore Roosevelt's administration barred immigration of Japanese laborers
1907-13	Spanish immigrants arrived to work Hawaiian sugar plantations
1909	Siberians began to work in the cane fields of Hawaii
1910	New Orleans had highest percent of Italians living in America
1910	One thousand Molokans were living in San Francisco & five thousand in California
1910	Mexicans fled to America during a revolution
1911-13	More than 23 thousand from southern Italy & 21thousand From northeast & central Italy arrived in the US
by 1914	One million Poles had come to the US
by 1914	Croatians had settled in Calumet, Michigan
1914-18	Mass migration to the US was halted by World War I
1914-18	Syrians & Lebanese settled in New York City, Detroit, Washington, D.C., & Iowa
by1920	Most Spaniards living in Hawaii migrated to California
1920	Large groups of Portuguese could be found in New Bedford, Lowell Cambridge, Boston & Fall River, Massachusetts & Oakland, California
1920	The largest Greek populations were in New York, Detroit, San Francisco, Providence & New York City
1920s	About 800 thousand Italians, 160 thousand Scots, 500 thousand Mexicans & 400 thousand Germans arrived in US
1922	A wave of Russian immigrants settled along the Pacific Rim of US & Canada & in Toronto, New York, Philadelphia & Chicago

Before 1660, most of America's immigrants came from England and, like those who would follow them, they brought their beliefs and traditions with them. They established the language, the laws and the culture which would evolve into America.

Meanwhile the French snaked their way from Acadia and Quebec through the St. Lawrence across the Great Lakes and down the Mississippi River, taking control to the Northern and Western British colonies. The Dutch were the first to settle the land between the Delaware and Connecticut River and called the area New Netherlands, although Scandinavians, Germans, French, Walloons and English also made their homes there. Then in 1664, the English conquered that region and renamed it New York.

But the Dutch continued to immigrate. Swierenga[12] reported that when the 20th century arrived, 90% of all Dutch emigrants settled in America. The few who did not, migrated to Dutch colonies or South Africa. When they arrived in the US, the Dutch settled in "only twenty-two counties in seven Midwestern and two mid-Atlantic seaboard states." The largest group settled within fifty miles of Lake Michigan's shoreline -- in or near Muskegon, Grand Rapids, Holland and Kalamazoo, Michigan; Milwaukee, Sheboygan and Green Bay, Wisconsin; and Chicago, Illinois. Instead of trying to escape their " social order," they brought it with them, transplanting churches and villages while keeping almost segregated communities continuing life much as it had been in the Old Country.

The economic effect of Spanish immigration on America cannot be denied either. Eight states -- California, Nevada, Arizona, Colorado, New Mexico, Texas, Montana and Florida -- have Spanish names. Many Spaniards came directly to America from Galicia and Basque in northern Spain and Andalusia in the southwest. They worked on sugar plantations in Hawaii, as cigar makers in Florida, and in coal mines in West Virginia. Many of the Basques settled in Idaho and Nevada sheep ranges.

Mexicans of Spanish descent flooded into the US following the Mexican Revolution. Coming from eastern and central Mexico, economics was the primary reason for leaving Mexico. Although El Paso, Texas became a prime entry point, they fanned out through the

---

12 Swierenga, Robert P. "Dutch Migration to the United States." A Century of European Migrations, 1830-1930. Rudolph J. Vecoli and Suzanne M. Sinke (eds). Urbana: University of Illinois Press, 1991.

Southwestern states, working on railroads and in mines. It was not until after 1910 that most Mexican immigrants found work in agriculture.

But they were not the only ones who brought a new flavor to the culture of America. Hispanic culture has also spread with the introduction of immigrants from South and Central America, Cuba and Puerto Rico.

Early settlement of Russians in Alaska began the tide of Russian immigration. Between 1909 and 1912, Siberians found their way to the sugar cane fields of Hawaii., before resettling in California and throughout the West. When a leader was exiled to Siberia in 1887, Russian Doukhobors arrived en masse and settled in Canada after receiving three blocks of land in Saskatchewan (then part of the Northwest Territories) from the Canadian government. Russian Molakans of Transcaucasus went to East Los Angeles before fanning out across California and into Oregon, Washington, Arizona and Mexico. A few even made their way to Galveston, Texas; Australia, Panama and Chile.

Czechs went to Wisconsin, Texas and Nebraska, while Dutch and Scandinavians could be found in Ogden and Salt Lake City, Utah. Poles established large communities in Buffalo and Brooklyn, New York; Detroit, Wyandotte and Hamtramck, Michigan; and Chicago, Illinois. Although Germans made up one-fifth of the white population of Texas as early as 1847, they also dominated in St. Louis, Chicago and Milwaukee.

Scots-Irish and Dutch became mill workers. Chinese on railroad construction crews or in mines. Norwegian fishermen became North Dakota farmers. Basque immigrants became sheep farmers of the American West, while Japanese became truck farmers in California. Immigrants from the British Isles, Germany and Russia worked in coal mines in southeastern Oklahoma. Irish and French Canadians could also be found in American mining communities. In 1890, foreigners outnumbered Americans in Oklahoma coal fields two to one.

Alanen[13] found that 65% of the residents of the copper mining area of Michigan in 1860 were immigrants -- mostly from Cornwall and other mining regions of England. Because of their shared language, many of these skilled English miners received key positions with their companies. Scandinavians soon followed.

The percentage of urban immigrants in the twenty largest cities in the US in order of total population in 1870 was[14]

City	% Irish	% German	% English
New York	21.0	16.0	02.5
Philadelphia	14.0	07.5	03.3
Brooklyn	19.7	09.8	05.0
St. Louis	10.4	19.0	01.7
Chicago	13.4	17.5	03.4
Baltimore	05.6	13.2	00.8
Boston	22.7	02.2	02.4
Cincinnati	08.6	22.9	01.6
New Orleans	07.7	07.9	01.0
San Francisco	17.3	09.0	03.5
Buffalo	09.6	18.9	03.0
Washington, DC	06.4	03.8	06.1
Newark	11.9	15.1	03.8
Louisville	07.7	14.3	00.9
Cleveland	10.7	17.1	04.8
Pittsburgh	15.2	10.1	03.3
Jersey City	21.4	08.6	04.9
Detroit	08.7	15.9	04.1
Milwaukee	05.2	31.6	01.9
Albany	19.1	07.4	02.3

13 Alanen Arnold R. "Companies as Caretakers in the Lake Superior Mining Region." A Century of European Migrations, 1830-1930. Rudolph J. Vecoli and Suzanne M. Sinke (eds). Urbana: University of Illinois Press,1991.

14 Dinnerstein, Leonard and David M. Reimers. Ethnic Americans: A History of Immigration. New York: Columbia University Press, 1999.

But while, for one reason or another, certain areas of the country attracted certain immigrants, no place was ignored. As Dinnerstein and Reimers[15] pointed out

> "one could find -- then as now -- Italians in Louisiana, Michigan, and Colorado; Hungarians and Greeks in Florida: Slavs in Virginia; Mexicans in Illinois; Irish in Montana."

To Canada and Back

Sometimes it appears that war is one of the deepest connections the United States has with its neighbor Canada.

- When the French controlled Quebec, Canada, they rained havoc on the British Colonies to their south throughout the French and Indian Wars.
- During and following the American Revolution, British fled the US to Canada when they were threatened and their land confiscated.
- During the War of 1812, families living on both sides of the Canadian-US border found themselves torn apart.
- In 1839, the Aroostook War broke out when both Maine and New Brunswick claimed the valley of the Aroostook River.
- The only Civil War battle fought north of Pennsylvania occurred when Confederates raided Vermont from nearby Canada
- And, more recently, American men fled to Canada to evade the draft during the Vietnam War.

In spite of this, through the years until 9/11 terrorists entered the United States through Canada, the border between these two counties was inconsequential. In fact, the border between the state of Washington and Canada was not even set until 1848. For a while, Acadia was a borderland between Maine and Canada. The French had included Maine as part of the province of Acadia, while the British gave it to the Plymouth Colony.

When Vermont became a state in 1791, it included land acquired from Canada. Perhaps that was why Theron Balch listed his birthplace as Canada in the US census while his brothers Aaron and Simeon listed Vermont.

The fluid aspect of the Canadian border was important to the Daniel Landon and John Askin families. The Landons had been happy with their lives in Litchfield, Connecticut when the American Revolution

---

15 Dinnerstein, Leonard and David M. Reimers. Ethnic Americans: A History of Immigration.

broke out. Some Landons fought for the Rebels, others for the British, and a family was divided. The sons of Daniel Landon supported the British and ended up having their land confiscated by their new government. While Daniel and his wife remained behind, son Oliver took his family through the wilderness in to Canada and settled in Lansdowne, Ontario with several of his siblings and cousins. Just about one hundred years later, Oliver's great-great grandson John Landon was living in Thamesville, Ontario, when he received an opportunity to manage a hotel in Romeo, Michigan. He took the job and moved his wife and three children to the US where his children eventually married and raised their children. Meanwhile, John's siblings remained in Canada.

As a young man, John Askin, who was born in 1739, came to the New World from Ireland. He ultimately made his way to the Detroit area where he purchased and was granted land on both sides of the Detroit River. In due course, his children married residents on both sides of the river. Everything changed when the War of 1812 arrived and family loyalties became divided. Askin's sons and several of his grandsons fought with the British. Meanwhile, son-in-law, Elijah Brush, fought with the Americans. Askins who were loyal to the British but living in Detroit had to flee across the river to Canada.

Since movement between these two countries has always been uncomplicated, Canada became an obvious destination for many traveling the Underground Railway to escape slavery. Then, after the Chinese Exclusion Act was passed in the US, Chinese took advantage of the liquid border by entering the United States through Canada. Although French-Canadians began immigrating to the US in the 1830's, it was not until 1860 that they began leaving Canada in great numbers to settle in mill towns in New England. Ramirez[16] approximated that between 1840 and 1940, 2.8 million Canadians, of which 900 thousand were French-Canadians, immigrated to the US. The largest number of

---

16 Ramirez, Bruno. "Quebec and International Migrations." A Century of European Migrations, 1830-1930. Rudolph J. Vecoli and Suzanne M. Sinke (eds). Urbana: University of Illinois Press, 1991.

Canadians left for the US between 1890 and 1900 and between 1920 and 1930, with 450 thousand leaving Canada each of those decades.

Canadian emigrants did not go to America's rapidly expanding areas. Instead they stayed close to the Canadian border. For instance, most of those from eastern Ontario went to New York. In 1850, almost 65% of the population of the Pembina District of the then Minnesota Territory were Canadian born, with the largest number from Manitoba. Pembina eventually became a county in North Dakota. Even more Canadians went to North Dakota during its 1879-1886 and 1898-1915 land booms.

Some may have been transient. Before the Canadian Pacific Railway, the only way for settlers to get to Manitoba land given through Canada's Homestead Act of 1872, was to travel through the US. When Manitoba land closed, everyone looked to the Dakotas. While American land was filling, the Canadian prairies west of Manitoba remained unsettled. But once the American land had begun to fill and prices there had risen, the Canadian prairie land became more attractive to Americans and Canadians alike. Although percentage-wise it was not the peak year, in raw numbers, the highest number of emigrants from the United States to Canada was in 1912 at more than 139 thousand.[17]

America's Historic Migration Patterns

Since Jamestown's first trail, Americans have been on the move. Between the settlement of Jamestown in 1607 and the California Gold Rush of 1849, Americans went from that one small settlement in Virginia, into the valleys of the Appalachians, through the Mohawk Valley or Cumberland Gap, to the Mississippi River and all the way to California. Along the way, that migration to the American west had many stops. At each stop, towns sprang up, people raised families and some moved on.

---

[17] Randy William. With Scarcely a Ripple: Anglo-Canadian Migration into the United States and Western Canada 1880-1920. Montreal: McGill-Queen's University Press, 1998.

Early settlement came in three phases. Those of primarily English descent settled from the coastal plain to the foothills of the Appalachians. Non-English primarily Germans and Scots-Irish, moved into the back country and valleys of the Appalachians. The next phase saw migration into the land between the Appalachians and the Mississippi River.

Those from New England went to the Midwest; the Mid-Atlantic States to Tennessee, Kentucky and southern Ohio, Indiana and Illinois; and the coastal South into the rich soil of the Deep South. Whether they were Indians forced from their land, solitary fur trappers or farmers looking for tillable land, they moved when conditions at home were not such to keep them and hoped that opportunities lay over the next hill.

It has been found that those who were more likely to migrate fit into certain categories. They were more likely to be middle class rather then the poor or wealthy, Irish or Scandinavian rather than English those with family who had made the trip ahead of them, and farmers in search of more fertile land rather than shopkeepers who lacked the necessary skills for pioneering

Timothy Bosworth's study[18] compared various categories of people and he determined the likelihood that they might migrate. Below are the categories he studied with the more likely to migrate listed at the top down to the least likely at the bottom.

National Origin	Religion	Occupation	Age
Scots	Presbyterian	Agriculture	20-29
Irish	Baptist	Artisan	30-39
Scots - Irish	Congregational	Professional	0-19
English	Lutheran	Mercantile	40-54
French	Huguenots	Maritime	55+
German	Anglican		
Welsh	Quakers		

18 Bosworth, Timothy W. Those Who Moved: Internal Migrants in America Before 1840. Madison: University of Wisconsin (Thesis), 1980.

Generally older people who were native born and had ties in their communities were more likely to remain when economic times were bad. However, younger, landless children of migrants duplicating their parents behavior were the most likely to move on when faced with the economic insecurity of the mid-1800s.

Studies of the effect of events on populations show that even before there were automobiles or moving vans, changes in transportation methods, such as the invention of steamboats or opening of the Erie Canal, encouraged the westward movement. Partially due to improved ports, in 1650, more people arrived and lived between Virginia's James River and New York City then in the South or New England as might be expected. As they began to head north, south and west, most pioneers found themselves in areas with no governments. Generally, land was free to whoever got there first. Sometimes there were claims offices. Some just settled in and waited to see if anyone would try to kick them off the land and never bothered to register their claim.

Revolutionary War veterans received certificates redeemable for "western" land. Not all veterans had the means or urge to migrate. So in 1787, members of the Ohio Company from the Atlantic states bought up veteran certificates and, the next year, they arrived at the Ohio River. The route they took became the modern-day Pennsylvania Turnpike.

Land became available through acts of Congress, such as the Homestead Acts and military warrants. The idea was to promote the move west by providing people with free land or selling the land for as little as $1.25 per acre. A land patent transferred ownership from the federal government to individuals.

Eventually the General Land Office (GLO) of the Bureau of Land Management (BLM) would take over disposal of public lands. Today they oversee in excess of two million Federal land titles from 1820 to 1908 in Public Land States. These records are searchable on the Internet.

Historians have long placed an enormous importance of climate. Generally Scandinavians were lured to the northern states and the Great Lakes of America. Most people did not remain in low, hot, malarial-ridden swampland for long. Conversely, they were attracted by fertile valleys where natural water was abundant. The majority followed the old Indian paths while some hacked their way through the wilderness and looked for peninsulas or ridges which were more defensible in an attack.

Understanding America's historic migration patterns can yield information leading to where ancestors originated in the United States and to stops along the way west where their descendants settled.

Years	**Who or Where from**	**Moved to**
1620-40	Virginia	Rappahannock, James & Potomac Rivers & across Chesapeake Bay
1640	Salem, Massachusetts	Long Island, New York
1661	Massachusetts/Virginia Quakers,	Maryland
1670	Virginia	Blue Ridge Mountains
1675	New England	South Carolina
1680	New England Quakers	Pennsylvania
1680s	Maine	Massachusetts
early 1700s	Virginia	Maryland
1700-1800	Rhode Island	Renssellaer County, NY
1700-1800	Pennsylvania	Southwestern New York
1700-1800	Southwestern New York	Pennsylvania & New Jersey
1700-1800	Long Island, New York	Monmouth, New Jersey
1700-1800	New England	Oneida County, NY
1719	New Jersey Quakers	Frederick County, VA
1727	Pennsylvania Palatines	Virginia
1730	Virginia	South Carolina
1738	New Hampshire	New York
Late 1700's	Maryland	Virginia
1784	Loyalists	Canada
1788	Atlantic Coast States	Western Pennsylvania & Ohio
1790	South Carolina	East Tennessee
1790-1812	Connecticut	Western New York
1800	Soldiers	Lake Champlain area of New York
1800	South Carolina	Middle Tennessee
1810	Tennessee	Alabama
1810-20	Virginia and the Carolinas	Alabama
1818-25	New England and New York	Illinois & Michigan
1819	New England	Indiana & Illinois
1820	South Carolina	West
1830s	Alabama	Mississippi
1867	Northern carpetbaggers	Deep South

Despite common belief, everyone was not moving west or south. Bosworth[19] wrote that between 1732 and 1754, North Carolina's population doubled and between 1760 and 1776, Vermont claimed seventy-four new towns.

The East

Early migrations to New England were conducted by sea or coastal trails, such as the Kennebunk Road which followed the coast from Boston to southern Maine. But as pioneers discovered fertile inlands, and Indians became less of a threat, the settlers began to move up and down the river valleys. The Mohawk (Iroquois) Trail led people through the Mohawk and Hudson River Valleys. One Balch family migrated to Massachusetts, then New Hampshire, then Vermont, then New York; settling in each place for several years before moving on again.

Meanwhile, Pennsylvania and New York became pass-through states for newly arrived immigrants on their way west, New Englanders moving south and Long Island Tories heading north to Canada.

Eastern trails and roads

Trail or Road	To	From	Misc.
Bay Road	Boston	Tauton	
Boston Post Road	New York City	Boston	
Catskill Road	Boston	Wattles Ferry	
Coast Path	Boston	Plymouth	
Cumberland Road/ National Pike	Cumberland , Maryland	Wheeling , West Virginia	later to St. Louis
Forbe's Road	Philadelphia	Pittsburgh	
Great Valley Road	Southeast Pennsylvania	Cumberland Gap	via Shenandoah Valley
Great Conestoga (Lancaster Pike & Pennsylvania Road.)	Philadelphia, Pennsylvania	Lancaster Pennsylvania	later to Pittsburgh
Great Genesee Road	Utica, New York	Cleveland, Ohio	

19 Bosworth, Timothy W. Those Who Moved: Internal Migrants in America Before 1840.

Greenwood Road	Hartford	Albany	
Hudson River - Lake Champlain Trail	New York	Canada	followed waterways
Iroquois Trail or Mohawk Trail	Hudson River	Niagara River	via Hudson & Mohawk Valleys
Kennebunk Road	Boston	Southern Maine	along the coast
King's Highway	Boston	Charleston	later connected to Boston Post Road
Kittanning Path	Frankston, Pennsylvania	Ohio River	via Kittanning Gorge
Nemacolin's Path or Braddock Road	Baltimore (Potomac River)	Pittsburgh	eventually to Ohio River
Old Roebuck Road	Boston	Providence	via Boxboro & Attleboro
Old Connecticut Road or Bay Path	Cambridge Massachusetts	Albany, New York	via Grafton & Springfield
Portage Path	around Niagara Falls		via Hudson & Mohawk Valleys
Tobacco-Rolling Road	Northern Virginia	near Richmond	via Culpepper & Hanover

* became the 1st designated postal road

The Mountains

In Virginia and the Carolinas, the Blue Ridge and Appalachian Mountains presented a natural barrier. Then the 1763 Proclamation Line set a no settlement zone for territory across those same mountains and South Carolina was settled by residents of North Carolina and Virginia.

A series of treaties signed between 1816 and 1821 finally opened Indian land in Georgia and Tennessee. Some realized the land received in the Georgia Land Lottery was worthless, or became concerned living so close to Spanish Florida, took one of two migration paths -- either Tennessee or into the Deep South of Alabama and Mississippi.

One Lampkin family took the Tennessee route, settling in Washington County, before moving on to Alabama, then Mississippi. While Tennessee's first white settlers had already come from Virginia or North Carolina, a few from southeastern Pennsylvania, Maryland and New Jersey also arrived early. Most were of English or Scottish heritage, with a small mix of French Huguenots.

Appalachian trails and roads

Trail or Road	To	From	Misc.
Boone's Wilderness Trail	Fort Chiswell Wythe Co., Virginia	Central Kentucky	via Cumberland Gap
Great Warrior's Path	Philadelphia	Chattanooga	via Maryland & Virginia
Jonesborough	New Bern NC	Knoxville Tennessee	
Kentucky Road	Virginia	Kentucky	via Cumberland Gap
Nashville Road	Knoxville	Nashville	
Old Northwestern Turnpike	Winchester , Virginia	Parkersburg on the Ohio River	
Old Walton Road	Knoxville	Nashville	
Old Northwestern Turnpike	Westchester Virginia	Parkersburg West Virginia	
Robertson's Road	Cumberland Gap	Nashville	via Cumberland River
South Carolina State	East Tennessee	Charleston	
Unicoi Road	Maryville , Tennessee	Tugaloo Georgia	over Smokey Mountains
Zanes Trace	Pittsburgh PA	Ft. Gillad , Kentucky	eventually to Lexington & Nashville

The South

Migration into the Mississippi Territory was slow until after the 1814 Treaty of Fort Jackson when the Creeks ceded much of present-day Alabama to the United States. Most who moved into the territory came over the Federal Road, Lower Creek Trading Path, Natchez

Trace or Jackson Military Road, while some came by boat. Many who moved directly from Georgia into Alabama settled along Alabama's western border, waiting for Mississippi Indian lands to open for settlement. That came with a series of Indian treaties.

Years	**Treaty of**	**Area of Mississippi land opened**
1801	Fort Adams	southwestern
1805	Mount Dexter	southeastern
1820	Doak's Stand	parts of west central
1830	Dancing Rabbit	eastern to western borders in central
1832	Pontotoc Creek	northern

Unfortunately, Mississippi Territory land records can be confusing. Land offices in what would become Alabama and Mississippi sold land in both states. In addition, the Florida line originally extended all the way to the Mississippi River, cutting Alabama and Mississippi off from the Gulf of Mexico except by river down the Tombigbee through Spanish territory or the Mississippi River through French territory.

Every southern state eventually sent pioneers into Arkansas and Texas - some from the north via the Ft. Smith Trail from Arkansas or down the Red River Trail from Oklahoma. Others took the path Gideon Lincecum took from Maryland to North Carolina, to Georgia. His son Hezekiah continued the migration pattern into eastern Mississippi, then his son Gideon migrated on to Texas, through Louisiana.

Southern trails and roads

Trail or Road	To	From	Misc.
Carolina Road (Rogues Road or Upper Road)	the Virginia / Maryland line near Leesburg	Charlotte North Carolina	later on to Georgia , Alabama & New Orleans
El Camino Real	Mexico	Louisiana	reached St. Augustine by 1836
Fall Line Road	Fredericksburg Virginia	Georgia	
Federal Road	Washington, D.C.	New Orleans	via Alabama & Mississippi
Gaines Trace	Florence , Alabama	Cotton Gin Port on the Tombigbee	
Jackson Military Road *	Nashville , Tennessee	New Orleans/ Madisonville Louisiana	via Muscle Shoals , Alabama

Lower Creek Trading Path	Greenville , Mississippi	Augusta, Georgia	branches to Savannah & St. Augustine
Natchez Trace	Nashville	Natchez	created by Choctaws
Occaneechi/ee Path	James River, Virginia	Augusta, Georgia	
Richmond Road	Central Maryland	Ft. Chiswell (Cumberland Gap)	via Richmond, Virginia
Salada Road	Augusta , Georgia	Jonesboro Road, North Carolina	via South Carolina
Three-Chopped Way	Georgia	Natchez	via Fort Stoddart
Upper Road	Fredericksburg Virginia	South Carolina	via Old Occaneechi/ee

* built by Andrew Jackson

The Midwest

As early as 1612, the Great Sauk Trail took the French and English into Detroit. The Northwest Ordinance of 1787 opened additional land by declaring all land north of the Ohio River and east of the Mississippi River would be settled as part of the United States. Much of Michigan, Ohio, Indiana, Illinois and Wisconsin were settled by pioneers from New England and the Mid-Atlantic especially once the National Road was finished all the way to Vandalia, Illinois.

Settlers from Virginia, Ohio and Kentucky traveled over the Old Chicago Road into the unpopulated Northwest. Others followed the Great Trail from Fort Pitt (Pittsburgh) to Detroit. Ohio, in particular, attracted settlers from the East, the South and the West, while the General Land Office maintained Revolutionary War bounty warrants for Ohio, the Cincinnati land office also gave out land patents for southeastern Indiana.

Midwestern trails and roads

Trail or Road	Began	Ended	Misc.
Buffalo Trace (Kentucky Road)	New Albany Indiana	Louisville & Vincennes	via Greenwich & Vincennes
Fort Miami Trail	Ohio River	Detroit	via Valley of Maumee
Great Trail	Pittsburgh	Detroit	via Northern Ohio
Michigan Road	Madison on the Ohio River	Michigan City, Indiana	via South Bend & Indianapolis

Old Chicago Road	Indianapolis Indiana	Chicago , Illinois	via Williamsport , Indiana
Pottawatomie Trail (Great Salk Road *)	New France, Canada	Mississippi River	another branch went to Wisconsin
St. Croix Road	Lake Superior	Mississippi River	improved by US Army Engineers

* by 1833 stagecoaches took this route from Detroit and Chicago

The West

Fur traders began the western push into the Great Plains. They were followed by cattlemen, miners and farmers. Some homesteaders went to Kansas before continuing on to the Dakotas or Montana, while others migrated to Colorado from Alabama, Georgia, Wisconsin, Illinois, Ohio and New York. The Federal Government encouraged the expansion through a series of acts.

- The Pre-Emption Act of 1841, which was repealed fifty years later, gave everyone with cultivated federally-owned land (squatters) the right to purchase 160 acres for just $1.25 per acre.
- The Graduation Act of 1854 reduced the price of public land depending upon how long it had already been up for sale.
- The Homestead Act of 1862 opened a lot of western land by providing one quarter section of land for seven years for a $10 filing fee.
- The Timber Culture Act of 1873 augmented the Homestead Act by giving homesteaders an additional quarter section of land. In exchange, the homesteader had to plant a number of those acres with at least 2700 trees per ten acres.
- To encourage economic development of the West's arid and semi-arid public lands, the Desert Land Act of 1877 allowed for the purchase of 640 acres at $1.25 per acre if the homesteader agreed to irrigate a portion of the land.
- The Timber and Stone Act of 1878 allowed individuals to purchase 160 acre blocks of western land deemed "unfit for cultivation" for $2.50 an acre, to be used for logging and mining.

Although many from Ohio settled in Missouri, St. Louis and Independence also became important stopping points on the trip west. It was the Santa Fe Trail that took them from Independence, Missouri to

Santa Fe, New Mexico. Meanwhile, the Oregon Trail took settlers from Independence to Wyoming and Idaho. The Missouri River took them from any point along the Mississippi River into Montana and the Dakotas.

Of course, it seemed everyone headed to the gold fields of California (1849), Nevada (1851), Colorado (1858), Alaska (1861) and South Dakota (1874). Sometimes all these miners could only claim was a couple hundred feet of creek bed. But it was all theirs.

The Gold Rush of 1849 sent nearly one hundred thousand from every state in the Union to California. That trend was to continue even after the gold no longer drew them. Dinnerstein and Reimers[20] estimated that as late as 1939, 90% of the field workers in California were refugees from the Dust Bowl states.

Western trails and roads

Trail or Road	To	From	Misc.
Boseman Trail	North Platte River	Montana Gold Mines	
Butterfield Overland Mail Route	Eastern Missouri	San Francisco California	
California Trail	Independence Missouri	California	one prong of two-prong trail
Canadian River Trail	Fort Smith, Arkansas	Santa Fe, New Mexico	via south bank of Canadian River
Cherokee Trail	NE Oklahoma	Santa Fe Trail	
Deadwood Stage Route	Deadwood, SouthDakota	Fort Mandan , North Dakota	to Missouri River & Oregon Trail
Goodnight / Loving Trail	Young Co., Texas	Pueblo , Colorado	originally a cattle trail
Mormon Trail	Council Bluffs, Iowa	Great Salt Lake, Utah	via North Platte & Fort Bridger
Mullan Road	Columbia River in Washington	Fort Benton, Montana on Missouri River	military road
Old Southwest Trail	St. Louis	Texas	via Arkansas
Old Spanish Trail	Santa Fe	Los Angeles	
Oregon Trail *	Independence Missouri	Willamette River, Oregon	one prong of two-prong trail
Overland Stage Route	St. Louis , Missouri	San Francisco California	offshoot to Ft. Smith & Memphis

20 Dinnerstein, Leonard and David M. Reimers. Ethnic Americans: A History of Immigration.

Pony Express Route	St. Joseph , Missouri	California	via Salt Lake City, Utah
Santa Fe Trail (over mountains)	Independence , Missouri	Santa Fe , New Mexico	via Kansas & across the Rockies
Southern Trail	Galveston	Los Angeles	
Upper El Paso Road	El Paso , Texas	San Antonio , Texas	
Western Trail	Central Texas	Ogallala , Nebraska	connected to Oregon Trail

*first wagon train of sixteen wagons and more than one hundred people left Missouri in May 1842

Long Distances

Many trails and roads these early settlers took connected with other roads. Boone's Wilderness Trail connected with the Great Wagon Road at Fort Chiswell. Zanes Trace connected with the Natchez Trace. Other trails were intended to take travelers over long distances and crossed several regions

Long distance trails and roads

Trail or Road	To	From	Misc.
Great Warrior's Path (Seminole Trail or Great Wagon Road)	Northern New York	Carolinas	via Kentucky & west of the Blue Ridge
Kenawha Road	Shenandoah Valley	Ohio River	
Maysville Turnpike	Zanesville, Ohio	New Orleans	via Nashville
National Road	Baltimore	St. Louis	via Vandalia, Illinois
Yellowstone Trail *	Massachusetts	Washington	via Yellowstone

*1st trans-continental highway

Trail of Tears

And finally, there were the four trails used to move the Cherokees west into Indian Territory in 1838-39 --

- The Northern Land Route ran from southeastern Tennessee through Kentucky, Illinois, Missouri and Arkansas.
- The Water Route proceeded down the Tennessee River to the Ohio, Mississippi and Arkansas Rivers.

- The Benge Route from Ft. Payne, Alabama, crossed the Tennessee River, through southeastern Kentucky, over the River, west to the Old Southwest Trail to Arkansas and west into Indian Territory.
- The Bell Route from Chattanooga, moved across the Mississippi River to Little Rock, Arkansas, along the Arkansas River to Ft. Gibson.

The Religious Factor

Many times the church rather than town was the keeper of the vital records and the parish is the logical place to look for the information.

Discovering the primary religion of the region where the ancestor originated can lead to new avenues of inquiry. However, in countries where records are kept by ecclesiastical rather than civil authorities, it is important to know the area of jurisdiction. For instance, a British parish could have been a group of hamlets, a town or a small portion of a much larger city.

When non-conforming religions developed in England, separate church records were kept for them by the governmentally "accepted" parish of the times, while the non-conforming churches maintained records of their own as well. Moreover, it was about that time that the Non-Conformists, Separatists and other persecuted religious groups began looking for someplace else to settle.

1492	Jews fled to Portugal after being expelled from Spain
by 1540	Catholicism had been introduced to Mexico by the Spaniards &began slowly spreading north into California
1540-1638	Portuguese Jews went to London & The Netherlands
1550	Edward VI gave Protestant emigrants a charter with the right to worship as they pleased, independent of the Church of England
1562	English Protestants fought the Wars of Religion in Normandy
1562-c1610	French Huguenots arrived in England
1607	Anglicans arrived at Jamestown, Virginia
1608-1759	French Catholics settled along St. Lawrence River Quebec
1609	Leiden/Leyden Holland offered English Separatists refuge from persecution
1620	Sephardic Jews migrated to Barbados
1620	Pilgrims landed in Plymouth
1630	English Puritans (Congregationalists) landed in Boston
by 1640	Sephardic Jews arrived in Nevis
1634	Catholic priests arrived in Maryland
1644	Non-Conformists migrated from New England to Maryland

late 1600s	William Penn offered religious sanctuary to German Mennonites, Dunkers & Schwenkfelders
1654	Sephardic Jews migrated to the Dutch West Indies
1654	Jews arrived in Barbados
1654	Brazilian Jews arrived in Dutch New Amsterdam (New York)
1657	Gov. Peter Stuyvesant reversed himself, allowing "Quakers, Jews " or Muslims " entry to New Netherlands after residents of Flushing protested.
1658	Jewish settlers arrived in Newport, Rhode Island
1670-90	French Huguenots arrived in US
1675	Salem, New Jersey settled by Quakers
1676	William Penn offered refuge to Quakers
1680	Quakers continued to arrive in Pennsylvania
1682	German Palatines immigrated to Pennsylvania
1685	Huguenots arrived in Virginia
1687	French Huguenots settled at the Cape of Good Hope
1687	A group of French Huguenots arrived in England
1688	Huguenots arrived in New York
1696	French Huguenots settled in South Carolina
1700	Huguenots arrived in North Carolina
1700	Two thousand Quakers settled in Pennsylvania
1710	German Palatines immigrated to North Carolina
1710	German Palatines arrived in England
1710	Another large group of Palatines arrived in Pennsylvania
1717	German Mennonites migrated to Pennsylvania
1717	German Reformed & Lutheran groups arrived in Pennsylvania
1722	Moravian settlement was established in Saxony
1730	First large group of Amish arrived in the US& settled in Lancaster, Pennsylvania
1732	Protestant Salzburgers migrated to England
1734	Eight thousand Salzburg Protestants immigrated to Georgia
1734	Moravian Brethren began to arrive in Georgia
1740	Moravian Brethren migrated from Georgia to Pennsylvania
1741	Moravians founded Bethlehem, Pennsylvania
1767	Amish arrived in Pennsylvania
1786	Central European Mennonites settled in Canada
1794	Ten Eastern Orthodox monks arrived in Russian owned Alaska
1800	Groups of Pennsylvania Mennonites immigrated to Canada
1800	Pennsylvania & New Jersey Quakers removed to Canada
1838	Scot Presbyterians from the Outer Hebrides arrived on the Isle of Lewis in Lower Canada (Quebec)
1847	Mormons arrived in Utah
1873	Russian Mennonites settled in South Dakota
1874	Mennonites moved into Kansas
1880-1924	Roughly 2.5 million East European Jews arrived in the US
1881	Russian Jews moved into other Eastern European countries
1881-1903	Northeastern US port cities of New York, Boston, Philadelphia, & Baltimore were flooded with Jewish immigrants
1883	Dutch Calvinists moved to Charles Mix County, South Dakota
1890-1900	Nearly 656,000 Italians (two-thirds of them men) arrived in US cities of New York, Detroit, Philadelphia, Chicago & Baltimore

1891	Russian Jews moved to North America
1907-14	Ten thousand Jewish immigrants came into the United States through Galveston, Texas
1945-68	The Los Angeles Jewish population quadrupled

As early as 1683, Mennonites followed William Penn and his talk of religious freedom to Pennsylvania. Once Penn gave sanctuary to non-conformist groups such as the Mennonites, Reformed and Lutherans; residents of German extraction jumped to one-third of Pennsylvania's population in the 1700's, before spreading out to the Midwest and Canada. Early German Lutherans also immigrated to Maryland and Virginia migrating through the Shenandoah Valley into western Virginia. Later, German and Scandinavian Lutherans moved into the Midwest, establishing communities in Missouri, Wisconsin and Minnesota .

Fleeing persecution in England in the 1640s, Quakers (Society of Friends) made their way to Massachusetts where they found more persecution. Many then migrated into Rhode Island. However, in the 1680s, Pennsylvania also attracted Quakers, as did the James River area of Virginia. Eventually they moved into South Carolina, Georgia, western Pennsylvania, eastern Tennessee; and then into Illinois, Indiana and Ohio. Meanwhile, Pilgrims and Puritans arrived in Massachusetts, Narragansett and Connecticut before spreading up and down the Atlantic Coast and onto Long Island. With Scots came the Presbyterian Church. In 1750, one-fifth of New Jersey's population was Presbyterian. Similarly, wherever the Dutch settled, the Dutch Reform Church followed.

Between 1829 and 1903, Jewish immigration to the US averaged 37,000 a year. They settled in large American cities such as New York, whose Lower East Side was home to more than 350,000 in 1916. Dinnerstein and Reimers[21] estimated that the Jewish population of the United States skyrocketed from 250 thousand in 1877 to 4.5 million by 1925, while others migrated to Canada, Australia, South Africa and Argentina.

Spanish Catholics arrived early in Florida and along the shores of the Gulf of Mexico. French Catholics migrated to Maryland Pennsylvania, and upper New England. Other French Catholics made their way across

21 Dinnerstein, Leonard and David M. Reimers. Ethnic Americans: A History of Immigration.

Canada through the Great Lakes and down the Mississippi River. Before the Irish Potato Famine, America's Roman Catholics were primarily socially prominent English Catholics. Suddenly with the famine, the Catholic population went from 5% of the population in 1850 to 17% in 1906, making them the largest religious denomination in the US

The new American Catholics were unbelievably diverse -- urban and rural immigrants who spoke different languages and belonged to different social statuses. It was not just the Irish who changed the religious scenery of Catholic America. It was the Catholic Italians and Germans too .

Although the Northeast first attracted Congregationalists and the South became home to Anglicans, the Middle Colonies attracted setters from countries displaced by the Reformation and its religious wars. Those colonies also attracted the smaller groups -- the Portuguese Jews, the German Baptists and the Dutch Mennonites, in addition to the slightly larger Dutch Reformed and Quakers. Added to the mix were the beliefs and traditions of the black slaves many of whom were Muslim, and the Native Americans.

In the colony of York, religious groups settled together in a patchwork pattern with the Dutch Reformed along the Hudson River, German Reformed and Lutheran along the Mohawk River and west of Albany, Congregationalists on eastern Long Island, and French Huguenots at New Rochelle in Westchester County.

Although Pennsylvania was founded by Quakers, their religious tolerance attracted other persecuted sects; such as the Reformed Germans, Lutherans, Amish, Dunkers, Schwenkfelders, Mennonites and Moravians. Meanwhile, Delaware was settled by members of Scandinavian Lutheran and Dutch Reform Churches which were shortly joined by others. Yet, by the American Revolution, the Anglican Church had grown the most in Delaware.

One misconception is that the Amish settled only in Pennsylvania. In reality, the Amish have settled in twenty-four states and Canada. The largest groups are not in Pennsylvania: they are in northern Ohio and northern Indiana.

Early North American churches were transient by nature. The Mormon movement which began in Fayette and Palmyra, New York in

1830, moved to Ohio, Missouri, and Illinois before finally going on to the Great Salt Lake

Understanding an area's religious trends lead a genealogist to church records -- from baptisms to marriages to funerals -- which sometimes are the only sources of the information. Each of the early colonies began attracting members from the various religions and, by 1820, the populations of the states had developed into pockets of specific religions.

State	**Religions with greatest number of members in Colonial (pre-1776) Era**[22]	**Religions with greatest number of members in 1820 (the first being the largest)**[23]
Connecticut	Congregational	Congregational, Anglican, Baptist
Delaware	Anglican, Dutch, Lutheran, Presbyterian	Presbyterian, Anglican, Quaker, Baptist Methodist
Georgia	Anglican, Moravian	Baptist, Methodist, Baptist, . Presbyterian
Kentucky		Methodist
Louisiana	Roman Catholic	Roman Catholic
Maine	Congregational	Congregational, Baptist, Roman Catholic
Maryland	Roman Catholic, Presbyterian	Roman Catholic, Anglican, Baptist, Quaker, Presbyterian
Massachusetts	Congregational	Congregational, Baptist, Quaker, Anglican, Presbyterian
Missouri		Methodist, Roman Catholic, Baptist
New Hampshire	Congregational	Baptist, Congregational
New Jersey	Dutch Reform, Lutheran, Quaker, Presbyterian, Catholic	Dutch Reform, Baptist, Anglican, Congregational, Quaker
New York	Dutch Reform	Presbyterian, Dutch Reform, Anglican, Baptist, Methodist, Quaker, Lutheran, Roman Catholic
North Carolina	Anglican, Presbyterian	Methodist, Baptist, Anglican, Presbyterian in western region
Rhode Island	Congregational	Baptist
Pennsylvania	Quaker, Lutheran, Reformed, Amish, Brethren, Moravian, Presbyterian, Schwenkfelder	
South Carolina	Anglican, Huguenot	Methodist, Baptist, Presbyterian, Anglican
Vermont	Congregational	Congregational, Baptist
Virginia	Anglican, Presbyterian	Baptist, Presbyterian, Anglican

22 Noll, Mark A. A History of Christianity in the United States and Canada. Grand Rapids, Michigan: William B. Eerdmans Publishing Company, 2000.
23 Kirkham, E. Kay. Research in American Genealogy: A Practical Approach to Genealogical Research. Washington, D.C.: 5th Institute of Genealogical Research, 1954.

6

Myths, Confusions, Secrets and Lies

> If you are afraid of skeletons, stay out of closets. And if you are ashamed to have ancestors who do not meet your own social standards, then stay away from genealogy.
>
> -Val Greenwood *Researchers Guide to American Genealogy*

Each piece of information collected about an ancestor, every story handed down is not necessarily correct. This is especially true of a family's oral history which may contain embellishments or omissions. The story was gradually changed as it was passed down from generation to generation. Perhaps embellishments were added to make it more interesting, or facts were omitted to hide a secret. Blind acceptance can easily lead a in the wrong direction. Usually there is a truth in there somewhere. All a researcher needs to do is look to history to find the answers.

Myths

Webster defines myth as "a popular belief or tradition that has grown up around something or someone" and "an unfounded or false notion." History is filled with myths. Paul Revere only made it twenty miles on his famous ride before he was arrested. And he was not shouting "The British are coming:" he was shouting "The Regulars are coming." No little Dutch boy stuck his finger in a dike. Robin Hood was probably a compilation of "Robin Hoods" who may, or may not, have been common thieves. Catherine the Great was not Russian at all. She was a German who took control of Russia after having her husband imprisoned and, possibly, murdered.

Genealogy also has its myths. There's the myth of two brothers who came to America -- one went to Virginia, while the other went to Boston. Then there is the myth of being descended from Charlemagne, always through an illegitimate child because the legitimate ones have been documented by historians. With this myth there is usually a family castle in Europe. There are also those who claim descent from an Indian princess or a plantation owner.

Genealogist John Colletta related his grandmother's story of an ancestor being a plantation owner in Mississippi. Upon researching the man, Colletta discovered his ancestor was a carpetbagger from the north who journeyed south and opened a store following the Civil War.[24]

Despite these flights of fancy, history does teach us the Pennsylvania Dutch were German, names were seldom altered on Ellis Island, a five-year-old in the 1860 census did not fight in the Civil War, everyone named Lincoln was not descended from Abraham, records were kept concerning children on the Orphan Trains.

If a story sounds outlandish, ask if history supports it. And remember, although myth is one resource to be considered, it needs to be based on historical fact and logical deduction, also known as "common sense."

Confusion

Webster defined "confused" as "disordered or mixed up." Since there is usually some truth mixed in with the confusion, at least these genealogies or oral histories can provide clues.

This is where a timeline is indispensable.

One story passed down through my family was that John Reynolds helped build the Erie Canal then took his family to Michigan where his grandson William married Jennie Smith in 1885.However, the dates and places of John's marriage and the births of his children compared with the history of the Erie Canal, were inconsistent with that story. After my great-aunt died and left me the Smith Family Bible, I discovered in the front, Jennie Smith's grandparents Nathaniel and Ruth Smith had lovingly recorded the dates and places of birth of each of their children. Making a timeline and comparing the information in the Bible with the building of the Erie Canal, it became clear that somehow the children or grandchildren of William and Jennie Smith Reynolds had confused the story their parents

---

24 Colletta, John Philip. Only a Few Bones: A True Account of the Rolling Fork Tragedy and Its Aftermath. Washington, D.C: Direct Descent, 2000.

had passed down to them. It was not Grandpa John Reynolds who had worked building the Erie Canal: it was Grandpa Nathaniel Smith.

Names cause confusion. The Smiths had two sons named Edwin. The first died before the second was born. Another family produced Margaret Mary, Margaret Anne and Margaret Amelia. The family referred to the girls by their middle names. Boxer George Forman named all his sons "George."

Secrets

The word "secret" can mean "kept from, hidden" or "marked by the habit of discretion: closed mouth" or "working with hidden aims." When the word "secret" is used in connection with genealogy, usually a family secret is an act of self-preservation or a means of protecting the family from harm or humiliation. Secrets might be related to anything, including adoption, adultery, desertion, divorce, handicaps, illegitimacy, imprisonment, incest, mental illness, poverty, rape and "shot-gun wedding."

Many times the "family secret" was kept to save someone from unnecessary pain. My mother was told her father died accidentally. As an adult she discovered her father committed suicide after her mother left him, taking their young daughter (my mother) with her across country.

Some secrets were kept for survival. During the World Wars, a number of descendants changed their names to avoid discrimination in the US. During World War II, a number of European Jews lied about their religion.

Elizabeth Shown Mills,[25] one of the most widely respected and scholarly professional genealogists in the nation, noted that because of the sensitivity and personal nature of family history, omissions, myths and misconceptions concerning racial ethnicity have had far reaching ramifications. Mills pointed out that America's "melting pot" did not cross "color lines."

Although public people have been eminently researched, late US Senator Strom Thurman is a good example that even they can have

---

25 Mills, Elizabeth Shown. Ethnicity and the Southern Genealogist: Myths and Misconceptions, Resources and Opportunities. Generations and Change: Genealogical Perspectives in Social History. Robert M. Taylor, Jr. And Ralph J. Crandall (eds). Macon, Georgia: Mercer University Press, 1986.

secrets. After his death in 2003 at the age of 100, a mixed-race, 78-year-old woman stepped forward acknowledging that she was the daughter of Thurman, an avowed segregationist. After an investigation and DNA testing, the Thurman family finally acknowledged her.

Racist practices frightened or shamed many localized populations of mixed black, white and Indian origins into denying their heritage, making it difficult to trace their history. Although terms, such as "Mulatto" for a person who had white and black parentage, and "Mestiz," for a person who had white and Native American parentage, made identification easier, other populations were less easy to define. Some family members distanced themselves from the "secret" while others lied to themselves and everyone else. Unfortunately, the truth has been lost through the generations.

Some of the groups frequently referred to as "Mestee" are discussed elsewhere in this book. They established themselves in remote regions of the US and include the Cane River Creoles of Louisiana, the Brown People of Kentucky, the Nanticokes and Moors of Delaware, the Wesorts of southeastern Maryland, the Brass Ankles and Turks of South Carolina, the Buckheads and the Carmel Indians of Ohio. While several had Indian blood mixed with whites, blacks or both, others, like the Issues of the eastern Blue Ridge of Virginia, were primarily Mulattos with just a remote possibility of Indian blood.

Elizabeth Shown Mills[26] reported that between 1714 and 1803, 49% of native-born whites living in northwest Louisiana "boasted Indian blood." At one point, some southern states defined a "Negro" as anyone with one-eighth or more African blood. As Mills suggested, with statistics like those, "a 'white' genealogist would be naive ... assuming that he will find nothing but 'white' ancestors."

Lies

A lie is "an assertion of something known or believed by the speaker to be untrue with the intent to deceive." Because of the stigma attached to divorce, a woman might have listed herself as a widow when

26 Mills, Elizabeth Shown. Ethnicity and the Southern Genealogist: Myths and Misconceptions, Resources and Opportunities.

in reality her husband deserted her or she "kicked the bum out." Couples listed themselves as husband and wife when in reality they had never bothered to marry. Women shaved years off their ages. Older men who married sweet young things did the same thing.

In the 1980's, an elderly African-American woman from Mississippi, enlightened me with her tales of growing up black in the South. Sadye Wier's husband Robert had been the product of a local white pharmacist and his black maid. Whenever Sadye and Robert traveled in the Deep South in the earlier years of their marriage, they had difficulties finding restaurants that would serve them. However, since Robert Wier was so light skinned, he could go into the "White's Only" restaurants, eat, and bring food back to his wife.

More recently, a man researching his family could not find any information about his grandmother from before her marriage to his grandfather. He found census after census describing his "white" grandparents after their marriage. However, when he ordered his grandmother's death certificate with the informant listed as his grandfather, he discovered his grandmother listed as "Mexican."

The 10,000 to 20,000 "near white people" in Virginia known to posses even the slightest amount of "colored blood" were a problem in the eyes of Dr. W.A. Plecker[27], Virginia State Registrar of Vital Statistics from 1912 to 1936. In an attempt to protect "racial integrity," Dr. Plecker declared "war" on racial mixing. In order to keep the white race pure, Plecker proposed a law passed by the Virginia legislature in 1924, making it unlawful for any white to marry anyone other than another Caucasian. According to the legal definition, "one with no trace of the blood of another race, except that a person with one-sixteenth of the American Indian, if there be no other race mixture, may be classed as white."

In order to truly describe a person, race-wise, Virginia physicians who reported marriages and births were required to use terms such as

- Mulatto for offspring of a white and a black,
- Quadroon for offspring of a mulatto and a white,

27 Plecker, W.A. "The New Virginia Law to Preserve Racial Integrity." Virginia Health Bulletin vol. 16: 2 1924. <www.eugenicsarchives.org> Printout dated 05/04/2006.

- Octoroon for offspring of a quadroon and a white,
- Black, Negro or Colored for offspring of black parentage.

The term "Indian" was no longer to be used except for those with "known" pure Indian blood. Japanese, Chinese and "other Mongolian and Malay races" were to be listed as the birth country of their ancestors.

As lethal as Walter A. Plecker was, he was only following in footsteps of many who had gone before him. In 1786, Maine voided all marriages between whites and blacks or mulattos. When Virginia passed its law, Ohio already had a statute forbidding marriage between a "pure white" and a person "of visibly African blood."

Several signals a researcher can look for that indicate a family has hidden their racial or ethnic origin include --

- Family tales of having Indian, Black Dutch or Black Irish ancestry,
- Varied racial designations within families (siblings, aunts, cousins) in the Federal censuses,
- Different race designation in censuses (i.e. mulatto in 1880, Indian in 1900),
- Change of surname for no clear reason,
- Vague family traditions that do not "check out",
- Rejected Indian land claims
- A lack of any family history.

To uncover the truth, researchers need to knock away the false foundations on which the myths, confusions, secrets and lies have been built.

7

Even Harder to Find Missing Persons

"The same lady loved genealogy as much as she loved detective fiction. Genealogy is a pursuit of hidden knowledge, and success at the end of the search is like the perfect outcome of a mystery murder."

-Graham Landrum, *The Famous DAR Murder Mystery*

Some ancestors just don't seem to want to be found. When encountering a difficult ancestor, just as police do today when looking for a missing person -- look at the personal history. What was happening in their world when they disappeared? Migration could be the consequence of conflict of some sort -- conflict in the broadest sense, not just war.

For example, when Capt. John Underhill, an honored military man, was declared a "debaucher" and banished from the Massachusetts Bay Colony, he moved his wife and children to New Hampshire. However, the same problem of infidelity followed him there and he deserted his wife and moved to Connecticut. Underhill returned to Boston, confessed the original adultery then attempted to commit adultery once more and was banished yet again. Running out of places to go, in 1644 Underhill made his way to what would become Flushing, Long Island and pled his loyalty to the Dutch.

There are those people who have simply been misplaced. A child is adopted. A woman gets married and changes her name. A divorce occurs. Sometimes the surname is so common that a person can be lost in the midst of a mass of people with the same name. People seldom disappear alone. Trace family members, friends and neighbors. Look for the one with the oddest given name. It is much easier to find Absalom Smith than his brother John Smith in New York.

Then, there are those who really are missing. Some have disappeared with good reason, like runaways, military deserters, victims and those trying to evade the law. They do not appear in tax, census or vital records. They may show up in newspaper ads of the time, looking for runaway slaves, or in news articles as criminals or their victims. Others have disappeared against their will, such as those forced into slavery.

And mistakes are made.

In 2004, a group of professional genealogists had a lively discussion on an online news list. One of the professionals had been searching the Ancestry.com census database when she noticed a number of people in the 1850 census listed as being born in India. In a search asking only for those born in India, she received 106,000 hits, but the surnames did not seem to be Asian or even American Indian. Upon going to the enhanced view of the actual censuses, the genealogist discovered that the enumerator had written "Ind," for Indiana in most of the cases checked.

Another genealogist openly wondered if Ancestry had "outsourced" the indexing.

Two years after this open discussion, only five people in the US were still listed in the 1850 census as being born in India. Obviously, Ancestry had learned of its error and corrected it. However, for the five listed the actual census read "Ind Ter" for "Indian Territory " as their birthplace, not India. Unfortunately, there were still 9,023 people listed in the United States as being born in India in the 1860 census. As before, the actual census clearly read "IN" or "Ind." The 1860 census also listed 1592 people as having been born in Kenya. Upon looking at the actual digitalized census records, most were like 53-year-old Capander Reeves of Alabama who actually was enumerated as having been born in "Ken" for "Kentucky".

Name Changes - Legal or Not

The most obvious reasons for a name change are a woman who takes her husband's surname and an adopted child who takes the new parents' surname. However, a person might legally change their name for other perfectly understandable reasons. Immigrant Andreas Peter found Americans became confused by his name, frequently referring to him as Peter Andreas. After legally petitioning the court for a name change, he became Andreas Peters. Simply adding a legal "s" to the end of his name cleared up all the surname confusion.

Spellings of surnames changed over a period of time. For some reason, one Machen brother changed the spelling of his surname to Matchen. French "Morin de Loudons" changed their name to Morin, Loudon and de Loudon. Some eventually moved to England and became Landons.

Any number of shadier reasons might result in a complete change of identity. Attempting to escape capture, bad credit and lawsuits come to mind. These were the people who did not want to be found then, and may still be impossible to find now.

Females

Historically, laws and traditions have made females notoriously difficult to trace. In addition to changing their surname when they married a number of other road blocks have been placed in the way to tracing them.

- Fewer than 10% of women left wills.
- Women had to sign away their dower rights.
- Men owned land and paid the taxes.
- Women were not allowed to vote.
- Pre-1850, Federal censuses listed only adult male as head of the household. The few females who were named usually were widowed heads of the household.

Many women traveled alone to America. Sirianna Hendreksen left Norway after her husband died and traveled to America to be with several of her children who had already settled there. Others came as indentured servants. These women have been especially difficult to trace.

Naturalization laws of the United States also worked against them. A woman's citizenship designation was derived from her husband. An immigrant female became automatically naturalized by marrying an American or when her immigrant husband or father became naturalized. But before 1906, they were not listed on their husband's or father's records.

Conversely, a 1907 law ruled that a wife's citizenship was determined by her husband's. In other words, a female born and raised in the United States to American-born parents would lose her citizenship upon her marriage to an alien. That law was in affect until 1922 when Congress passed the Cable Act, also known as the Married Women's Act. However, it was not until 1940 that those women who had lost their citizenship between 1907 and 1922 were allowed to apply for repatriation in a local court.

The only way to find a missing female is to study each and every document that surfaces with her name on it. Read all letters and journals from the time and area. Check divorce, not just marriage records. Early divorces were generally granted by State Legislatures. Baptismal records of children frequently contained the mother's maiden name, and those named godparents of her children might be her relatives? Who were the informants on the death certificate? Was there an obituary? If so, were surviving brothers named?

In censuses, who were the neighbors? Who was living with the married couple? Frequently elderly or widowed in-laws were taken into the home. During a search for the ancestry of Frank Fergusons maternal grandparents, it was discovered that in 1860, Frank's parents, William and his 23-year-old wife "Amelia", had two boarders -- an older woman named Elizabeth Sams and a 17-year-old named William Bennington. Ten years earlier, Elizabeth Sams and her second husband were raising Elizabeth's children by her first husband. They included 7-year old William Bennington and his 13-year-old sister "Permelia" Bennington.

Slaves

As daunting the task of tracing a slave back to Africa, a few records were kept. The majority of the slaves that ended up in America came from West Africa. Some who arrived had been sent by way of other colonies, North America's off-shore islands, South America or England. Certain American destinations received more slaves from specific regions of Africa.[28,29]

---

28 Rawley. James A. The Trans-Atlantic Slave Trade: A History. NY: W.W. Norton & Company, Inc, 1981.

	Georgia	Maryland	Mississippi	North Carolina	South Carolina	Virginia
Angola			X		X	
Barbados					X	X
Bight of Biafra					X	X
England	X			X	X	
Gambia	X	X	X	X	X	X
Gold Coast /					X	X
Jamaica	X	X		X	X	X
Senegal	X	X	X	X	X	X
Sierra Leone			X		X	
South Carolina	X	X		X		X
Windward Coast*					X	X
Whydah					X	X

*approximately the coast of modern Liberia

In 1780, 85% of all mainland slaves lived in just four colonies -- Virginia, South Carolina, North Carolina and Maryland. Although most researchers look to the South as the probable American genealogical starting point for today's African-American family, it must be remembered that the North may also have been the beginning point. Rawley discovered that in 1780, New York had approximately 21,000 slaves, putting it fifth of the thirteen colonies having slaves.

Rawley[30] reported that between 1715 and 1761, New York and New Jersey imported more then 4500 slaves. By 1790, nearly 8% of New Jersey's population was black and it was not until 1804 that New Jersey passed a law gradually abolishing slavery. In fact, according to Wacker,[31]

29 Schaefer, Christina K. Genealogical Encyclopedia of the Colonial Americas: A Complete Digest of All the Countries of the Western Hemisphere. Baltimore: Genealogical Publishing Company, 1998.

30 Rawley. James A. The Trans-Atlantic Slave Trade: A History.

31 Wacker, Peter O. "Patterns and Problems in the Historical Geography of the Afro-American Population of New Jersey, 1726-1860." Pattern and Process: Research in Historical Geography. Ralph E. Ehrenberg (ed.) Washington, D.C: Howard University Press, 1975.

the 1860 census indicated that New Jersey still had eighteen slaves, although they were officially designated as 'apprentices'."

Americans also think of migrations as happening east to west. But if a slave came from an area not part of the British trade routes, the slave may have come to America via French, Spanish or Portuguese trading routes to Central or South America.

For instance, in 1776, the French began trading slaves from Tanzania. Any former slave who reported "Chamba" as his place of birth was from an area inland on the Ruvuma River of Tanzania when the French turned their attention to that region. That particular slave may have come through New Orleans and traveled up the Mississippi River. New Orleans was owned by France then Spain and slave trade continued through that city after the United States and Britain halted the trade. So, New Orleans became the entry point of slaves being sent to Louisiana, Mississippi or other points north.

During the Revolutionary War, the British tried to lure slaves to join them and quite a few did. Approximately three thousand accompanied the British home on defeat. The British kept records of those blacks that accompanied them home, including names, age and description. Other blacks followed the British to Canada, but their records are kept in the National Archives in Washington, D.C.

On the other hand, many African-Americans fought on the side of the rebels during the revolution and their pension records lay in the National Archives and their descendants are becoming members of organizations such as the Daughters of the American Revolution (DAR). The DAR maintains records of many of America's first African-American soldiers.

While the new nation was beginning to deal with slavery and freed slaves, some were thinking about returning to Africa. The American Colonization Society was formed to transport freed slaves back to Africa and begin an African colony for the United States. Initially they were trying to aid both abolitionists who wanted to free all slaves and allow those who wanted to return "home" and slave owners who feared "mischief" freed men could bring upon those still enslaved.

The Republic of Liberia was established on land purchased by the society for those freed US slaves who wished to return to Africa. Their first settlement began at Cape Mesurado in Liberia in 1821. By 1860, more than eleven thousand had been transported to Liberia and more would follow. However, at the conclusion of the Civil War, financial aid waned. Passenger lists and land grant records from those days have survived. All the society's records were donated to the Library of Congress and are available to the public.

Actual enslavement officially ended with an 1865 constitutional amendment and the last legal slave ship arrived in the US at Mobile Bay in 1859. But black-market slave entries were still made in more clandestine landings after that.

Following Reconstruction, race riots, massacres and lynchings became common place. The Library of Congress American Memory website listed lynchings based on race occurring yearly.[32]

Year	Lynchings Nationwide
1885	74
1890	85
1900	106
1905	57

Lynchings certainly did not stop in 1905. In fact, 1919 became known at the year of the "Red Summer." Inflation, unemployment and competition for jobs led to unrest. Seventy-six black Americans were lynched and twenty-six race riots broke out across the nation during the Summer and Fall of 1919.

One of the most violent was on July 19 in Washington, D.C., where six were killed. In Chicago on July 27, thirty-eight blacks and whites were killed, more than five hundred were injured and one thousand black families were left homeless. Problems in Elaine, Arkansas, were aggravated in October by outside agitators. Finally the Army restored order in Elaine, but not before thirty blacks and whites had been killed.

An understanding of the history of the African-American in the United States can lead a family researcher to insight into the slave experience and, perhaps, find some family history. One of the best places is the American Memory website prepared by the Library of Congress entitled *Born in Slavery: Slave Narratives from the Federal Writers Project.*

---

32 African American Perspectives: African American Pamphlets - Timeline <memory.loc.gov/ ammenem/aap.html>

Between 1936 and 1938, the Works Progress Administration (WPA) traveled the country interviewing Americans about their lives and pasts. More than 2300 of those interviewed were former slaves. The collection also contains 500 black-and-white photographs of people interviewed. An example of the type of material included in them is a portion of an interview with former slave Prince Johnson of Clarksdale, Coahoma County, Mississippi, chosen at random from the *Mississippi Narratives Volume IX* to be included here.

> "My gran'pa, Peter, gran'ma Millie, my pa, John, an' my ma Frances, all come from Alabama to Yazoo County to live in de Love fam'ly. Dey names was Denis when dy come, but, after de custom o'dem day, dey took de names o' Love from dey new owner. Me an' all o' my brothers n' sisters was born right dere. Dey was eleven head o' us. I was de oldes' Den come Harry, John, William, Henry, Phillis, Polly, Nellie, Virginny, Millie, an' de baby, Ella.
>
> "Us all lived in de quarters an' de beds was home made. Dey had wooden legs wid canvas stretched 'crost 'em. I can't 'member so much 'bout de quarters 'cause 'bout dat time de young miss married Colonel Johnson an' moved to dis place in Carroll County. She carried wid her over one hund'ed head o' darkies.
>
> "den us names was changed from Love to Johnson. My new marster was sure a fine gent'man. He lived in a big two-story white house dat had big white posts in front. De flowers all 'roun' it jus' set it off...
>
> "Marster an Old Mis' had five chillun. Dey is all dead and gone now, an' I's still here. One o' his sons was a Supreme Judge 'fore he died.[33]

After the war, Prince Johnson went to live with the "Supreme Judge" Jim Johnson who had moved to South Carolina.

> "Us got dere in time to vote for Gov'nor Wade Hamilton. Us put 'im in office, too. De firs' thing I done was join de Democrat Club an' (helped) 'em run all o' de scalawags away for de place. ..."I'se seen many a patrol in my lifetime, but dey dassent come on us place. Now de Klu Kluxes was diff'ent. I rid wid 'em many a time. 'Twas de only way in dem days to keep order.
>
> "When I was 'bout twenty-two, I married Clara Breaden. I had two chilluns by her, Diana an' Davis. My secon' wife's name was Annie Bet Woods. I had six chillun by her; Mary, Elle, John D., Claud William, an' Prince, Jr. Three boys an' two gals is still livin'. I lives wid my daughter, Claud

33 Born in Slavery: Slave Narratives from the Federal Writer's Project, 1936-1938 <memory.loc.gov>

One thing history teaches us is that some assumptions can be wrong. Since a number of southerners moved north, the assumption has always been that most African-American Southerners, who moved, headed north.

Earl Lewis[34] hypothesized that any black migration to northern and mid-western cities was associated to a sort of American Industrial Revolution which sent rural blacks into Southern cities as well. He actually discovered that more blacks moved to cities in the south than the north in the decade between 1910 and 1920. While 1.5 million left the rural South, half of them went to southern cities of Norfolk, Virginia; Houston, Texas; Jacksonville, Florida; Birmingham, Alabama; Baltimore, Maryland and Atlanta, Georgia, to fill the demand for labor. During those years, the black population grew

While black families may be difficult to trace, the study of history can lead to an understanding of what life was like for them at various times in American history.

by 1500 African servants & slaves had arrived with Spanish & French explorers in the Western Hemisphere.
1517 Spanish settlers received consent to take fifteen African slaves to America
1562-68 John Hawkins took slaves from western Africa to Hispaniola
1619 Twenty male & female Africans arrived in Jamestown when Dutch slavers traded them for food
1623 First black child born in English Colonies was in Jamestown.
1624 Dutch imported Africans to the Valley
1634 African slaves arrived in Maryland & Massachusetts
1641 Massachusetts made slavery legal
1642 Virginia passed a law to fine anyone harboring a runaway
1645 African slaves arrived in New Hampshire
1649 Three hundred African slaves arrived in Virginia
1652 Rhode Island passed the first anti-slave law in North America, limiting slavery to ten years.
1663 Maryland legalized slavery
1664 Maryland law prohibited marriage between a white woman & a black man
1664 New York & New Jersey legalized slavery
1671 Two thousand African slaves arrived in Virginia
1675 While North America had 5,000 slaves the West Indies had 100,000

---

34 Lewis, Earl. Expectations, Economic Opportunities and Life in the Industrial Age: Black Migration to Norfolk, Virginia 1910-1945. The Great Migration in Historical Perspective: New Dimensions of Race, Class, and Gender. Joe William Trotter, Jr. (Ed.) Indianapolis: Indiana University Press, 1991.

1682	South Carolina legalized slavery
1688	Pennsylvania Quakers signed the first written protest of slavery
1691	Virginia Colony banished freed slaves
1700	Rhode Island & Pennsylvania legalized slavery
1708	Carolinas had more African slaves then free or bonded whites
1738	Fugitive slaves sought refuge with the Creek Indians in Georgia & the Spanish in Florida
1750	English colonies had more that 236,000 slaves, with more than 200,000 of them south of Pennsylvania
1756	Virginia had 100,000+ slaves
1765	South Carolina had 90,000 blacks & 40,000 whites
1766	New York Methodist congregation received blacks in their flock
1780	Pennsylvania passed gradual emancipation
1790	Blacks made up 19% of total US population
1790	Virginia had 290,000+ slaves
1793	Fugitive Slave Act became law allowing slave owners to take back their slaves from free states
1793	Virginia law forbade free Blacks from entering the state
1808	Banned importation of slaves, but illicit importation continued
1816	Slave rebellion failed in Virginia
1821	First colony of freed slaves settled in Liberia
1831	Nat Turner's slave rebellion in Virginia failed
1833	Slavery was abolished in British Colonies
1833	An anti-slavery convention was held
1847	Liberia declared its independence
1857	Supreme Court 's Dred Scott Decision stated blacks were not US citizens & slave owners could take their slaves from free areas.
1859	Last slave ship to the US arrived in Mobile Bay, Alabama
1859	Abolitionist John Brown raided Harpers Ferry
1861	Civil War broke out
1862	District of Columbia abolished slavery
1863	Emancipation Proclamation freed slaves in Confederate states
1863	The all black 54th Massachusetts Volunteers charged Fort Wagner in Charleston, South Carolina
1864	Maryland freed its slaves
1865	Constitutional amendment abolished slavery.
1865	Nearly four million slaves had been freed
1865	General Sherman set aside land in South Carolina & Florida for former slaves but President Andrew Johnson later vetoed it.
1865	Freedmen's Bureau established to help former slaves
1866	New Orleans police stormed a Republican meeting of blacks & whites, killing forty.
1866	Congress overrode President Andrew Johnson's veto of Civil Rights Act.
1866	Ku Klux Klan was founded
1866	Southern Homestead Act opened public land in Alabama, Mississippi, Louisiana, Arkansas & Florida to settlers of all races.
1866	Racial violence in Memphis ended with forty-six blacks & two whites dead & hundreds of black homes & churches destroyed

1868 Between two & three hundred black Americans were massacred in Opelousa, Louisiana
1873 Slavery was abolished in Puerto Rico
1875 Twenty black Americans were massacred in Clinton, Mississippi
1875 Civil Rights Act guaranteed equal rights to black Americans in public accommodations
1881 Tuskegee Institute was founded in Alabama
1881 Tennessee instituted segregation of public transportation (Jim Crow Laws). Other southern states followed.
1883 Supreme Court overturned Civil Rights Act of 1875
1883 Supreme Court upheld Tennessee's Jim Crow Laws separate public facilities for blacks & whites
1886 Twenty black Americans massacred in Carrollton, Mississippi
1890 Mississippi instituted literacy tests to disenfranchise black citizens. Other southern states followed.
1896 Supreme Court denied argument that Southern segregation practices (Jim Crow Laws) conflicted with the 13th & 14th amendments, formulating the "separate but equal" doctrine.
1898 Louisiana introduced the "Grandfather Clause" which allowed automatic voter registration of only males whose fathers or grandfathers were qualified to vote on January 1, 1867.
1899 Afro-American Council set aside June 4 as a day of protest against lynchings & massacres.
1906 Black soldiers rioted against segregation
1909 NAACP (National Association for the Advancement of Colored People) formed
1910 Blacks made up 10.7% of the US population
1910 City Council-designated segregated neighborhoods began in Baltimore, followed by Dallas, Greensboro, Louisville, Norfolk, Oklahoma City, Richmond, Roanoke & St. Louis
1913 President Wilson's administration instituted government-wide segregation of facilities.
1915 Ku Klux Klan reactivated in Stone Mountain, Georgia
1917 Supreme Court struck down Louisville's city-designated, segregated neighborhoods
1917 Major migration of southern blacks to northern industrial hubs.
1917 In World War I, 370,000 African-Americans served in military
1917 NAACP protested in Manhattan
1919 Seventy African-Americans lynched, including returning soldiers still in uniforms
1919 Twenty-five race riots in the North & South
1922 A filibuster in the Senate killed a Federal anti-lynching law
1924 Ku Klux Klan reached its peak of influence
1930 Black Muslim movement founded in Detroit
1944 US Navy commissioned its first black officers

Isolated Societies

When one thinks of isolated or closed societies in America, their mind usually goes to one of the religious groups such as the Amish or the

Shakers or to a modern-day cult. But those are not America's only closed societies.

Our early history is filled with runaway slaves, indentured servants, and Indians disappearing into the forest just ahead of the colonials. Should it be of any surprise that escaping Spanish or British prisoners, indentured or slave servants and Native Americans might find themselves together in some Appalachian valley beginning a fugitive community, hiding from the white settlers steadily moving westward?

As many as two hundred multiracial groups of isolated societies could exist in the United States. Most are made up of persons of mixed races who are referred to as "Mestee." In many cases, the groups deny their identity. The Brass Ankles and the Turks of South Carolina claim Mediterranean descent. In fact, the Turks have been recognized as white since the time of the Revolutionary War.

Typically these mestee groups live in their own communities in rural areas, where they provide farm labor. Most are found east of the Mississippi River: many on the edges of Appalachia. Because mestee groups tended to be geographically connected, many of these groups that follow are lumped under the Melungeon name.

The Melungeons of Appalachia were possibly the people French explorers encountered and recorded in Appalachia in 1654. These dark skinned people of uncertain origin were definitely discovered living in cabins in Hancock County, Tennessee, as early as the 1790's. They spoke an Elizabethan form of English and called themselves "Portyghees." The *Dictionary of the English Language* reported the name may have originated with the French "melange" meaning "mixed", the Greek "melas" meaning "dark" or "black" or the Afro-Portuguese"mulango" meaning "shipmate."

While Melungeons who live primarily in Lee, Scott County and Wise County, Virginia; Hancock County (Hawkins County), Tennessee ,Ashe County, North Carolina and Letcher County, Kentucky, can resemble Indians, their white ancestry is also evident. They seem to have some Mediterranean features and suffer from genetic diseases distinctive to the Mediterranean region. At various times, Melungeon ancestors have been thought to be descendants of the lost colony of Roanoke and Native

American; Portuguese or Moors brought to the New World by the Spanish to build roads to forts and missions; colonists who came with Welsh explorer Madoc; products of African-American, Native American and Caucasian intermarriage; shipwrecked Portuguese sailors; Turks, African and South American natives left on North American soil by Sir Francis Drake. It is far easier to say what they are not. They are not uniquely Native American, Caucasian or African. Although they were designated as "Free Persons of Color," Melungeons received none of the basic rights of White America.

It is possible the Melungeons and other closed societies originated on or near a coast, then as the Whites moved further West, so did these groups -- just ahead of settlers - until they were finally detected. In many cases, localities might be the only clues to placing an ancestor in a specific group. They include -

- The "Cajans" of the Spanish frontier of Alabama (as opposed to the Cajuns of Louisiana) purportedly sprang from the intermarriage of children of a Mulatto family and a free black family which settled in the Lower Tombigbee River Region of rural southern Alabama. Indians and white loggers, cattlemen and railroad men apparently added genes to the mix.
- The Guineas of north central West Virginia have been regarded as blacks or mulattos on official records, but could also carry some Indian blood. Found in the western portion of Virginia before the 1800's, they have survived as farmers, day laborers, coal miners and servants.
- Jackson Whites / Ramapo (Ramapough) of New York and New Jersey were a reclusive mountain group with Dutch sounding names. They considered themselves descendants of the Delaware and Tuscarora tribes. Still, their hermitic ways led to intermarriage and genetic abnormalities. Although mostly Caucasian in appearance, they attended segregated black schools in New York as late as 1947. In reality, the Jackson Whites also have features of Mohawk Indians. Blacks, Dutch and, possibly Hessian soldiers or deserters may also have added to their gene pool.

One story postulated that Jackson Whites were descendants of runaway slaves and white female followers of Washington's forces. When Washington retreated, these outcasts took refuge on Ramapough Mountain where they insulated and armed themselves against the rest of the world.

- The Wesorts of Maryland are a distinctly multiracial group which was first identified circa 1800 but did not give itself its name until circa 1890. Many reorganized in the 1970's as an Indian tribe. Despite romantic lore of shipwrecked sailors, the Wesorts have been traced back to 17th century English who arrived in Maryland as indentured female servants who became pregnant with multi-racial babies.
- The "White Creoles" of Louisiana are French and Spanish with some Indian and, perhaps African American, in the mix. The "Colored Creoles" of Mississippi, Alabama and Louisiana are a mixture of French and Spanish with a great deal of black and, perhaps some Indian, in the mix.
- The Issues of Amherst County, Virginia, were as early as 1785 at the foot of the Blue Ridge. "Issue" was a term given free blacks before the Civil War and bi-racial children afterwards. Possibly they carry some Indian blood. A few Issues who have left Virginia, migrated to New Jersey.
- Lumbees or Croatans of North Carolina were discovered living along the Lumber River in the Robeson County area as early as the 1730's. In the 1990 census, 90% of Pembroke in Robeson County, North Carolina, identified themselves as Lumbees. Others were found in Hoke, Scotland and Sampson Counties, North Carolina and Bulloch and Evans Counties in Georgia. Although labeled as Indians by the North Carolina and South Carolina State Legislatures in the late 1800's, the Croatans or Lumbees were not recognized by the Federal Government until 1956. Some researchers have suggested that they may have been related to the Cheraw Indians who left the area circa 1703 to go to South Carolina.

- The Redbones of southwestern Louisiana and Texas were probably of mixed white and African-American descent but may also have had Asian, Native American, Basque, Spanish, Gypsy, Moor or Portuguese blood. Redbones were first considered to be freed blacks with English surnames. Depending upon the source of information, Redbones may have originated in Georgia or the Carolinas.

  In 1806, the United States and Spain agreed to set-up a Neutral Zone in Southwestern Louisiana while talks were conducted setting a boundary between their two territories. Although populated chiefly by Indians and having no law in the area, outlaws, stray Mediterranean seamen, runaway slaves, Texans fleeing the Spanish and privateers sought refuge in the area. The Neutral Zone became the home of the Redbones. It was there that they farmed and became a socially isolated society. Although today most are cooper-colored skin with high cheekbones and dark hair and eyes; light skinned, blond-haired, blue-eyed Redbones and Redbones with prominent Negroid features are also found.
- The Dead Lake People of Gulf and Calhoun Counties, Florida, have been traced back to South Carolina and may have been related to the Brass Ankles or Redbones.
- The Catawba of South Carolina and the Black Seminoles still speak an Indian language. Although racially considered black, the Black Seminoles are culturally Native American.
- The Haliwa Indians of Halifax and Warren Counties, North Carolina are less black and more white then the nearby Lumbees. They are suspected of being the people who remained behind when the Melungeons crossed the mountains.
- The Moors and Nanticokes, whose origin has long been a matter of speculation, reside primarily in southeastern Delaware. They descended from Moorish crew of a pirate ship wrecked off Delaware who were taken in by the Nanticoke Indians, or English soldiers who had been stationed in Tangiers, and with Moorish,

who were given land in Delaware for their service to the Crown. Or perhaps they were descendants of a wealthy Spanish or Irish woman who purchased a slave who turned out to be a Moorish prince and fled the white community with him. Meanwhile, the Nanticokes have been attempting to be recognized as Indians, but, as with the Moors, they are clearly a mixed race people.

- As with the Nanticokes, many claim to be Native American groups who have lost their native language or communal land. They include the Mashpee, Pequot, Wampanog, Mattapony, Nansemond and Pumunkey who not recognized by the Bureau of Indian Affairs. Some are apparently interconnected. The Magoffin County People of Kentucky are thought to be related to the Carmel Indians who overlap them in the south central hill country of Ohio. Also among the nearly two hundred mestee groups found in the United States are the Sabines, Houmas, Rockingham Surry Group, and Brown People of Virginia

Perhaps someday DNA testing will bring an answer to the questions surrounding these mysterious groups. But in the meantime, isolation, inter-marriages, "passing" as white, and members moving away have proven to make research of these people's true ancestry very difficult.

Orphan Trains

When New York City found itself drowning in immigrants, poor access to medical care, appalling living conditions, homeless people, gangs and no social services, the American Female Guardian Society and Connecticut minister Charles Loring Brace stepped up to help get children into better conditions. Or that was the plan. Some have called it the earliest attempt at "foster care".

In 1854, the first group of "orphans" was sent by train to Dowagic, Michigan. In the next 75 years, more than 200 thousand homeless children were sent west on what became known as the "Orphan Trains." By 1910, children had been sent to 47 states, the District of Columbia, Indian Territory and Canada. The top ten destinations were New York, followed by Illinois, Ohio, Iowa, Missouri, Michigan, New Jersey, Kansas, Indiana and Nebraska.

They traveled in groups of ten to forty, accompanied by at least one agent. Some were orphans: others unwanted. Some were sent in order to rescue them from sick or addicted parents: most were homeless.

Agents planned the route, sent flyers to towns along the route and arranged for committees to screen possible parents. These "parents" were notified of the expected time of arrival. Upon delivery of the children, the new parents signed their contract. Some of these children were adopted: others were indentured. Indentured children did not have the rights of inheritance that adopted children did.

These children are difficult to trace. The adopted ones usually had their names changed to their new parents' surname. The agent could move a child from one home to another and the surname could change with each move. Since birth certificates did not exist for the most part, sometimes baptismal certificates were the only source of birth information. Records of those who were indentured are easier to trace since their records do not have to remain sealed as adoption records do. In addition, the indentured children could keep their birth names and show up in census records.

The Orphan Train Heritage Society has an incomplete list in its database and will search for information. The names in their database have been collected from books, magazines, newspapers and memories. The New York Children's Aid Society will also search, but for only those who can prove direct descent from a suspected Orphan Train passenger.

While most of the "orphans" were gathered in New York, other big cities facing similar problems followed New York's example. Among those groups were Boston's Baldwin Place Mission and Home for Little Wanderers, the Minnesota Home Society, the Chicago Home Society, and even Canadian groups.

No Records At All

One of the most unmanageable problems faced by genealogists are people who lived and died in the United States without leaving a trace.

These are men who arrived without families (may have even jumped ship) and married American women. Some had appeared on wanted posters in their homeland: others may have been military deserters. For whatever reason, they renounced their ancestry and told their children little about their backgrounds while totally assimilating into American culture.

According to Clifford Neal Smith,[35] the 1806 German conscription laws for Wurttemberg were an attempt to gain soldiers to fight for Napoleon, leading many able-bodied young men to turn to America. Some of these southwestern Germans were already serving in the Austrian, Prussian and even Spanish military. Those drafted who did not show up for induction were listed in a gazette in 1807 and their land was confiscated. If they were from Wurttemberg going to America, they probably sailed from northern Germany, Holland or England which were friendlier to their cause. Those historical records have survived.

Unfortunately, the story surrounding ancestor James Montgomery has made it almost impossible for Montgomery researchers to find out much about him. The story passed through four or five generations was that as a boy in Ireland, James had become fascinated with tales of foreign ports told by an old sea captain and decided to stow-away on a ship to America. So, of course, there are no emigration, immigration or ship records.

Montgomery had made it inland to "Skillet" (which turned out to be Lick Skillet, Webster County), Mississippi, where he married Azalean Stewart. Fortunately, marriage records have been found.

The story continued that during the Civil War, James enlisted in the "Mississippi Rebels" (5th Mississippi Infantry) and by November 21, 1861 had received a serious injury to his lung. A year later, he still was unable to perform his duties and was discharged.

A doctor advised James to move west for his health. So in 1863, with the war going on all around them, James and Azalean packed up their small children and began the journey to Arizona. Somewhere along the route, possibly north of Dallas, Texas, James' health turned worse.

35Smith, Clifford Neal. Missing Young Men of Wuertemberg, German, 1807: Some Possible Immigrants to America. German-American Genealogical Research Monograph Number 18. McNeal, Arizona: Westland Publications, 1983.

According to the story, the only help Azalean could find was at a single Indian teepee, out in the middle of the prairie. James died in that teepee in November 1863. After burying him the Indian told Azalean to go home, which she did.

The only documents found for James were military and marriage records. So fewer than five years of his life is documented, the rest remains a mystery. Assuming the family lore is correct, any hope of learning,

- where he came from in Ireland,
- how old he was when he arrived in America,
- what ship he stowed away on,
- what port he arrived at,,
- what year he arrived,
- how or when he arrived in Lick Skillet, or
- where and when he was buried,

is almost non-existent and, in this case, history may not be able to help.

Places That Changed Their Names

Governmental names change. In many cases, the person has not moved, his county has changed its name. Place names change. Duncanville in Dallas County, Texas, has at various times been named Indian Springs, Penn Springs and Duncan Switch.

Place names changed to make them "politically correct" -- less racially or ethnically offensive. "Squaw" and the infamous "N-word" have disappeared from modern American maps. Other, bawdier names, such as Whorehouse, have also disappeared.

Place names changed to honor people and places. Boardwalk, Mississippi, was changed to Starkville to honor a Rev. War brigadier general from New Hampshire who had never been to the town. Nearby Possum Town became Columbus, Doaks Ferry became Lincoln. Following the Crimean War, Pine Grove, California changed its name to Sebastopol. Rome is in Georgia and Athens, Paris and New York are in Texas.

Places changed names when they merged with another place, as when Tanganyika and Zanzibar became Tanzania. Other places changed names when they divided, such as Virginia and West Virginia and North and South Carolina. Just a small taste of place name changes includes --

Old Name	**New Name**
Abyssinia	Ethiopia
Acadia	Prince Edward Island, New Brunswick, Nova Scotia
Cape Breton	Nova Scotia
Ceylon	Sri Lanka
Chosen	Korea
Dearborn	Chicago
Dohomey	Benin
Edo	Tokyo
Fort Orange	Albany
Fort Duquesne	Pittsburgh
Friendly Islands	Tonga
Gold Coast	Ghana
Gran Columbia	Venezuela, Ecuador, Columbia, Panama
India	India, Pakistan and Bangladesh
Kampuchea	Cambodia
Knik Anchorage	Anchorage
Kristiania	Oslo
Leningrad	St. Petersburg, Russia
Livonia	Estonia and Latvia
Losantisville	Cincinnati
Lower Canada	Quebec
Maritime Provinces	Prince Edward Island, New Brunswick, Nova Scotia
Martin's Vineyard	Martha's Vineyard
New France	Canada
New Amsterdam	New York City
New Granada	Venezuela, Ecuador, Columbia
Nueva Espana	Mexico
Peking	Beijing
Persia	Iran
Petrograd	St. Petersburg, Russia
Pig's Eye	St. Paul, Minnesota
Prussia	Germany
Rupert's Land	Northern and Western Canada
Siam	Thailand
Stalingrad	Volgograd
Trucial States	United Arab Emirates
Transjordan	Jordan
Transvaal	South Africa
Upper Canada	Ontario
Urbana-Shari	Central African Republic
Willemstad	Albany
Yerba Buena	San Francisco

Excellent sources are readily available in bookstores, libraries and on the Internet to aid in finding out if an ancestor's native city, county or country ever changed names or was once part of another political division.

Ghost Towns

Sometimes the problem is not that a town's name has changed or its boundaries have moved. Sometimes it is that the town no longer exists. The words "ghost town " conjure up visions of dry Western towns with tumbleweed blowing across the dusty road and saloon doors hanging askew. Thoughts do not go to Maryland and land along the Upper Potomac River -- a mining and lumbering region with lots of little "company towns" that popped up along the river. But the disastrous flood of 1924 forced some of the mines to shut down, while others were simply mined out. Lumbering companies moved away. All those communities became ghost towns when their residents moved away to find employment elsewhere.

Every state has dozens, if not hundreds, of communities that have disappeared for one reason or another. When Hartford lost Pulaski County 's courthouse and jail in 1837, the downhill spiral began. When the railroad was built in Amory, Mississippi in 1887, the businesses and population of nearby Cotton Gin Port were quickly absorbed. Eddyville, Kentucky was moved to make way for a Barkley Dam. Citizens of Calabasas, Arizona were either killed or run-off by Indian raids. A combination of Indians and constant flooding of the Virgin River brought the end to Grafton, Utah. Gold miners deserted Liberty, Washington when they heard about the discovery of gold in Alaska.

But states have varied regulations concerning inclusion or exclusion of communities on their official maps. Texas, for instance, is less likely to delete one of its over 2000 cities or towns then some other states. As recently as 2006, Georgia's Department of Transportation removed nearly five hundred communities from the official Georgia map. They claimed that towns fewer than 2500 residents; like Poetry, Tulip, PoBiddy, Hickory Level, Crossroads, Due West, Hemp, Sharp Top and Roosterville; needed to be dropped to make the map easier to read.

The Three Lost States

Four areas attempted to become the nation's fourteenth state. Vermont succeeded and the other three -- Franklin, Transylvania and

Westmoreland (Wyoming) -- were gobbled up by neighboring states. However, years after they had disappeared, many of their citizens still gave the lost states' names as their place of birth.

Franklin

After the French and Indian War, the British forbade settlement west of the mountains. Many saw that as a good reason to do the exact opposite. Others fled to the northeast corner of present-day Tennessee after the defeat of the Regulators in the Carolinas.

And, as with the Regulators, the people in Upper East Tennessee came to hate their North Carolina leaders so much, they refused to pay their taxes. North Carolina became so disgusted it ceded its western territory. With no more interference from North Carolina, the movement gained momentum with a 1784 meeting in Jonesborough and within several months the state of Franklin was born. They even invited Ben Franklin to live there: the elder statesman declined.

This vast area in the bend of the Tennessee River was probably the most significant of the failed states. It made laws, chose a governor and assembly, organized a court system, collected taxes and wrote a constitution which included a declaration of independence from North Carolina. Soon more settlers arrived. The government was functioning and the settlers were happy.

Eventually, leaders began bickering. They could not agree whether to become a state in the new Union or remain as an independent country. After 1785, the government barely functioned amid continual clashes with officials over the mountains in North Carolina who suddenly wanted the land back and with in-fighting of Franklin's own leaders. The Franklin legislature met for the last time in 1787. Indians began attacking, settlers fled, taxes went unpaid.

In February 1790, North Carolina formally ceded their claim to the land to the new United States of America. It remained a territory until 1796 when it became part of the new state of Tennessee. Franklin's governor during its short life was John Sevier who became the first governor of the Commonwealth of Tennessee.

Transylvania

Transylvania began as pure land speculation, but evolved due to a desire for independence. Circa 1769, jurist Richard Henderson and others from Salisbury, North Carolina formed the Transylvania Company and purchased land between the Kentucky and Cumberland River from the Cherokee. This land; which purposely did not fall under the authority of England or any of her colonies, was intended to be a state of leaseholders.

The Transylvania Company sent Daniel Boone to lead a group of men in search of a path into the land, a route which would eventually become known as the Wilderness Road. The frontier settlement of Boonesborough, with its nearly thirty cabins and one general store, became Transylvania's capital. It had an assembly which made a few laws before being claimed by Virginia following the American Revolution.

Westmoreland

Originally the land was granted by King Charles as part of Connecticut. In late 1768, the Susquehanna met in Hartford to arrange settlement of the twenty mile long by three to four mile wide Wyoming Valley region and the land surrounding it, including all or part of the present Pennsylvania counties of Bradford, Cameron, Centre, Clearfield, Columbia, Elk, Lackawanna, Luzerne, Lycoming, McKean, Montour, Northumberland, Potter, Sullivan, Susquehanna, Tioga, Union and Wyoming.

The first permanent Connecticut settlement in the valley was not established until 1769. When the Connecticut Yankees began to filter into the Wyoming Valley, they discovered that Pennsylvania had also received a grant from King Charles. Pennsylvania's settlement had begun in the mid-1750's, mainly by pockets of farm families.

The settlers on both sides found themselves caught up in a land dispute involving Connecticut, Pennsylvania and the Native Americans. The first Yankee-Pennamite War lasted from 1769 to 1771. Another followed in 1775 and the Third Yankee-Pennamite War was fought in 1783 and 1784. Between these brutal wars the area faced constant, low-grade conflicts.

In the meantime, a government of sorts was put in place. In 1773, an agreement, rather then a constitution, provided for the election of "directors," constables and tax collectors. Public schools were established. Yet, despite the region's declared independence, criminals were still turned over to Connecticut for trial.

The makeshift government lasted only until 1774, when Connecticut assumed jurisdiction and designated a town named Westmoreland stretching from the Delaware River to fifteen miles west of the Wyoming Valley along the New York state line.

In December 1775, Westmoreland was invaded by the Pennsylvania militia and Pennsylvania was granted lands in the Wyoming Valley. In 1776, Connecticut named Westmoreland a county. But in July 1778, the area was the site for the Battle of Wyoming when colonials were defeated by one thousand British, Iroquois and Loyalists who massacred their captives.

After the American Revolution, no one seemed to have authority over the region, so movement for statehood for Westmoreland began in earnest. But a court decree settled the land dispute between Connecticut and Pennsylvania by ruling in favor of Pennsylvania which the settlers in the Wyoming Valley considered an invader.

Meandering Boundaries

Genealogists need to understand the history of the land if they hope to find those ever-important original records. Just because a town is in a certain county, does not mean it has always been in that county, or even the same state. Boundaries grow and shrink with the passage of time.

Take, for instance, Sumner County, in east central Mississippi, which was established in 1874 out of Choctaw County and Montgomery County. But in 1882, Sumner's name was changed to Webster. Prior to 1874, Greensboro had been the county seat for Choctaw County. Suddenly it found itself part of the new county which preferred the more centrally located Walthall to serve as county seat. So, while the records at the former county seat of Greensboro may be in the Webster County courthouse at Walthall, they may also be found in the new Choctaw County courthouse in Ackerman. In addition, when looking for Webster County records, the name Sumner County must remember too.

Likewise, nearby Clay County formed in 1872 out of Mississippi land taken from Lowndes, Oktibbeha and Chickasaw counties, and was originally named Colfax County. The name was changed to Clay in 1876.

While most of those parent counties had been formed out of Indian Territory given up in the Treaty of Dancing Rabbit, in 1830 Lowndes was carved out of Monroe County. To complicate matters even more, Monroe County had been part of Alabama until February 1821, after a survey uncovered a discrepancy and ended up placing it in Mississippi. So, there are parcels of land on which a person could have been born in 1820, lived and died in sixty years later having lived in both Alabama and Mississippi and, at one time or another, in Monroe, Lowndes, Colfax and Clay Counties and while never moving from the family farm.

Further south in Mississippi, most of the land has been in British hands and part of Spanish West Florida. At points, Pennsylvania claimed Buffalo, New York; Massachusetts claimed Maine and New Hampshire claimed Vermont. Connecticut and Pennsylvania, Michigan and Ohio disagreed over their border for years. Maryland gave land to form the District of Columbia. Before the Civil War, Virginia included the area now known as West Virginia

Internationally, the history of Alsace-Lorraine is a perfect example. Whenever a birthplace flip flops on a censuses between France and Germany chances are the birthplace if Alsace or Lorraine. The complex history of this region - sometimes French and sometimes German - has ping-ponged the provinces through the centuries since they was taken from the Romans by the Franks in the late 5th century. More recently the provinces have lived under eight centuries of German influence under the Holy Roman Empire followed by -

1618-1648 Owned by Holy Roman Empire occupied by France
1648-1871 France
1871-1918 German Empire
1919-1940 France

1940-1944	Third Reich (Germany)
1945-	France

To complicate matters even more, since the region was bi-lingual, there were two names for the regions, towns and even surnames.

Alsace (French)	Elsass (German)
Lorraine (French)	Lothringen (German)
Strasbourg (French)	Strassburg (German)

Passenger records might show one family from Lothringen while another passenger record might show a family from Lorraine. Only with the understanding of the history does a researcher realize both families came from the same province.

While always the battleground between two nations, during the Thirty Years War (1618-1648) Alsace-Lorraine saw its population massacred and its land decimated. After so many years of Germanic influence the change to French loyalties came slowly but it did come. During the 1870 Franco-Prussian War, Alsace-Lorraine again became the battleground between two powers. By then patriotically French, thousands migrated to America when Prussia defeated Napoleon II and took the region once again. Schrader-Muggenthale[36] approximated 125,000 people emigrated from Alsace-Lorraine had immigrated to Algeria and America in the 1840's. Then yet again, in World Wars I and II the battlefield was Alsace-Lorraine and many more fled.

Anton and Louis Stoll left Kesseldorf, Alsace in 1850. In the 1860 and 1870 US census, Anton (b. 1816) and his wife Maria (b. 1833) Stoll of Columbia, Monroe County, Illinois, gave France as their places of birth. In 1880, with Alsace under German control, the Stolls listed the German "Elsas" as their birthplaces. However, in the 1900, after Anton and Marie had died and their many children had married, those children listed the birthplace of their parents as Germany. Each response, while confusing to a researcher who did not know the history, was correct at the time it was given.

Unfortunately, Alsace-Lorraine is not the only place where similar confusing conquests have taken place. Just a few include

---

36 Schrader-Muggenthaler, Cornelia. The Alsace Emigration Book. Appolo, Pennsylvania: Closson Press, 1991.

- <u>Korea</u>, also known as Chosen, was taken by the Mongols, made a Kingdom, fought over in the Russo-Japanese War, annexed by Japan and, finally, partitioned into North and South Korea.
- <u>Slovakia</u> began as an independent country, was conquered by the Austro-Hungarian Empire, joined with the Czech Republic to become Czechoslovakia, occupied by German and dominated by the Soviets before becoming an independent Slovakia again.
- <u>Latvia</u> was settled by the Balts, taken over by the Vikings, dominated by the Germans, split between Poland and Sweden, annexed by Russia, given its independence, invaded by the Soviets, occupied by Nazi Germany, incorporated into the Soviet Union, and, finally, received its independence again.
- <u>Tibet</u> was a powerful Buddhist kingdom which was conquered by the Mongols, annexed, given independence after the Chinese Revolution and, invaded by the Chinese Communists
- Similarly, between 1756 and 1870, the Pope had authority over the Papal States which were only part of many small states which would become the country of Italy.

Just as the United States began with colonies joining together, Germany's small states, dukedoms, tribes or principalities eventually united to become confederations and, eventually, countries. German states were not united into the German Empire until 1871. After the 1815 Congress of Vienna, Germany was simply a group of thirty-nine independent states, including the free cities of Luebeck, Bremen and Hamburg. That lasted until the mid-1800s when Bismarck managed to unite Prussia with the collection of kingdoms, provinces, duchies and electorates. Although in 1871 the confederation became the Second German Reich, it was not until after World War I that kingdoms, duchies and earldoms were outlawed and these states were totally absorbed by Germany.

After World War II, Germany was partitioned into East and West Germany and Poland managed to take in parts of Old Prussia. Even Denmark took in the part of Schleswig-Holstein north of Flensburg. The fall of the Berlin Wall signaled the beginning of the end of two Germanys and in 1990 the country was once again united.

This kind of reshaping of countries has happened time and again on continent after continent.

Historical Maps

One of the best ways to understand a region is to collect and study its maps - be they modern or old. Knowing that Great Grandma Thea was born in 1877 to a large family of fishermen in Ärberg, Norway tells us little about her life. Looking at a modern map, Ärberg does not exist anymore. But an historic map shows that Ärberg was once a small village on the tip of Senja Island, sticking out into the Arctic Ocean above the Arctic Circle. The same map reveals that in Thea's day there was just one footpath which led to the nearest village, but no roads. Travel was done by sea. During the long, dark, harsh winters they must have faced incredible hardships? Could enough food be stored during what must have been a very short growing season to feed that large family for the entire winter? Words like "isolated," "frigid," "desolate," and "bleak" suddenly add new dimensions to Thea's childhood. It was a dangerous sea her father and brothers fished and a stark existence her family lived.

County lines were not walls keeping people in for legal and religious services. Learning the roads, paths, towns and borders of an area in which an ancestor lived as they were in his time could reveal that it might have been closer or easier for him to get to a neighboring county seat to file papers or take out a marriage license then to get to his own county seat. No matter how crudely drawn and despite inaccuracies, historic maps could indicate which paths were heavily traveled. When it comes to life's social aspects, as the old saying goes, "Its location, location, location."

Less than a mile from the English border, Gretna Green, Scotland, has been the place young British went to elope since the 1700s. The Marriage Act of 1753 required the English to post banns, secure a license, and hold a service conducted by the clergy in a church or chapel during daylight hours. Those under 21 needed parents' consent to marry. Meanwhile, Scottish law only required that vows be exchanged in front of witnesses. In 1856, Scotland enacted a law requiring a three week residency for marriage in Scotland. While not put completely out of business, Gretna Green saw a drastic drop in marriage from the nearly eight hundred performed in 1855.

Similarly, Maryland developed into a favorite spot for couples from New York and New Jersey to elope to since it had no waiting period. Angola, Indiana, had the first Justice of the Peace over the state line from Michigan at a time when Indiana had "no waiting" marriage licenses and lenient age and parental consent requirements. Las Vegas, Nevada still attracts couples from Southern California, while Reno, Nevada, attracts couples from Northern California. Other elopement destinations like Carson City and Sparks, Nevada, became very popular during wartime.

Despite intending to map all of Britain, including London, and publishing a six volume road atlas, John Ogilby died having completed only one volume and the map of London which were published by 1675. The single volume containing maps of the counties of Kent, Middlesex and Essex, the towns of Canterbury, Ipswich and Maldon, and 7500 miles of road set the bar for Western European maps that followed. Surveyors for Ogilby noted bridges, wall hills, landmarks, inns and, even hedges. Although each map covered about seventy miles in width, the map of London to Landsend was depicted through a series of sheets.

Each historic British Ordnance Survey map covers a 40 km by 40 km area in great detail and reveals changes in every town and village in the country beginning in the early 1800s. Some are so detailed; they indicate who owned which pews in the local church.

Maps from 17th, 18th and 19th century America draw a distinct picture for solving genealogical problems. But the value of maps lies in supplementing or confirming information and as a means to uncover records. The closeness of villages to towns, the closeness of towns to county or even state lines give indications of where records might be hiding. Paths between towns at the time an ancestor lived there lead to churches, schools, and future spouses.

Locating the farm of William Fleetwood in Armuchee, Georgia proved difficult. Several early censuses reported the farm was on Floyd Springs Road. Two later censuses gave "Old" Bells Ferry Road as the location of the Fleetwood home. Yet neighbors remained the same. When the farm was finally found by means of land records, it was on Turkey Mountain Road.

Using old maps of Floyd County, it soon became evident that initially the front of the house was the present-day back and the entrance to the house was from a road 1/4 mile through farm land to the present side of the house. That side road was Floyd Springs Road.

A series of maps indicated that through the years, Bells Ferry Road had changed its course. When new sections were built, the parts of roadway left behind became known as "Old" Bells Ferry. In the meantime, the Fleetwood house went through some remodeling and the back of the farm house became the front, looking out on to "Old" Bells Ferry.

Apparently having a Bells Ferry and an "Old" Bells Ferry in the same area became confusing. So "Old" Bells Ferry Road going past the new front of the Fleetwood house, was renamed Turkey Mountain Road.

Old maps of regions can be found in courthouses, local history museums, local libraries, state libraries, state archives, university libraries, the Library of Congress and, sometimes, online. Among the most useful sorts of maps are -

- Land Office plats at the National Archives were large scale maps of land ownership and allotments which included patentees' names
- Survey maps were the official documentation used to transfer and locate land by giving the legal description.
- Plat maps in courthouses showed ownership, property lines, neighbors and land handed down through the families.
- Sanborn Fire Insurance Maps numbered one million maps covering twelve thousand towns and cities issued and updated by the Sanborn Company at regular intervals from 1867 until 1961. The maps were produced to scale to aid insurance underwriters in determining fire risk and establishing premiums. Changes made between maps were evident. Small villages grew, others disappeared. Streets changed their routes and their names.
- Post route maps illustrated communications beginning in 1839
- Regional planning maps demonstrated population trends, such as race and country of origin, from 1790-1930. The Ohio Valley Regional Planning Committee produced seventy-five large scale

maps of Illinois, Indiana, Kentucky, Ohio, Pennsylvania, Tennessee and West Virginia and even indicated Ohio River flooding of 1936 and 1937. Similar maps have been produced for New England, the Southeast and the Pacific Northwest.

It is not just the old maps that can be beneficial when researching ancestors. Thousand of modern maps have been drawn showing historical migration routes and the demographics of a region. Complete atlases have been published on such diverse subjects as congressional districts, war and ethnicity.

8

Social History and Community Genealogy

"People are the fundamental building blocks of society, and therefore, also are the starting point of all social sciences."

-Robert Charles Anderson "The Place of Genealogy in the Curriculum of the Social Sciences" *Generation and Change: Genealogical Perspectives in Social History*

In his *Dictionary of Concepts in History,* Harry Ritter[37] defined "social history" as "historical writing that concentrates on ... social groups, their inter relationships and their roles in economic and cultural structures and processes..." According to Taylor and Crandall,[38] social history examines "lives & institutions of the common folk" while exploring "patterns of daily life in the context of community; workplace and family."

That is what genealogists do! We have learned that neighboring families attend the same church, intermarry and even migrate together. Using land and census records to find out who were the ancestor's neighbors has become just one technique genealogists use in researching.

Call it "community genealogy."

Our history is our heritage. It is the collected memories of our parents and grandparents and great-grandparents. Social historians study those "memories" that define our beliefs, customs, behaviors and rituals. We act the way we do because our "memory" guides us in that direction. Like the recipe originated with our ancestors and passed on to us, a lot of what we do, how and why we react, comes from incidents in our ancestors' lives.

Generations of a family went to jail. Bigotry continued. Farmers had farmers. Miners had miners. Generation after generation of other families were in the military. Values and beliefs, work ethic and financial responsibility, alcoholism and temperance. "We're dog people." "We're cat

---

37 Ritter, Harry. Dictionary of Concepts in History. New York: Greenwood Press, 1986.
38 Taylor, Robert M. Jr. And Ralph J. Crandall (eds) Generations and Change: Genealogical Perspective in Social History. Macon, Georgia: Mercer University Press, 1986.

people." "We don't hug." "We don't cry." "We've always done it that way!" The circle remains unbroken and few, if any, know where in the family it began

It all depends on the recipe for life passed on to the next generation.

With German air raids during World War II, British cities became dangerous places. In 1939, London became a childless city when over a four-day period the government evacuated two million urban English and Scottish children age 16 and under and mothers of children under five to the countryside. Nine roads were made one-way heading out of the city of London for the period of the evacuation. However, the disruption of Britain's transportation system lasted far longer than the four days.

Likewise, some of the social problems that followed the evacuation had only a short term effect, some much longer. Many were the poor from the congested urban slums. Suddenly the cities' poor were living in the middle and upper class rural homes that received them -- a mix that did not always work well. Both sides -- evacuees and welcomers -- had to make major adjustments.

The influx also put a strain on the infrastructure of the receiving communities. Suddenly they had to provide medical care, food, water, schooling and sanitation to the community's newest residents.

The social historian looks at the interactions of communities of multi-class groups like the poor of London in the countryside and of multi-ethnic groups, like the Melungeons; the effects of urbanization or industrialization on people, like Southern rural African-Americans who moved to the North for work; and the outcome of social dissent like striking mine workers. Social historians know it would be wrong to study plantation life of the antebellum South and ignore slavery.

The community does not have to have geographical boundaries. Just because a particular group is in a particular place at this time does not mean that is the way it has always been. Today's Caucasus have twenty-eight ethnic groups, all or part of whose territory has been fought over and been claimed by the Mongol, , Ottoman and Russian Empires. Although united by geography, the Kurds have never had a nation of their own. Instead, they have been part of Kurdistan, Turkey, Syria and Iraq.

Then in 1944, the Soviets moved the entire Chechen nation into central Asia. Those who wished to return to their land were not allowed to go home until 1957.

Using social history places an ancestor in the context of the world in which he lived and the people he associated with through his work, ethnic, religious or geographical communities, not in the context of the world of today with its computers and air conditioning and cell phones and automobiles.

The lynchpin of both genealogy and social history is people. But as Robert Charles Anderson[39] pointed out, the difference is that genealogists use specific tools to uncover a "body of facts" while social historians produce interpretations in addition to a body of facts. Genealogists look at individuals, while social historians look at populations. Genealogists study only one type of relationship, familial; while social historians study many types.

Immigration

We joke that everyone brings some "baggage" into a relationship. We seldom realize how true that saying is and how that "baggage" comes into our family and our history. As librarian and genealogist Lloyd Bockstruck[40] wrote

> "each of us is affected by decisions made by others in our past. Sometimes we regret those choices of our ancestors. Sometimes we are unaware that they explain a lot about us until we learn who our ancestors were. Simply understanding why you were born in a certain locality and not another can have ramifications."

For instance, take the life changes of Albert Jakobsen, a fisherman born on Senja Island in Norway, who took his young family to join his brother Jens on a farm on the prairies of North Dakota, far from any sea. Another brother followed, and a sister, and an uncle and cousins. Because of that first migration made by Jens and the wonderful tales he sent back

39 Anderson, Robert Charles. "The Place of Genealogy in the Curriculum of the Social Sciences." Generations and Change: Genealogical Perspectives in Social History. Robert M. Taylor, Jr. And Ralph J. Crandall (eds). Macon, Georgia: Mercer University Press, 1986.

40 Bockstruck, Lloyd. "All the king's descendants." Family Tree. Dallas Morning News. Saturday, December 14, 2002. p 8C.

home, the lives of so many changed. Instead of being born to the sea, the next generations were born to the plow. Instead of Norwegian, they were born Americans.

While generally encouraging immigration, through the centuries Americans have looked suspiciously at groups perceived as different because of their in languages, customs, religion or race. From the beginning of our country, immigrants experienced disdain -- first the Quakers, then the Scots-Irish. Suspicion and resentment have fallen at various times on the Italians, Chinese, Africans, Irish, Polish, Japanese, Germans, Puerto Ricans, Cubans, Vietnamese and Mexicans. Provisions of the United States immigration laws made this possible.

1790	Congress adopted the rule that "any alien, being a free white person" could apply for citizenship after two years residency & swearing loyalty to the US Constitution
1795	Act of 1790 was amended to require a five year residency for citizenship rather than two
1798	Alien and Sedition Acts required fourteen years residency before citizenship & permitted deportation of "dangerous" aliens
1800	Required residency before citizenship was changed to five years
1806-14	Immigration slowed amid hostilities between France & England
1819	The Steerage Act required the enumeration of immigrants
1850	The California Foreign Miner's Tax imposed a $20 per month tax on foreign miners.
1851	California Foreign Miner's Tax was repealed because miners were leaving the state.
1852	California Foreign Miner's Tax reinstated at $3 per month
1854	California Supreme Court ruled testimony Chinese concerning whites was invalid. Previously that law applied to Indians & blacks
1857	Dred Scott Decision declared slaves were not citizens
1860s	Homestead Act of 1862, granting citizens 160 acres, attracted approximately two million immigrants -- primarily Irish, English & German -- and encouraged naturalization
1862	California imposed "police tax" of $2.50 a month on each Chinese
1864	Act allowed employers to recruit labor from Northern & Western Europe when the Homestead Act of 1862 & the Civil War depleted urban areas of industrial workers
1864	Congress passed a law making the importation of laborers easier
1864	An attempt to encourage immigration centralized immigration authority with the Federal government
1868	Burlingame Treaty gave commercial advantages in exchange for free migration & emigration of Chinese
1870	California Foreign Miner's Tax was eliminated after begin repeatedly raised
1870	Naturalization Act gave right of citizenship to those of African birth or descent
1873	Injunctions against Chinese testimony was repealed

1875 Residency permits required of Asians
1875 Court found state immigration laws were unconstitutional
1875 Congress passed the first law restricting immigration by prohibiting prostitutes or convicts from entering the country
1882 Chinese Exclusion Act curtailed the immigration of Chinese for ten years and barred Chinese from US citizenship
1882 Congress barred convicts, lunatics, idiots & people expected to Be public charges & placed a head tax of fifty cents on immigrants
1885 Contract labor laws allowing importation of unskilled aliens ended, Although crossing land borders was still allowed.
1886 Washington State barred Asians from owning land
1888 Provisions for expulsion of aliens were updated
1890 Congress appropriated $75 thousand to build a Federal immigration station on Ellis Island. Meanwhile, the Barge Office at Manhattan processed immigrants.
1891 Immigration placed under the Treasury Department
1891 Federal government assumed responsibility of overseeing immigration
1892 Citizenship was granted to Native Americans
1892 Ellis Island opened, replacing Castle Garden in New York City
1897 Buildings on Ellis Island burned, destroying numerous immigration records dating from 1855 & closing the immigration center
1898 *US v. Wong Kim Ark* found that a child born in the United States to Chinese people residing in American was a citizen of the US
1900 Ellis Island reopened
1902 Chinese Exclusion Act renewed
1903 Angel Island Detention Center, where Chinese immigrants were detained, was declared unfit for human habitation
1903 Congress added epileptics, beggars, polygamists, anarchists & other radicals to the list of excluded immigrants
1905 Construction began on new Angel Island Immigration Center in San Francisco Bay
1906 San Francisco school board ordered segregation of Orientals
1906 Naturalization Act required the ability to speak & understand English as a qualification for citizenship & changed the Bureau of Immigration to the Bureau of Immigration and Naturalization which was to keep all naturalization records
1906 Immigration Act prohibited migration of Japanese & Koreans from Hawaii
1907 Congress raised the head tax on immigrants
1907 People with physical or mental defects that could affect their ability to earn a living, those with tuberculosis & unaccompanied children were added to list of excluded immigrants
1907 The United States & Japan reached an agreement limiting Japanese immigration
1907 Ellis Island 's peak year, with over one million immigrants
1910 Congress' Dillingham Report suggested a literacy test to restrict immigrants from eastern & southern Europe
1910 Angel Island reopened
1915 State of Washington barred Asian immigrants from taking salmon or shellfish for sale or profit
1917 Congress included a literacy test which banned anyone over 16

years of age who could not read in some language & everyone from Asia from immigrating.

1918-19 Ellis Island became a stop for wounded US servicemen after immigration declined during World War I

1921 Law passed setting quotas, based on foreign born of that nationality already in US in order to limit European immigration

1921 Washington State law prevented non-citizens from owning land

1922 Japanese declared ineligible for citizenship

1924 Immigration Act changed quotas from being based on the 1910 census to the 1890 census

1924 Oriental Exclusion Act banned immigration from Asia

1924 Johnson-Reed Act set annual quotas for each nation.

1924 Border Patrol established

1924 National Origins Act

1927 Immigration quotas were reduced again

1929 Law declared re-entry of a deported felon to be a felony, entry of an alien by fraud a crime while adding additional categories of those ineligible to enter

1930 President Hoover directed strict enforcement of the provision barring people who might become a public charge

1930s More than 100 thousand Mexicans were forced to return to Mexico

1931 Law provided that any alien guilty of violating US law could be deported

1932 Provided that quota limits did not apply to spouses of US citizens

1933 More than thirty thousand illegal Mexican aliens were deported

1934 Filipino immigration was reduced to fifty per year

1937 Washington extended alien land restrictions to Filipinos

1940 New law required fingerprinting & registration of aliens

1940 Immigration and Naturalization was transferred to Department of Justice

1941 Ellis Island became a detention center for suspected enemy aliens

1941 Washington State Supreme Court ruled against the 1937 amendment to the state's Alien Land Law

1942 Franklin Roosevelt signed an executive order sending persons of Japanese ancestry on the Pacific Coast to internment camps

1942 The US & Mexico agreed to allow temporary foreign laborers to work in the United States

1943 Congress repealed the ban on Chinese immigrants

1944 Korematsu v. the US ruled the exclusion of Japanese from West Coast was justified

1945 The War Brides Act allowed the entry of spouses & children of US military personnel

1946 Luce-Cellar Bill granted naturalization to Asians, Filipinos & Indians

1948 Displaced Persons Act allowed the entrance to the US of an additional 205 thousand displaced persons

1950 All aliens were required to report their address annually

1950s Because of shortage, special immigrant laws were passed to allow Basque sheep herders into the US on non-quota visas

Understanding the history of immigration is vital when searching for immigration and naturalization records. Prior to 1906, no Immigration and Naturalization Bureau existed. Earlier records lay with the court.

Following the Immigration Act of 1924, all aliens entering the United States were required to present a visa. The type of visa required depended upon the country of origin and the reason for entry.

Type of visa	Qualifications for visa
Quota	Applicant was native of a country subject to quota. This included most European & Asian Countries.
Non-Quota	Applicant was a native of a country not subject to quotas. Between 1924 & 1944, this included all North, Central & South American countries.
Immigrant	Applicant wished to move to the US permanently.
Non-Immigrant	Applicant wished to vacation, attend school or conduct business in the US on a temporary basis.

A French fisherman wishing to settle in the United States applied for a Quota Immigrant visa. A Brazilian wishing to attend a business conference would apply for a Non-Quota Non-Immigrant visa.

Beginning in 1940, all resident aliens over 14 years of age were required to be fingerprinted and registered. Since 1944, alien files have been maintained on all individual, documented immigrants.

The American Industrial Revolution

While the arrival of a large numbers of immigrants created new social problems, industrialization and economic expansion with the accompanying radical fiscal changes, escalated into the economic boom of the Industrial Revolution of the 19th century. Changes coming out of the Industrial Revolution had wide ranging repercussions. Socially, people migrated from rural to urban areas. Technologically, spinning machines of the 1730s and 1740s advanced the textile industry as did Cartwright's power loom of the 1780s. And on it went.

Year	Inventor	Invention
1712	Newcomen	First practical steam engine
1733	Kay	Flying shuttle for weaving (power loom)

1764	Watt	Improved steam engine
1769	Arkwright	Spinning frame
1781	Watt	Improvements to steam engine
1789	Slater	Mass production of thread
1793	Whitney	Cotton gin
1801	Fulton	Submarine & torpedo
1807	Fulton	Commercial steamboat
1827	Walker	Matches
1831	McCormick	Mechanical harvesting machine
1844	Morse	First practical telegraph system
1844	Howe	Sewing machine
1852	Otis	Elevator
1853	Strauss	Blue jeans
1856	Bessemer	Improved steel manufacturing
1867	Latham	Typewriter
1876	Bell	Telephone
1877	Edison	Phonograph
1879	Edison	Incandescent light bulb
1903	Wright	Airplane
1908	Ford	Model T & assembly line

In addition to the inventions of the period, the United States saw the building of the Erie Canal (1818-1825), America's first oil well (1859), and the completion of a transcontinental railroad (1869). Financially, the United States revolutionized its economic base in less than 200 years. Politically, the disparity in the rate of industrialization changed the balance of power. The Ottomans lost their hold on Europe while English, Dutch and French production exploded.

Associations, Brotherhoods, Societies and Unions

While the Industrial Revolution pulled people to cities, factory workers earned miserable wages for a long day's work and no voice. When workers died, dependants were left destitute. Meanwhile, farm families similarly faced losing their land and livelihood when the head of the family died. Following the Civil War, two major depressions brought people together to form fraternal brotherhoods or benevolent associations based on insuring and providing mutual aid for members. Next came the coupling of issues, such as wages and hours, in an attempt to provide economic stability through unions.

By 1896, at least one in fifteen Americans belonged to a fraternal organization. The largest of them were

Ancient Order of United Workmen
Ancient Order of Foresters of America
Ancient Order of Hibernians of America
Improved Order of Red Men
Junior Order of United American Mechanics
Knights of the Maccabees
Knights of Honor
Knights of Pythias
Modern Woodmen of America
Odd Fellows
Royal Arcanum

Organizations, like the Freemasons, had lodges in communities of every size and the state lodge retained information concerning members of lodges under their charter. Some state lodges have even published books, such as the *Annual Returns: Mississippi Free and Accepted Masons,* which was filled with genealogically helpful information. By contacting a lodge at the state level, a researcher might find an ancestor's

Date of death
Place of residence
Approximate age
Dates of membership
Names of family members
Obituaries of recent & past officers

Other types of organizations united people with similar needs and interests. Some began as hereditary organizations dependant upon an ancestor, frequently centered on a military, as was Grand Army of the Republic, or an historical event, as was General Society of Mayflower Descendants. There were groups for tavern owners and temperance advocates. There were organizations based on nationalities and occupations. Steelworkers, auto workers, cigar makers, iron molders and granite cutters all organized. While some became unions and others became insurance companies, many remained social. They all seemed to fall into certain categories.

Early settlers
Ethnic groups
Family names
Geography
Hate
Lineage
Local history
Masonic
Military
National origin
Professional
Religion
Secret societies
Security (such as, insurance)
Social
Time period

Members of organizations similar to the Daughters of the American Revolution (DAR) have carefully documented each member's lineage back to at least one particular ancestor. Cemetery associations have kept records of who have been buried in their local cemetery. Military units have published reunion books. Ethnic societies have published research guides and record abstracts. Many groups have even put some of their records on the Internet. Alumni associations, medical and dental societies, the Boy Scouts, and even purported secret societies have kept records.

Secret societies have existed for thousands years. Freemasonry is one of the oldest to survive to the present day. Some secret societies were the beginning of religious sects: others became political movements.

To determine which organization may have information, a researcher may need to know the ancestor's occupation, ethnicity or religion and what military events occurred during his lifetime. Although there are far too many to list here, a brief sampling of societies include

Adirondacks Historic Society
African Blood Brotherhood
Afro-American Historical & Genealogical Soc.
Aid Association for Lutherans
Alabama Baptist Society
Albanian Catholic Charities
Alliance of Transylvania Saxons
Amalgamated Assoc. Of Iron, Steel & Tin Workers
Amalgamated Clothing Workers
American Federation of Labor
American Foundrymen's Assoc.
American Indian Historical Society
American Woman Suffrage Assoc.
Ancient Arabic Order of the Nobles of the Mystic Shriners
Ancient Mystic Order of Bagmen of Baghdad
Ancient Order of United Workmen
Anti-Horse-Thief Association
Anti-Thief Association
Arctic Brotherhood
Asia Society
Association of Lithuanian Workers
Association of Union Veterans
AztecClub of 1847
B'nai B'rith
Bavarian National Association
Beavers Reserve Fund Society
Benevolent Order of Buffaloes
Benevolent Order of ScottishClans
Black Archives in Mid-America
Black Railroad Workers
Black Rev. War Patriots Foundation
Brotherhood of Electrical Employees
Brotherhood of American Yeoman
Brotherhood of Locomotive Engineers
Byelorussian Congress
Carpenters Union
Catholic Family Life Insurance Society
Catholic Total Abstinence Society
Chicago Marble Setters Union
Children's Aid Society
Chinese Society of America
Clan Carmichael USA
Civil War Descendants
Civitan
Colonial Society Sons of Indian Wars
Columbian Knights
Court of Honor
Croatian Fraternal Union
Czech Heritage Foundation
Czechoslovak Society of America
Dames of Malta
Danish Brotherhood of America
Danish Refugees Council
Daughters of Scotland
Daughters of Rebekah
Daughters of the Republic of Texas

Daughters of Union Civil War Veterans
Degree of Pocahontas
Descendants of Colonial Tavernkeepers
Descendants of Mexican War Veterans
Descendants of Whaling Masters
Exhausted Society of Order of Hounds (Salesmen)
Farmers Alliance & Industrial Union
Fenian Brotherhood
First Catholic Slovak Union
First Families of the State of Franklin
Foresters of America
Fraternal Order of Bears
Fraternal Order of Police
Fraternal Order of Orioles
Free Sons of Israel
French Heritage Society
Friends Historical Society
Genealogical Soc. of Flemish Americans
General Soc. of Mayflower Descendants
German Freedom Society
German Order of Harugari
Gideons
Gleaners
Grain Dealers Association
Grand Army of the Republic
Greek Catholic Union
Grotto
Hadassah
Hawaii Sugar Planter Association
Homesteaders' Life Association
Huguenot Soc. of the Founders of Manakin in the Colony of Virginia
Hungarian Reformed Federation
Immigrant Genealogical Society
Improved Order of Red Men
International Black Sheep Society
Intern'l Brotherhood of Old Bastards
Intern'l Brotherhood of Blacksmiths& Helpers
Intern'l Order of Hoo-Hoo
Intern'l Order of Oddfellows
Independent Order of Puritans
Independent Order of Vikings
Irish Protestant Association
Italo-American National Union
Jewish Genealogical Society
Jewish War Veterans
Job's Daughters
Johannes Schwalm Historical
Jovian Order
Kiwanis International
Knights of Columbus
Knights of Labor
Knights of Loyola
Knights of the Golden Circle
Knights Templar
Lancaster & Mennonite Historical Society
League of Foreign-Born Citizens
Legion of Honor
Lions International
Lithuanian Alliance of America
Loyal Order of Buffaloes
Lutheran Brotherhood of America
Maine Boys Sweet Corn Club
Melungeon Heritage Association
Mennonite Historical Society
Merrill's Marauders Association
Mexican Veterans Association
Michigan Cock Fanciers Association
Military Order of the Purple Heart
Mineral Mine Smelters Association
Molly Maguires
Mutual Benefit Society
Nantucket Historical Association
National Catholic Society of Foresters
National Fed. of Temple Brotherhoods
National Fraternal Society of the Deaf
National Huguenot Society
National Grain Dealers Association
Nat'l Japanese American Historical Society
National Military Family Association
National Slovak Society
National Soc. Daughters of the American Revolution
Native Sons of the Golden West
Nobles of the Mystic Shrine
Odd Fellows
Ohio Genealogical Society
Old Time Telegraphers
Order of Anti-Poke Noses
Order of Artistic Typists
Order of Bugs
Order of Daedalians
Order of First Families of Mississippi

Order of Hibernians
Order of Houn' Dawgs
Order of Scottish Clans
Order of the Bath of the USA
Order of the Eastern Star
Order of the Sons of Hermann
Order of the Sons of Italy
Order of Yellow Dogs
Orphan Train Heritage Society
Orthodox Society of America
Patrons of Husbandry (Grange)
Pilgrim Society
Pioneer Fraternal Association
Point Lookout POW Descendants
Polish Beneficial Association
Portuguese Continental Union
Protestant Knights of America
Quarrymen's Association
Red Cross of Constantine
Rotary International
Royal Neighbors
Royal Order of Scotland
Scandinavian American Fraternity
Serb National Federation
Showmen's League of America
Slavonic Catholic Society
Slovene National Benefit Society
Soc. for the Preservation & Encouragement of Barbershop QuartetSinging
Society of Loyalist Descendants.
Society of United Irishmen
Society of the Whiskey Rebellion
Sons of Abraham
Sons of Confederate Veterans
Sons of Italy
Sons of Malta
Sons of Norway
Sons of Temperance
Sons of the American Revolution
Sons of the Republic of Texas
Spanish-American War Veterans.
St. Andrews Society
States' Rights Association
Tall Cedars of Lebanon of the USA
Temple of Honor & Temperance
Travelers Protective Association
Tuskegee Airmen Inc.
Ukrainian Historical Association
United Ancient Order of Druids
United Commercial Travelers of America
United Daughters of the Confederacy
United Mine Workers
United Order of True Sisters
United Paperworkers International
United Spanish War Veterans
United States Letter Carriers Mutual Benefit Association
Veterans of Foreign Wars
Vietnam Veterans of America
Volstead Volunteer Vigilantes
Volunteers of America
Welsh Society
Western Bohemian Fraternal Assoc.
White Rats of America (Vaudeville)
White Shrine of Jerusalem
Woman's Christian Temperance Union
Woman's Missionary Society
Women Army Corps veterans
Women's Benefit Association
Woodmen of the World
Workmen's Circle
Young Men's/Women's Christian Assoc.
Xavier Society for the Blind
Zionist Organization of America

Some are now extinct, others have combined. Many have sister societies similar to the Ladies' Society of the Brotherhood of Locomotive Firemen and Enginemen. The *Encyclopedia of Associations* with its handy keyword index, available at most university and large public libraries, can help find organizations still around today.

The Rise of Labor Unions

Eventually some fraternal organizations based on occupations turned into labor unions. Membership lists varied since a myriad of industries organized unions early. They sprang up amid tenements and sweat shops of the cities and children in southern mills and coal miners of Appalachia. In the early 19th century workers attempt to unite in bargaining or dealing with employers was short lived and related to specific problems. But, by the end of the 19th century unions were entrenched in our psych.

1648 Shoemakers & coopers in Boston formed guilds.
1677 Cartera strike in New Yorkled to 1st US court case involving strikes
1770 Conflict between rope workers & British soldiers set off the Boston Massacre
1806 Philadelphia Journeymen Cordwainers Union charged with criminal conspiracy after a strike
1824 Mill workers protested in Pawtucket, Rhode Island
1825 Boston carpenters went on strike for a 10-hour work day
1827 City-wide labor council formed in Philadelphia
1828 Women mill workers struck in Dover, New Hampshire
1831 United Tailoresses' Society went on strike in New York
1834 National Trades' Union became 1st nationwide union
1834 Eight hundred female mill workers in Lowell, Massachusetts went on strike
1853 The General Trades' Union founded in Cincinnati
1853-54 More than four hundred strikes nationwide
1859 Mill workers in Lowell, Massachusetts on strike
1860 Nearly fifty thousand working men & women marched during a Lynn, Massachusetts shoemakers' strike
1866 National Labor Union (NLU) formed
1869 The Knights of Labor was founded by Philadelphia tailors
1874 Cigar Makers International Union used a union label for first time
1877 First nationwide strike stopped trains & incited riots across the country
1877 Coal-mining activists (Molly Maguires) were hanged in Pennsylvania
1877 "The Great Uprising" of railroad workers
1882 First Labor Day Parade in New York City
1884 Federation of Organized Trades & Labor Unions called for an eight hour work day
1886 Bomb exploded during a labor demonstration in Chicago. Rioting followed.
1886 Two thousand Polish workers marched through Milwaukee speaking out against the ten-hour work day
1886 Samuel Gompers founded the American Federation of Labor (AFL)
1886 Knights of Labor marched, demanding an 8-hour work day

1886 Fights broke out between unionists & non-unionists hired to replace them in Haymarket Square riot in Chicago (4 died & 7 policemen were killed)
1887 Thirty-five unarmed black sugar workers were shot & two were hanged by Louisiana Militia during a strike
1888 Railway car men united to provide death & disability benefits.
1890 New York garment workers won right to unionize after seven month strike
1892 Strikers at Carnegie Steel Plant in Homestead, Pennsylvania held out for five months
1892 Frisco Mine in Coeur d'Alene, Idaho dynamited by striking miners
1894 Federal troops called in for fifty thousand involved in the Pullman Strike (34 railway workers killed)
1896 Colorado state militia called on to break a miners strike in Leadville
1897 Nineteen unarmed striking mine workers were killed by a sheriff-lead posse in Lattimer, Pennsylvania
1898 Two hundred non-union, black mine workers went on strike (14 killed)
1899 Members of Western Federation of Mines dynamited Idaho mill
1899 Federal troops occupied Coeur d'Alene, Idaho mine region
1902 Fourteen miners killed in Pana, Illinois
1903 Child workers led by "Mother" Jones demanded 55-hour work week
1904 Dunnville, Colorado mining strike (6 union members killed, 15 taken prisoner & 79 deported to Kansas)
1905 The radical International Workers of the World (IWW) formed with the aim to replace capitalism with a socialist system.
1906 International Typographical Union went on strike calling for an eight-hour day
1909 Female garment workers walked out on strike in New York
1910 Llewellyn Ironworks in Los Angeles was dynamited during a strike
1912 National Guard called out for coal miners strike in West Virginia
1912 Police beat women & children during a textile strike in Lawrence, Massachusetts
1913 US established the Department of Labor to protect worker's rights
1913 Silk Workers Strike in Paterson, New Jersey
1913 Three maritime workers striking against the United Fruit Company in New Orleans were shot
1914 Clayton Antitrust Act legalized non-violent strikes & boycotts
1914 Militia halted Western Federation of Mines Strike in Montana
1914 Company guards attacked a striking union's tent camp with machine guns & set fire to it (19 men, women & children killed)
1914 Amalgamated Clothing Workers organized
1916 Strikebreakers beat picketing strikers in Everett, Washington while police looked on
1918 United Mine Workers organizers were killed
1919 Boston police called for a work stoppage after attempts to join the AFL were thwarted
1919 Roughly 350,000 steel workers walked off their jobs demanding recognition of their union
1919 Four million workers went on strike over the year

1920 In "Palmer Raids" federal agents seized union leaders & literature
1920-21 Army troops intervened in West Virginia miners' strikes
1922 Coal miners strike in Herrin, Illinois (36 died in violence)
1924 Child labor amendment to Constitution failed
1925 Company houses of non-union members were dynamited in Wheeling, West Virginia
1926 Textile workers in Passaic, New Jersey held a year-long strike
1927 Picketing miners massacred in Columbine, Colorado
1930 Farm workers from Imperial Valley, California were arrested for attempting to unionize
1931 Vigilantes attacked striking miners in Harlan County. Kentucky
1932 Striking Ford auto workers killed by police in Dearborn, Michigan
1933 About 18,000 cotton workers went on strike in Pixley, California
1934 Textile workers in Woonsocket, Rhode Island went on strike
1934 National Guard killed strikers at Electric Auto-Lite in Toledo, Ohio
1935 Wagner Act (National Labor Relations Act) gave workers the right to unionize
1935 Taft-Hartley Labor Act limited some powers of unions & circumstances under which they could strike
1935 John L. Lewis broke with the AFL & formed the Committee of Industrial Organization, later named the Congress of Industrial Organizations (CIO)
1937 United Auto Workers (UAW) signed first General Motors contract
1938 Fair Labor Standards Act & its later amendments established a minimum wage, banned child labor & set the forty-hour work week.
1943 Amalgamated Clothing Workers set-up an insurance fund
1946 Twenty-state strike of oil refineries
1946 Nation-wide packinghouse strike
1950 President Truman ordered the army to seize all railroads nationwide to ward off a general strike.
1952 Truman ordered army seizure of US steel mills to prevent strike.
1955 AFL & CIO merged forming the country's largest labor union

Unionization was not solely an American phenomenon. Deplorable working conditions could and still can be found worldwide. Alan Campbell[41] studied Lanarkshire, Scotland, mines and their unionization. He compared wages for Govan and Lanark miners and discovered they peaked in 1825 and 1836, while they dropped drastically in 1816, 1827, 1831 and 1839, which would explain migrations to England and the US.

The colliers' discontent had been long coming. According to Campbell, as early as the late 1500s,

> "a miner named John Henry ... set fire to the coal pit of his master Mungo McCall. Because he didn't have the freedom he had under his previous master, "Johnne Levingstoun." Henry

---

41 Campbell, Alan. The Lanarkshire Miners: A Social History of their Trade Unions, 1775-1874. Edinburgh: John Donald, 1979.

was hanged, beheaded and his head stuck on a stake as a warning to others who might rebel."

During the 1816-17 decline in wages, the Ayrshire secretary of the Colliers Association put together a budget for a family of five which included one pound of meat per day for the family and two shillings six pence per week on such luxuries as clothing, tea, sugar and tobacco which added up to a good deal more than the miners were making.[42] Reasons for emigrating from Scotland might be found in these statistics.

Salary	1811	1839
weekly wages	22s 1 ½d	15s 9d
value of free house	1s 2d	1s 0d
value of free coal	1s 5d	0s 6d
Total Salary	**24s 8 ½d**	**17s 5d**

Genealogical Material Found in Books

Local Histories

A new genealogist is told local newspapers are good sources - places to learn who came to town to visit, who married whom and what relatives attended the ceremony. In reality, the average man of the 1800s did not live in town: he was a farmer who raised a bunch of kids, struggled to pay his bills, nearly broke his back tilling his fields, and never appeared in the local newspaper. As with most people who lived in the area, he also did not end up being mentioned in the local history book. So when his descendant finds that local history and turns to the index, if there is one, his name will not be listed. At that point, his descendant usually says "Darn" or something more colorful, shuts the book and returns it to its shelf.

Instead, the researcher should still study an area's local and geographic histories and look for settlement patterns to understand what was going on when the ancestor lived there even if the ancestor was never mentioned. Local or county histories tell what groups arrived and when the community was established, where ethnic clusters settled, what and where churches were established, what occupations the first residents

42 Campbell, Alan. The Lanarkshire Miners: A Social History of their Trade Unions, 1775-1874.

followed, how lives were affected by local events, where canals were built and railroads went through, when mines opened up and closed down, what the settlement pattern was. Did all the Norwegians end up around one community in the county, as they did in Henderson County, Texas? Did a congregation arrive together? If so, where did they originate? Was the Catholic Church a fairly recent addition or was it one of the first churches built? What transportation systems helped shape the growth pattern? What epidemics and conflicts occurred in the area?

While state, national and international history is important, generalizations cannot be made without understanding local history, culture and traditions. The introduction of the Scots-Irish to Appalachia, the mixture of French, Spanish and English in Louisiana, the blending of French and English cultures in Eastern Canada have made those areas of North America unique.

This is social history or community studies.

The local histories of John Winthrop (*History of New England* or *Winthrops Journal*), John Smith (*A Generall Historie of Virginia*) and William Bradford (*History of Plymouth Plantation*) have become more important to the study of those early colonies than most of the more recent publications.

Admittedly, that has not been the case with all local histories. In *The Past Before Us*, historian Kathleen Neils Conzen[43] wrote that

> "after almost a century in the historigraphical wilderness, the history of life at the local level emerged in the 1970's as one of the most lively and promising areas of historical inquiry in the United States ... Not that America has been without a local history tradition. Until very recently, however, it has not been an academic one."

While interest in urban history has led to a large number of studies and dissertations, post colonial rural communities have received very little attention from historians. Agricultural specialists documented more of the changes then historians.

Conzen went on to explain that for some reason, in the 19th century "numerous gifted and not-so-gifted amateurs" became "compulsive

---

43 Conzen, Kathleen Neils. "Community Studies, Urban History, and American Local History." The Past Before Us. Michael Kammen (ed.) Ithaca: Cornell University Press, 1980.

chroniclers of local history" and went on to found historical collections, societies and journals. Although insulated from standards set by academic historians, and driven by unfettered bias, unchecked heroic tales, misguided enthusiasm; sometimes these "amateurs," as Conzen called them, were the only ones recording local history. It really was not until the country's Bicentennial that professional historians really took an active a role in the study of communities. Before then, local, and even regional, history had often been considered by historians as less than relevant to history on the grander scale and academic historians often saw local or regional historians on the same footing as they viewed genealogists.

A true local history balances generalizations with detail. Even though Conzen does not say it, scores of early local histories were anecdotal. While the social historian might not find that sort of writing beneficial, the genealogist does.

Today, states have begun digitalizing all their county histories. Small Henderson County, Texas has several local histories and biographies and is home to a local history museum. Its active historical commission and its local historical and genealogical societies have their own web sites.

Social History Books

Alan Campbell's social history of miners of Lanarkshire, Scotland[44] examined an entire shire. In one chapter, two hamlets -- Coatbridge with 29.1% of its adult population working in the mines in 1861, and Larkhall with 26.8% -- were compared. As a descendant of Larkhall miners, I found this chapter especially interesting

The difference between the two towns came with the remainder of the male working population. Coatbridge workers were largely unskilled while Larkhall had 31.1% who were skilled weavers and 4% who were employers or professionals. Campbell found an 1869 description of Coatbridge by a David Bremner who wrote that the hamlet was

> "within a crescent of blast furnaces and in the town are a large number of rolling mills, forges and tube works, the

44 Campbell, Alan. The Lanarkshire Miners: A Social History of their Trade Unions, 1775-1874.

> hundred chimneys of which form quite a forest of brickwork capped with fire ... it is anything but beautiful.

Despite the conditions, the outlook for trade unionism in Coatbridge was bleak at the time.

On the opposite end of the spectrum, Larkhall became one of the best organized union districts in Lanarkshire and a description Campbell found showed life in that hamlet still hard but more pastoral with Thomas Stewart, a Larkhall collier describing

> "Mrs. McGuil, a housewife in a neighboring cottage, would regularly thresh corn along with her daughter in their barn and even plough their plot of land while her husband and sons worked the mine."

Campbell even described the marriage customs of the Lanarkshire region.

> The bride and groom were escorted to the church by a fiddler and other couples. After the service, they paraded through the countryside, their friends firing shotguns in the air in celebration. The wedding supper was followed by dancing and drinking followed by the ceremony of "bedding" the newlyweds.[45]

Another example of a social history study useful to the genealogist is a Masters Theses at the University of Mississippi by John Cooper Hathorn[46] which documented the social and commercial life of Lafayette County, Mississippi landowners. To that end, Hathorn searched records to determine who they were, where they settled, slave holdings size of land holdings, agricultural activities, trade and commerce, and schools and churches. That one historical study gives the genealogist researching a family in Lafayette County an abundance of information.

A study by Robert Charles Anderson[47] attempted to identify and describe all Europeans who had migrated to New England by 1635. His sources included passenger lists; court and church records; letters, such as Roger Williams correspondence; and journal, much like that of John Winthrop.

---

45 Campbell, Alan. The Lanarkshire Miners: A Social History of their Trade Unions, 1775-1874.

46 Hathorn, John Cooper. Early Settlers of Lafayette Co., Mississippi. Columbia, Tennessee: P-Vine Press, 1980.

47 Anderson, Robert Charles. The Great Migration Begins: Immigrants to New England: 1620-1633. Vol. I. Boston: New England Historic Genealogical Society, 1995.

Governor William Bradford's and Captain John Smith's records concerning the colonization of America were among the earliest historic writings in the US and are alive with information useful to the genealogist. Records of families which owned slaves are vital to persons descended from those slaves who are trying to reconstruct their family history.

Diaries and Journals

Historical diaries have long been used as a look into the social life of the time and place. In his journal, Judge Samuel Sewell[48] noted deaths and births and disease outbreaks in colonial Boston. The genealogical tidbits in the diaries are staggering. For example, on "Thorsday" November 9, 1682, Sewell wrote

> "Cous: Dan[l] Quinset marries Mrs. Anne Shepard Before John Hullesq. [Saml] Nowell, esq. And many Persons present, almost Capt. [Thomas] Brattles great Hall full; ... Cous. Savage, Mother Hull, wife and self came in ... In Singing Time, Mrs. Brattle goes out being ill; most of Comp[a] goe away, thinking it a qualm or some Fit; But she grows worse, speaks not a word and so dyes away in her chair ... and after a while [we] lay the corps of the dead Aunt in the Bride-Bed."

Any genealogist looking for ancestors in colonial Boston must take a look at Sewell's journal.

The study of diaries, journals and letters take on an important role in the search for female ancestors. For instance, the published multi-volume *John Askin Papers*[49] not only gave insight into the social life of early Detroit, Michigan and Windsor, Ontario, but provided important genealogical information. A 1795 letter written by Askin's daughter Archange, wife of David Meredith, reported that her

> "little Anne has grown into a pretty child ... My son David still looks the same ... I had a letter sometime ago from my little cousin, Therese Mercer ... Give my affectionate remembrances to the Commodor, Aunt Grant, Cousin Wright, My other little cousins, Uncle Barthe, the two who are in Mackinac, John and his wife."

---

48 Thomas, M. Halsey (ed.) The Diary of Samuel Sewell 1674-1729. Vol.1. New York: Farrar, Straus and Giroux, 1973.

49 Quaife, Milo E. (ed.) The John Askins Papers. Volume I: 1747-1795. Detroit: Detroit Library Commission, 1928.

Grant, Wright and Barthe were surnames of members of the family. Also, the letters of just this one daughter of Askin gave information about non-relatives, as well as insight into the social life of a military man's wife.

Other Sources

Social historians have long used sets of vital records, such as those at the in Boston, the DAR's Seimes Microfilm Library in Washington, D.C. and the Family History Library at Salt Lake City. Meanwhile, genealogists are using the Making of America Website (MOA) which makes available to the users a digital library of thousands of journals and books covering American social history during the 19th century. The continually expanding millions of pages from these historical texts have been digitalized thanks to a grant from the Andrew W. Mellon Foundation and hosted through the University of Michigan and Cornell University servers.

Oral History Projects

Oral history is the transmittal of history by word of mouth. When someone dies, they take their lifetime of experiences with them. To a genealogist, the names and dates of a person's life are skeleton bones. The places of birth, death and marriage are the muscle that give us something with which to work. The family, the community, the religion are the support systems or skin that holds the person together. But the high points and the low points of a person's life are the soul.

Oral history can put the soul and flesh on the skeleton of a pedigree chart.

The Library of Congress American Memory website contains a digitalized historical collection. Genealogists are using the transcripts of the Work Projects Administration (WPA) 2900 interviews of persons taken between 1936 and 1940 for an Oral History Project. Of those they can also read the 2300 first person accounts of slavery collected by the WPA.

But these are not the only oral histories that have been preserved. The Veterans History Project concentrates on wartime experiences of American veterans. The Smithsonian has oral histories taken from a variety of artists. Libraries, historical societies and history museums on town, county and state levels have become involved in recording oral histories. One named "Like a Family" interviewed Southern cotton mill workers, while another dealt with "Growing up in San Antonio

Keeping It All in the Family

Families are also passing along oral histories. Some purchase grandparent memory books, fill in the blanks, and give them to their grandchildren. Others sit with their children or grandchildren going through albums and tell tales about the pictures.

My husband's second eldest uncle (there were seven kids in the family and my father-in-law was the youngest) decided he wanted to pass on his boyhood memories. But he could not see himself writing it all down.

He was just a boy when the family left Norway and life was tough on the American prairie. Schooling was sporadic at best and the elder boys needed to work the farm from an early age. So Uncle Engvald got a tape recorder and told his story. A few copies were made and one of Engvald's sisters-in-law transcribed the tape and sent copies out to the rest of the family. For many of my husband's generation, that was the first time they heard the stories -- the ones from Norway, the arrival in America, the trip west by train, that first sod house.

People have been passing down family stories since the beginning of language. But recognize that when a history has been passed down orally, lapses or exaggerations can creep into the story. Ellen Robinson Epstein[50] told of a young man who went off to Vietnam to preserve the tradition that men of his family fought in wars, beginning with his great-grandfather who had fought in the Civil War. After returning from Vietnam, the young man became interested in genealogy only to discover his great-grandfather had never fought. Those wonderful military records he had hoped he would find did not exist.

Do It Yourself

A taped and transcribed oral history is the best way to avoid future misunderstandings. An audit check where someone else listens to the

---

50 Epstein, Ellen Robinson and Rona Mendelsohn. Record and Remember: Tracing Your Roots Through Oral History. New York: Monarch, 1978.

tape while reading the transcript lessens the chance of error. With today's video equipment the narrator comes more to life. In addition, pictures of family, friends and homes of the storyteller can be added to give the narration even more depth.

In preparation for approaching older family members, researchers need to educate themselves a little about the history of their subject's time and places they lived. Asking about historical events stimulates stories that help understand the narrator's personality and puts perspective on the event.

Keep in mind what larger circumstances and restrictions -- be they country, race, religion, community -- affect the narrator's feelings and thoughts. Those who fought in Vietnam cannot deny the enormous effect that war had on their lives -- the injured and dead, agent orange, anti-war riots, drugs, unfamiliar cultures, guerilla warfare, problems of returning to civilian life.

Questions should be open ended. These call for broader, more philosophical answers rather then closed ended question which require little thought and can be answered with a "yes" or "no."

Opened ended	**Closed ended**
Tell me about...	How many...?
Why did you...?	When ...?
What was ____ like?	Did you ...?
Then what happened?	Would you ...?
Describe how ...	Where did you...?

Follow-up by asking probative questions, such as "tell me more ..," "Describe...," "Explain...," How often...," "How did it look / feel / taste / sound?" Initial questions that could be asked, along with some follow-ups would include -

- Who was the first president you voted for? What were the issues of that election?
- What social changes have happened in your lifetime? Were those changes for better or worse?
- How is home life different now from when you were growing up?

- What was the best/worse part of being the oldest / middle / youngest
child in the family?
- How did you celebrate Christmas / Hanukkah / Fourth of July / Thanksgiving? What were your family's holiday traditions? What were family get-togethers like?
- What were your grandparents / parents like? What kind of work did your father / grandfathers do? How and where did they die?
- What do you remember about the town where you were born? What was it like growing up there? What was your house like while you were growing up?
- Why did your family move? How did they choose to settle where they did?
- What games did you play as a child? What did you do with friends on a nice summer day / Saturday night?
- What were the conditions in your country when you left?
- Tell me the new things you saw when you got here?
- How did you decide on an occupation / to move / to join the military?
- What was it like to have a husband / father / brother in the war? Did you know anyone who died in a war?
- Where were you when JFK was assassinated / FDR died?
- How did the Depression / World War II / Pearl Harbor / Vietnam / Gulf War / death of FDR / assassination of President Kennedy / 911 affect you?
- What was your wedding like? Who was your maid of honor / best man / bridesmaid / groomsman / flower girl / ring bearer? Where did you go on your honeymoon?
- What church / school did you attend?
- What countries / states / towns have you lived in / visited and which did you like best?

And probably the best follow-up is what Myers and Maze call the "silent question"[51] – keep quiet and wait, or smile and nod your head.

---

51 Myers, Lois and Elinor Maze. "Oral History Workshop." Henderson County Historical

Once a meeting or telephone call has been arranged, the planning begins. Questions can be asked in a letter or over the telephone when the relative lives a great distance away. Especially with older relatives or "newly- found" cousins, it might be easier to send the questions you plan to ask in advance.

- During the interview, make notes and afterwards, verify the spellings of the names of people and places. Years later you do not want to be asking "Was she saying that they lived on 'David's land' or 'Davis Lane'?"
- If an unknown phrase is used, ask what it means. I cannot help but wonder if my grandchildren will know what playing "45's on a record player" means or who "Uncle Miltie" or Frankie Avalon were.
- Choose questions carefully. Time may be limited that the interviewee will be able to work.
- Plan questions in advance s to maintain control and keep the conversation from wandering.
- Let them tell a story for a second time. The second time may have more or different information.
- Do not interrupt.
- Do not overwhelm the subject with too many questions at a sitting. Consider dividing questions into several sessions. Even a 15 minute interview is better than no interview at all.
- Never pass judgment. Different generations perceive events differently.

Despite a great deal of debate on whether to edit the transcript or not, it is important to keep it true to the interview. Even where opinions are expressed or epithets that are unacceptable by today's standards are used, they demonstrate something about the interviewee's life and we should not judge people outside the norms of their time. How would the Puritans judge modern man?

However, it is difficult to follow a completely unedited text with its crutch words such as "um" and "ah," its repetitions, its half sentences and meaningless false starts. Encouragements to continue and unnecessary

---

Commission and Baylor University Institute of Oral History. Athens, Texas. May 2008

comments by the interviewer can distract from the whole. The object is to produce as accurate and complete transcription while maintaining the integrity of the interview. Myers and Maze referred to it as transcribing "verbatim, more or less."[52]

52 Myers, Lois and Elinor Maze. Oral History Workshop. May 2008

9

State By State

"All of our people all over the country - except the pure-blood Indians - are immigrants or descendants of immigrants"

-Franklin Delano Roosevelt,
Campaign speech in Boston
November 4, 1944

Although knowing when a territory was organized or a state was admitted to the Union can be useful, even better for a Wisconsin researcher would be knowing that Wisconsin was part of the Michigan Territory in 1830, meaning that Wisconsin census information for 1830 was included in the Michigan census. Even better for a Wyoming researcher would be realizing that while Wyoming was not even a territory in 1860, neighboring Nebraska was and that the unorganized section of Nebraska Territory contained census information for what would become Wyoming. Similarly, within a four year period in the 1830's, portions of eastern South Dakota became part of three different territories -- Michigan, Wisconsin and Iowa Territories -- and South Dakota was part of five territories -- including Minnesota and Dakota Territories - before it became a state.

It all comes down to history, with a pinch of geography.

Colonial Differences

When studying colonial ancestors, Patricia Hatcher[53] pointed out that it should be remembered that differences between colonies determined how each pre-Revolutionary colony developed. Weather determined planting seasons. Location determined mortality rates. Colonies had their own form of government and their own state church. They had personalities of their own based on their founders.

---

53 Hatcher, Patricia Law. "Developing a Colonial Mindset" Lecture. Second Conference on Early American Genealogical Research. National Society Daughters of the American Revolution. Washington, D.C., October 2006.

Northeastern colonies were heavily influenced by Canada and France even though their earliest European settlers were primarily East Anglican Puritans. The area was also populated by family groups, but few infants or elderly.

The Middle Colonies were influenced by the Dutch and, to some extent the Swedes, and had a diverse population. However, the earliest settlers there were primarily single young men, especially in the Chesapeake Bay region. Germans and West Country British Cavaliers and their servants arrived a little later.

Southern colonies were fairly homogeneous, but with a higher mortality rate along the coast. The Spanish had some influence on British settlers of the South.

State Timelines

Even though it is hard to tell what made people move or disappear, these are just a few possibilities.

Alabama

1702	Capital of Louisiana moved by the French to near Mobile
1702	Spanish Catholics settled in Mobile
1703	French Huguenots arrived in Mobile
1717	Fort Toulouse built on Coosa River
1720	French Louisiana capital moved from Mobile to Biloxi
1721	More than one hundred slaves arrived in Mobile
1780	Spanish captured Mobile
1800-20	Migrations led from Virginia & Carolinas to south & into central Alabama
1803-11	Federal Road constructed from Milledgeville, Georgia to Fort Stoddert, north of Mobile
1805	Some Indian land opened for white settlement
1810	Migrations from Tennessee to Northern Alabama began
1812-16	Tuscaloosa founded
1813	US annexed "West Florida" from Spain
1813-14	Creek Indian War fought primarily in Alabama
1817	Territory of Alabama formed from Territory of Mississippi
1818	Areas first steamboat was the *Alabama*
1819	Alabama admitted to Union
1830	Gold discovered in Chilton County.
1832	First Alabama railroad opened
1833	Meteor shower
1835	Gold discovered in Verbena
1836-37	Second Creek Indian War
1837	Battle of Hobdy's Bridge

1840	Alabama's population -- 335,185 white, 253,532 slave, 2039 free black
1846	Montgomery selected as capital
1856	Alabama Coal Mining Company began mining near Montevallo
1861	State seceded from Union
1861-65	Nearly two hundred military events occurred on Alabama land during the Civil War
1864	Battle of Mobile Bay
1865	Magazine explosion in Mobile (300 died)
1868	Re-admitted to the Union
1871	Birmingham founded
1904	Tornado in Moundville (36 died)
1906	Hurricane hit the coast
1907	US Steel bought Tennessee Coal & Iron Co. in Birmingham
1908	Tornado in Birmingham (35 died)
1909	Boll weevil invaded state
1910	Coal mine fire in Palos (90 died)
1911	Coal mine explosion in Littleton (120+ died)
1917	Shipbuilding began to boom in Mobile
1920	Deadly tornado outbreak
1922	Coal mine fire at Dolomite (90 died)
1926	Hurricane
1932	Tornadoes in central & northeast Alabama (118 died)
1932	Tornado in Sylacauga (41 died)
1932	Tornado in Northport (37 died)
1934	Approximately 15,000 textile workers walked off the job at 30 mills, primarily in northern Alabama
1941	Huntsville received a $40 million war chemical plant
1944	First oil well
1947	Birmingham steel mills employed 30 thousand
1950's	Population & number of farms dropped due to black & white migration

Alaska

1741	Vitus Bering visited Alaska
1743-99	Russia occupied area
1784	First white settlement started at Three Saints Bay
1792	Fur monopoly granted to Grigorii Shelikov
1799	Russian-American Company began
1799	Russia established post in Old Sitka area
1801	Area settled by the Russians
1802	Russian fort at Old Sitka destroyed & up to 150 Russians & Aleuts massacred
1818	Russian Navy took control of Alaska
1821	Russian Navy banned foreign ships from Alaskan waters
1824	Russians explored Yukon, Nushagak, Kuskokwin & Koyuk Rivers
1835	United States & England received trading privileges
1839	Native Dena'ina population decimated by smallpox
1847	Fort Yukon established
1848	American whalers began fishing Alaskan waters
1853	Oil discovered at Cook Inlet

1857 Coal mining began on Kenai Peninsula
1861 Gold discovered
1867 Purchased by United States
1870 Gold discovered southeast of Juneau
1872 Gold discovered near Sitka
1876 Gold discovered at Windham Bay
1877 US troops withdrawn from Alaska
1880 Gold found at the headwaters of Gold Creek near Juneau
1882 First commercial herring fishing established
1882 Two salmon canneries built
1890 Larger salmon canneries began to be built
1890 Gold discovered along the beaches at Nome
1890 First missions established north of Bering Strait
1891 First oil claim made in Cook area
1892 Chinese began to arrive to work in canneries
1896 Gold discovered in the Yukon
1897-1900 Klondike Gold Rush
1898 Construction of White Pass & Yukon Railroad began
1899 Earthquake in Cape Yakataga
1902 Gold discovered near Fairbanks
1905 Telegraph linked Fairbanks & Valdez
1905 Tanana Railroad built
1907 Richardson Trail established
1907 Gold discovered at Ruby
1912 Representative territorial government formed
1912 Volcanic eruption at Novarupta
1917 Treadwell Mine Complex caved in
1918 First Seward to Anchorage train
1918 *Princess Sophia* sank near Juneau (350+ died)
1923 Anchorage-Fairbanks Railroad dedicated
1935 Federal government established 48 homesteaders in Matanuska Valley
1940 Soldiers arrived in Anchorage to build army base & airfield
1941-45 Anchorage population jumped from 7,700+ to 43,300+
1942 Alaskan Highway linked Anchorage to lower 48 states
1942 Japanese invaded Aleutian Islands
1944 Alaska-Juneau Gold Mine closed
1944 Oil & gas exploration began
1947 Alaskan Highway connected Dawson Creek, British Columbia to Fairbanks, Alaska

Arizona

1531 Spain began colonizing the region
1692 Guevavi Mission founded
1776 Spanish built fort at Tucson
1821 Mexico gained control
1821 American trappers & traders began to arrive
1832-36 Continuous general warfare with Apaches
1848 US gained control of portions of area as a result of Mexican War
1853 Gadsden Purchase presented US with the rest of Arizona
1854 Gold discovered around Tubac
1857 First stagecoach

1862 Beginning of ten year war between the Apaches & settlers
1862-65 Yuma settled & named Arizona City
1863 Territory of Arizona created
1879 Town of Tombstone founded
1881 First railroad crossed the state
1881-86 Geronimo led numerous attacks
1886 Indian fighting ended with Geronimo's surrender
1889 Capital moved to Phoenix
1911 Theodore Roosevelt Dam completed
1912 Admitted to Union
1916 Border skirmishes with Pancho Villa
1917 State immigration law passed defining a geographic zone from which no immigrants could come included India
1936 Los Angeles sent 125 policemen to Arizona & Oregon borders to keep "undesirables" out of California
1936 Boulder Dam completed

Arkansas

1682 LaSalle reached Arkansas on his way to the mouth of the Mississippi
1686 Henri de Tonti founded Arkansas Post
1721 Approximately 1300 starving settlers abandoned Arkansas Post
1762 France ceded Louisiana Territory to Spain
1803 Area purchased as part of Louisiana Purchase
1812 Made part of Missouri Territory
1818 Quapaw Indians gave US land between Arkansas & Red Rivers
1819 Area separated from Missouri & Arkansas Territories established
1820 Little Rock founded
1821 Capital moved from Arkansas Post to Little Rock
1822 Little Rock's first steamboat arrived
1832-39 Five Civilized Tribes moved from Southeastern US via Arkansas
1836 Arkansas admitted to the Union
1837 Major migration from the Deep South began
1846 Law passed barring establishment of a bank in the state
1859 All free blacks were ordered out of the state
1861 Seceded from the Union
1862-64 Battles at Pea Ridge, Jonesboro, Brownsville, Benton
1863 Federal troops occupied Little Rock
1864 Skirmish in Benton, Arkansas
1866 Former Confederates gained control of legislature
1868 New state constitution disenfranchised former Confederates & franchised blacks
1871 Railroad completed from to Little Rock
1874 President Grant sent troops during Brooks-Baxter War
1878 Construction began on first railroad in state
1887 Bauxite discovered southwest of Little Rock
1891 Legislation segregated railroad coaches & stations
1898 Tornado at Fort Smith (55 died)
1899 Bauxite mining started in Saline County
1906 Diamonds found near Murfreesboro
1909 Tornado in Brinkley (49 died)

1921 Tornados in Polk, Clark, Hot Springs & Garland Counties (11 killed, 39+injured)
1926 Deadly outbreak of tornados -- Heber Springs hit hard
1927 Mississippi River flooded one-fifth of the state
1927 Tornado at Poplar Bluff (98 died)
1942 Tornado at Berryville (29 died)
1947 Tornado at Pine Bluff (35 died)
1949 Tornado at Warren (55 died)

California

1578/9 Sir Francis Drake claimed California for Queen Elizabeth I
1768 Spanish King ordered settlement of region
1769 San Diego founded
1776 Spanish settlers reached San Francisco
1782 Los Angeles settled
1830 Russians began to settle
1841 First overland immigrant train reached California
1846 Mexico rejected US offer to purchase California
1848 San Francisco began attracting Chinese
1848 Gold found in western foothills of the Sierra Nevada Mountains
1848 Mexico gave up California
1849 Major Chinese immigration commenced
1849 San Francisco became supply point for 49er's
1850 Gold discovered near Columbia
1850 Admitted to Union
1857 Great Fort Tejon Earthquake (near San Bernardino) was estimated at 8.0 & affected Los Angeles
1857 *SS Central America* sank carrying thirteen to fifteen tons of California gold to New York (425 died)
1858 Chinese & "Mongolians" barred by law from entry
1859 Gold discovered at Brodie
1861 Fort Point built to protect San Francisco
1869 Dozens of Japanese sent to begin the Wakamatsu Tea & Silk Co.
1869 First west bound train arrived in San Francisco
1872 Earthquake
1877 Violence against Chinese in Chico
1877 Anti-Chinese riots in San Francisco
1890 Japanese immigration began
1892 Vacaville-Winters Earthquake in the Imperial Valley
1893 San Francisco Japanese formed their first trade union
1899 Oil discovered at Bakersfield
1900 Oil discovered on Kern River
1900 Increased number of Russians migrated to California
1900 Bubonic Plague scare in San Francisco led to quarantine & cordoning off of Chinatown
1902 Telegraph cable linked California with Hawaii
1904 *San Francisco Chronicle* published derogatory articles about Japanese
1905 California law forbade marriage between Whites & "Mongolians"
1906 Earthquake centered in San Francisco (475 to 3000 died)

1906 San Francisco Board of Education ordered segregation of Orientals from non-Orientals
1908 Asian Indians were driven out of Live Oak
1910 Iron works bombed during strike in Los Angeles
1913 California Alien Law prohibited Asian immigrants from owning property
1920 Large population of Portuguese in Oakland
1920's Population increased by 65%
1921 Japanese farm workers driven from Turlock
1928 St. Francis Dam disaster in Los Angeles
1930 Anti-Filipinoriot in Watsonville
1933 San Joaquin Valley turned into major destination for farmers fleeing Dust Bowl
1933 Long Beach earthquake
1934 San Francisco Maritime Strike
1934 Filipino lettuce pickers went on strike in Salinas Valley
1936 San Francisco -Oakland Bay Bridge opened
1937 Golden Gate Bridge completed
1938 Floods & landslides in Southern California (144 died)
1939 El Cordonazo / Lash of St. Francis / Long Beach Tropical Storm (45 died)
1939 World's Fair held in San Francisco
1940 Race riot in Los Angeles
1941 Japanese-Americans interned in guarded camps
1943 All-American Canal finished
1944 Port explosion (320 died)
1947 Industrial explosion (15 died, 150 injured, 55 buildings damaged
1947 Ship loaded with 3 million gallons of petroleum products exploded at Mormon Island

Colorado

1776 Father Escalante explored region
1803 US acquired as part of Louisiana Purchase
1806 Zebulon Pike explored
1822 First wagons crossed Colorado on Santa Fe Trail
1825 Small trading posts established
1832 Bent's Fort trading post completed
1840 New Mexicans entered southern region to farm
1848 Mexico ceded parts of Colorado to US
1850 US purchased additional Colorado land from Texas
1851 First permanent settlement established in San Luis Valley
1854 Utes attacked Fort Pueblo
1858 Gold discovered in Cherry Creek in now downtown Denver
1858 Boulder & Denver settled
1859 Pikes Peak Gold Rush
1860 Gold discovered in Leadville
1861 Indian raids killed settlers
1861 Colorado Territory organized
1863 Telegraph linked Colorado with the East
1864 Camp (Fort) Collins established to protect settlers on Overland Trail

1864 Sand Creek Massacre by Colorado Volunteers (800+ Indians died)
1864-65 Cheyenne-Arapaho Wars
1865 Indian attacks reached peak
1869 Last military battle against Indians in the eastern portion
1870 First railroad reached Denver
1871 Colorado Springs founded
1876 Admitted to Union
1879 Ute War
1881 Utes were removed to reservations
1882 Steel milled in Pueblo
1883 Narrow gauge line linked Gunnison & Grand Junction
1891 Gold discovered at Cripple Creek
1893 Acute unemployment statewide
1894 Strike at Cripple Creek mines
1899 Beet sugar refinery built in Grand Junction
1900 Gold production at peak
1903 Workers held strikes in mills & mines
1904 Strike at Cripple Creek Mines
1910 Coal mine fire at Dlagua (79 died)
1910 Coal mine fire at Primero (75 died)
1914 Coal miners held strike in South Colorado
1916 Tungsten mined in Boulder-Nederland area
1917 Coal mine fire at Hastings (120+ died)
1921 Arkansas River flood caused $15 million damage in Pueblo
1923 Oil discovered north of Fort Collins
1924 Pro Ku Klux Klan governor & US Senator elected
1942 Amache camp create to inter Japanese from West Coast
1944 Amusement park fire in Denver (6 died)

Connecticut

1620 Dutch arrived at the mouth of the Connecticut River
1630 English colonists from Massachusetts arrived at Saybrook
1633 English Puritans from Dorchester, Massachusetts Bay Colony, settled in Windsor
1633-35 Hartford settled by English colonists from Massachusetts
1635 English settlers from Nantucket, Massachusetts Bay Colony, arrived in Connecticut River Valley
1636-37 Pequot War
1638 New Sweden colonists arrived
1638 New Haven settled by colonists from Massachusetts & England
1658 New Haven passed severe laws against Quakers
1665 Hartford & New Haven united
1713 Connecticut Massachusetts boundary established
1729 Quakers & Baptists exempted from ministerial taxes
1739 Diphtheria epidemic
1740 King George's War
1742 Yellow fever epidemic
1747 Measles epidemic
1755 French Acadians began to arrive
1772 Scarlet fever in New Haven
1776 Joined to become one of the original thirteen states

1777 British raided Danbury
1781 New London became site of major Revolutionary War battle
1795 State sold Western Reserve territory
1815 First steamboat on Connecticut River
1824 Grant Enfield Canal by-passed Connecticut River rapids
1825 Construction of Farmington Canal began
1828 Farmington Canal opened
1828 Canal around Enfield Rapids opened on Connecticut River
1837 Railroad linked Stonington to Providence Rhode Island
1848 Slavery abolished
1854 Connecticut River flooded
1855 Samuel Colt completed armory in Hartford
1860 Connecticut had eighty-four woolen factories
1864 Massive fire destroyed half of Colts Armory in Hartford
1868 Groton gave land on which to build US Naval Station
1871 Hartford Insurance Co. filed for bankruptcy after the Great Chicago Fire
1872 Stricter liquor-licensing laws enacted in answer to Temperance Movement
1875 Textile workers strike in Taftville
1880 Disputed Long Island Sound border settled with New York
1897 Automobile plant opened in Hartford
1910 US Coast Guard Academy moved to New London
1915-16 Seventy-three strikes or lockouts in Bridgeport
1917 US submarine base opened at Groton
1920-30 West Hartford nearly tripled its population
1936 Connecticut River Valley flooded
1938 Hurricane caused $100 million damage in Old Lyme area
1944 Circus fire in Hartford (160 died)

Delaware

1627 Settled by Swedes
1629-30 Dover settled
1630 Dutch settled along Delaware River
1631 Town near Wilmington laid out
1638 Peter Minuit established Swedish settlement
1651 Dutch built Fort Casmir at Newcastle
1654 Swedes captured Dutch fort at Newcastle
1655 Dutch forced to surrender
1656 Finnish Lutherans began to immigrate
1657 Two hundred persecuted Italians arrived
1664 English took control
1673 Dutch regained control of Delaware River
1682 William Penn annexed Delaware
1692 England assumed control
1694 Restored to William Penn
1698 Scots-Irish arrived
1701 Welsh Protestants arrived
1701 Area split off from Pennsylvania
1717 Dover formally laid out
1730 French Catholics began arriving from West Indies
1732 Boundary with Maryland finally established

1754-63 French & Indian War
1776 First naval skirmish of Revolution occurred in Delaware Bay
1776 Became one of the original thirteen states
1777 Battle of Coochs Bridge
1777 Newcastle captured by British
1782 British ships attacked two French vessels in Delaware Bay
1790 French Catholics increased emigrating from West Indies
1798 British sloop sank off Lewes (40 died)
1802 Powder plant built on Brandywine by DuPont
1813 British bombarded Lewes
1813 Fort Union constructed
1822 Severe flooding in Brandywine
1829 Chesapeake & Delaware Canal opened
1832 Newcastle & Frenchtown Railroad opened
1838 Philadelphia, Wilmington & Baltimore Railroad opened
1854 Three wagon loads of powder exploded in Wilmington
1856 Delaware Railroad made first trip to Dover
1861 Although a slave state, Delaware remained in the Union
1863 Martial law proclaimed statewide
1871 Series of statewide earthquakes
1889 Three day hurricane
1891 Fire nearly destroyed Delmar
1909 Federal government became owner of Chesapeake Delaware Canal
1923 Broiler chicken industry began
1939 DuPont opened nylon plant in Seaford
1942 Air bases created at Newcastle & Dover

District of Columbia

1655 Georgetown area first settled
1752 Georgetown platted into eighty lots
1787 Constitution created a separate national capital
1788 Congress given authority over district not to exceed ten square miles in size
1789 Georgetown was incorporated
1790 Organized as a territory, seven square miles were named Federal City
1791 President Washington announced the site which included portions of Maryland & Virginia
1791 L'Enfant submitted his first formal plan for the city
1791 Residents of Rock Creek, Maryland & Virginia named to survey
1792 Cornerstone of White House laid
1793 Cornerstone of Capitol building laid
1800 Capital transferred from Philadelphia to Washington
1800 Washington Naval Yard established
1801 Congress took jurisdiction over the district
1801 District divided into Washington & Alexandria
1808 Construction of canal of Tiber Creek commenced
1812 War of 1812
1812 Tornado killed British soldiers occupying city
1814 British burned buildings, including the White House
1819 Congress moved back to Washington

1828 Ground was broken for Chesapeake & Ohio Canal to carry goods from Columbus to Georgetown
1835 Baltimore & Ohio Railroad opened to Washington
1835 Supreme Court Building completed
1846 Congress returned land Virginia had given in 1790 for the District
1849 Smithsonian Institution Building (the "Castle") opened
1857 "Know Nothing" riots
1862 Slavery abolished
1864 Confederates attacked Fort Steven in Brightwood section of the District
1867 Black males granted the right to vote
1871 Act of Congress annexed Georgetown to Washington City
1878 Establishment of present form of government
1879 Canal of Tiber Creek filled in
1881-1900Army Corps of Engineers dredged the Potomac River
1888 Blizzard downed telegraph lines & took off roofs
1889 District flooded
1894 Coxey's Army demonstrated for aid for unemployed
1919 "Red Summer Riots" (30 died)
1922 Blizzard dumped two feet of snow (nearly 100 died)
1924 Stone bridge across Potomac from Lincoln Memorial to Arlington opened
1931 Hunger marches
1932 Bonus Army encamped
1936 Washingtonians earned nearly twice what New Yorkers earned
1941 National Airport opened
1941-45 District suffered through nightly black-outs while average government employee worked more that ten hours a day

Florida

1513 Ponce de Leon explored Florida
1528 First Greek arrived
1564 French Huguenots established Fort Caroline on St. John River
1565 Spanish settled St. Augustine
1581 African slaves arrived in St. Augustine
1586 English burned St. Augustine
1594 Father Baltasar Lopez baptized eighty Indians
1702 Carolinians pillaged St. Augustine
1702-13 Queen Anne's War (War of Spanish Succession)
1703 South Carolinians raided Spanish missions
1739-42 War of Jenkins Ear
1752 Hurricane destroyed settlement on Santa Rosa Island & setters moved to Pensacola
1758 Gainesville settled by Spanish
1763 Spain ceded area to Great Britain
1767 Immigrants from Italy & Greece settled New Smyrna
1783 Great Britain ceded area to Spain
1812 British used Pensacola as naval base for War of 1812
1817-18 First Seminole War
1819 Florida purchased for $5 million & ceded to US
1822 Florida Territory organized

1832 Seminoles were offered a reservation in the western US
1835-42 Second Seminole War
1841 Seminoles attacked & burned settlement of Mandarin
1845 Admitted to Union
1851 Steamboat line began on St. John River
1856 Seminoles attacked Braden Plantation & stole livestock & slaves
1860 Railroad from Fernandina to Cedar opened
1861 Seceded from Union
1862 Confederate forces evacuated & Union occupied Pensacola
1864 Battle of Olustee
1864 Union army took control of Georgia
1865 Federal troops began to move inland from Cedar Key
1865 Battle of Natural Bridge
1868 Re-admitted to Union
1878 Statewide yellow fever epidemic
1880's Large phosphate deposits discovered in central Florida
1886 Yellow fever epidemic
1886 Most of Key West destroyed by fire
1886 The all-black community of Eatonville was incorporated
1888 Statewide yellow fever epidemic
1896 Regular rail service began from Jacksonville to Miami
1902 Slight earthquake near St. Augustine
1906 Hurricane in southeast
1910 Nine month cigar workers strike & accompanying violence in Tampa
1910 Hurricane in southwest of state (30 died)
1912 Railroad to Key West opened
1919 Hurricane in Keys (600 died in Florida & Texas)
1920 Economic depression
1928 Lake Okeechobee Hurricane (1800+ died)
1935 Labor Day Hurricane in Florida Keys (400+ died)
1936 Killer tornado in Gainesville
1947 Killer hurricane

Georgia

1732 Gov. Oglethorpe obtained patent from King George
1732 Oglethorpe settled Sunbury
1732 German Protestants & New Englanders arrived
1733 English arrived in Savannah
1734 Lutherans from Salzburg, Germany arrived in Effingham Co. area
1735 German Moravians arrived & established church at Savannah
1736 German Moravians arrived in Effingham
1736 Scot Highlanders arrived
1742 Spanish troops attempted to oust British settlers in Battle of Blood Marsh
1750 Ban on slavery was lifted
1752 Georgia made Crown Colony
1755 French expelled from Acadia by British arrived
1763 Land between Alatamaha & St. Mary's River annexed
1767 Pennsylvania Quakers arrived in Wrightsboro
1773 English & Scots settled in large numbers

1776 Became one of original thirteen states
1785-1820 Passports issued into Indian lands
1805 First Land Lottery
1805 Creek Nation ceded land to United States
1807 Land Lottery
1813-15 Creek War
1826 Creek Nation cedes land
1837-39 Atlanta settled
1838 Last of Cherokees removed from state
1861 Seceded from the Union
1861 Federal arsenal at Augusta surrendered to Confederates
1867 First appearance of Ku Klux Klan in state
1881 Hurricane hit Savannah & Augusta (700 killed)
1891 Jim Crow Law enacted
1893 Hurricane hit southern Georgia (2000 killed, 30,000 homeless)
1899-1901 Gold processing plants established near Dahlonega
1903 Tornado in Gainesville (98 died)
1912 Whites in Forsyth County drove out Black residents
1929 Tornado in Statesboro (40 died)
1930's Gold mining began
1936 Tornado in Gainesville (203 died) & Cordele (23 died)
1938 Hotel fire in Atlanta (35 died)
1946 Hotel fire in Atlanta (119 died)
1950's Lockheed Aircraft Corporation in Cobb County was the states' largest employer

Hawaii

1778 Capt. James Cook named them the Sandwich Islands
1779 Capt. Cook killed by natives
1782 Kamehameha began campaign to unite the islands
1790 Eruption of Kilauea volcano
1790 Battle of Kepaniwai on Maui
1795 Kamehameha led force to Oahu
1804 Kamehameha moved capital to Waikiki
1810 King Kamehameha united islands into a kingdom
1816 Russian American Co. began constructing fort at Honolulu
1817 Fort built at Kauai
1819 First missionaries embarked for Hawaii
1820 Calvinist missionaries arrived at Kauai
1824 Uprising bordered on Civil War
1827 French missionaries & artisans arrived
1829 Kaahumanu launched campaign to drive out Catholics
1830 Most foreign Catholics forced to leave
1830 Chinese arrived in Hawaii
1834 Steady decline of exports began
1839 Exports increased
1843 British navy seized Hawaii for five months
1848 Private ownership of land introduced
1850 Foreign ownership of land introduced
1852 Chinese contract laborers arrived
1860-80 Chinese subjected to public attacks

1870 Lepers were transported to island of Molokai
1878 Population -- 76% Native Hawaiian, 10% Chinese, 6% Mixed Hawaiian, 2% American
1880 Mauna Loa eruption added 24 square miles to shoreline
1881 Five hundred Norwegians brought on three year contracts
1885 First contract labor from Japan arrived
1886 Wave of Japanese arrived
1886 Chinese immigration ended
1887 Pearl Harbor was ceded to US
1889 Robert Wilcox Rebellion failed
1890s Japanese began to arrive
1893 Queen Liliuokalani was deposed
1893 US troops moved to annex Hawaii
1894 Republic formed
1895 Unsuccessful attempt to restore Queen (200 arrested)
1896 Honolulu's Chinatown was burned during a Bubonic plague scar
1896 Population -- 28% Native Hawaiian, 22% Japanese, 22% Chinese, 14% Portuguese, 8% Mixed Hawaiian, 3% American, 2% British
1898 Annexed by US
1900 Territory of Hawaii organized
1900 Laborers transported from Korea & Puerto Rico to Hawaii
1900 Threatened with plague, authorities burned down Honolulu's worst slums
1900 Lahaina's Japanese sugar plantation workers walked out
1900 Hawaii became a commonwealth state
1900 Ban on importation of contract labor led to major strikes & labor problems
1901 Hawaiian Pineapple Company (Dole) established
1902 Telegraph cable laid linking Hawaii with California
1904 Japanese plantation workers called for organized strike
1907 Filipinos arrived in Hawaii
1907-13 Immigrants from Andalusia, Spain, were recruited to work plantations
1909 Seven thousand Japanese laborers held four month long strike
1910 Picture brides arrived from Korea
1921 Hawaiian Homes Act granted forty acres to anyone at least 50% Hawaiian
1922 Hawaiian Pineapple Company purchased more of Lanai
1924 Sixteen hundred Filipino workers went on eight month strike against plantations
1929 First inner-island air flight
1935 First direct flight from San Francisco
1936-38 Sporadic strikes
1937 Last ethnic strike in Hawaii
1941 Pearl Harbor attacked by Japanese
1941 Japanese living in Hawaii were interned
1946 Tsunami hit Hilo (100+ died)

Idaho

1803 Became part of Louisiana Purchase
1805 Lewis & Clark reached Lemhi Pass

1809 First fur trading post established
1820 Fort Boise established
1834 Fort Hall constructed
1835 Martial law declared after rebellion of pea pickers in Teton County
1840's Additional military forts opened
1840-60 California Trails brought settlers
1853 Washington Territory established with part of Idaho included in it
1854 Snake River Indians massacred emigrants at Boise Valley (21 died)
1855 Mormons established Fort Lemhi
1860 Gold discovered near Pierce
1860 First permanent settlement established at Franklin
1860-62 Gold discovered in Elk City, Florence & Warren areas
1863 Idaho Territory established including Montana & Wyoming
1863 Mining began in Owyhees
1863 Boise Barracks established
1866 Gold discovered in Lemhi County
1869 Placer gold discovered at Oro Grande
1869 Transcontinental Railway completed
1870 Gold strike near Caribou Mountain
1873 Coeur d'Alene Indian Reservation established
1877 Nez Perce War
1878 Bannock War involved Bannock, Northern Piute & Cayuse Indians
1879 Silver strikes in Eureka, Nevada & Leadville
1879 Sheepeater War ended
1880 Coeur d'Alene settled
1883 Railroad arrived
1884 Silver operations commenced in Coeur d'Alene
1890 Idaho admitted to Union
1892 Martial law declared when striking miners dynamited Frisco Mill
1894 Gold discovered in Thunder Mountain area
1896 Clashes between cattlemen & sheep herders
1899 US Army troops called to Coeur d'Alene mining area
1901 US Army troops called to Coeur d'Alene mining area
1904 Twin Falls platted out
1906 Largest sawmill in US established at Oitlach
1910 In excess of three million acres in northern Idaho & western Montana in disastrous forest fire (86 died)
1924 Black Canyon Dam completed
1927 American Falls Dam completed
1932 Owyhee Dam dedicated
1935 Indian children integrated into public schools

Illinois

1682 Kalkaska settled
1720 French Canadians began to settle in the region
1757 Fort Massac constructed at the mouth of Tennessee River
1759 Fort Gage constructed at Kalkaska
1773 Land company purchased most of southern Illinois
1774 Quebec annexed Illinois

1778 George Rogers Clark claimed Kalkaska & Cahokia for American
1779 First American settlers
1780 English sent troops to recapture region
1783 Ceded by Great Britain to US as Old Northwest Territory
1787 Became part of Illinois Territory
1803 Fort Dearborn built on future site of Chicago
1809 Illinois Territory organized
1818 Admitted to the Union
1825 Settlers traveling overland through New York & the Erie Canal started to arrive
1832 Black Hawk War
1833 Chicago became a town & enormous growth period began
1845 Cook County had 23 settlements including Chicago
1848 Illinois & Michigan Canal linked Mississippi River to Great Lakes
1849-55 Cholera epidemic in Chicago
1865 Union stockyards opened in Chicago
1866-67 Cholera epidemic in Chicago
1871 Great Chicago Fire killed 250
1893 World's Columbian Exposition in Chicago
1896 Tornado in East St. Louis (255 died)
1903 Iroquois theater fire in Chicago (nearly 600 died)
1909 Coal mine fire in Cherry (250+ died)
1910-30 Chicago black population grew from 44,000 to 234,000
1915 *Eastland* sank in Chicago River (800+ died)
1916 Major black migration to Chicago began
1917 Tornado destroyed Mattoon (101 died)
1917 First US training base for military aviators opened
1918 Influenza epidemic (32,000 died in state)
1919 Chicago Race Riots (38 died)
1925 Tornados hit Franklin, Williamson, White, Hamilton & Jackson Counties in southern Illinois (800 died, nearly 3000 homeless)
1930 Largest ring of bootleggers exposed in Chicago
1933 Illinois & Michigan Canal closed
1940 Race riot in Chicago
1941 Train accident near Naperville (40+ died)
1946 Hotel fire in Chicago (60+ died)
1947 Coal mine fire in Centralia (100+ died)
1948 Tornado in Bunker Hill (33 died)
1949 Hospital fire in Effingham (77 died)

Indiana

1702 Vincennes settled
1790 General Joseph Harmar defeated on the Miami River
1800 Indiana Territory settled
1808 Shakers formed colony on the Wabash River
1809 Illinois Territory was divided off of Indiana Territory
1812 Last Indian fight in state took place near Peru
1813 Seat of territory moved from Vincennes to Corydon
1816 Admitted to Union
1824 Fort Wayne settled
1824 Several towns destroyed by tornados
1825 New Harmony Secular Utopian Society established

1835 Cicero settled
1853 Wabash & Erie Canal opened
1876 Gas discovered at Eaton near Muncie
1886 First gas well in state drilled at Portland
1889 Standard Oil Company built refinery in Whiting
1906 US Steel built a plant & founded Gary
1913 Floods in Indiana & Ohio (732 killed)
1917 Tornado in New Albany (46 died)
1918 Hammond circus train wreck (80+ died)
1925 Tornados in southwestern Indiana
1932 One-third of the workforce was unemployed
1946 Major strike at General Motors plant in Anderson

Iowa

1788 Frenchman Julien Dubuque became first white settler
1803 Became part of US with the Louisiana Purchase
1808 Fort Madison built
1812 Organized as part of Missouri Territory
1820 Missouri Compromise made non-slave state
1832 Black Hawk War
1833 Burlington settled
1833 Black Hawk cession land opened to white settlement
1834 Michigan Territory annexed Iowa District with two counties – Dubuque & Des Moines
1836 Wisconsin Territory annexed the Iowa District
1836 Census reported 10,500 living in Iowa District
1838 Iowa Territory organized
1839-41 Cedar Rapids settled
1840's Dutch began to arrive
1841 Fort Atkinson built
1842-43 Additional land was opened to white settlement
1846 Council Bluffs settled
1846 Mormons began to cross region
1846 Admitted to Union
1851 Sioux cession removed Native Americans from land
1856 Mormon converts from Denmark & Britain began to arrive
1857 Economic depression & bank failures
1862 Homestead Act increased settlement
1867 First railroad in region completed
1867 Grasshopper invasion severely damaged crops
1869 Pamphlets published in European languages to attract settlers
1873 Depression hit farmers badly
1880 Census indicated 262 thousand foreign born residing in state
1893 Pomeroy tornado (71 died)
1895 Tornado hit Sioux Center, Iowa
1895 Tornado hit school in Treton-Hull
1907 Last lynching in state
1913 Keokuk Dam completed
1918 Governor declared illegal the use of any language but English in public gatherings of two or more people
1926 Hybrid corn seed developed
1929-39 Farmers lost their land during Great Depression

1946	Hotel fire in Dubuque (19 died)
1950	Hospital fire in Davenport (41 died)

Kansas

1724	French explorer Bourgmont crossed Kansas to Rocky Mountains
1744	French built in area of future Fort Leavenworth
1767	French lost region to Spain
1803	Became part of Louisiana Purchase
1822	First time wagons instead of pack mules on Santa Fe Trail
1825	Indians gave right-of-way for Santa Fe Trail
1827	Fort Leavenworth established
1830	First wagons took Oregon Trail
1842	Fort Scott established
1843	First settlement of Kansas City area
1853	Fort Riley established
1854	Kansas Territory organized
1854	Topeka settled through Emigrant Aid Company
1854	Leavenworth established as an army post
1854	Swiss immigrants settled
1855-56	Wakarusa War in Lawrence
1856	Cholera at Fort Riley
1860-62	Abilene settled
1861	Admitted to Union
1869	Sioux& Cheyenne raided the northwest
1870-71	Families from Clermont County, Ohio settled in Ohio & Morris Counties
1871	Kansas Pacific Railroad sold 47,000 acres in Dickinson County to Scots, 32,000 in Clay County to English, & 19,000 in Riley County to Welsh
1871	Italians migrated to coal mine area in southeast of state
1871	First structure built in Dodge City
1874	Atchison, Topeka & Santa Fe Railroad sold Mennonites 100,000 acres in Harvey, Reno & Marion Counties
1874	Mennonites arrived
1874	Grasshopper plague consumed fields
1878	Several hundred Pennsylvania Brethren arrived in Abilene
1878	Czech community in Rawlins County suffered many losses from Cheyenne raids
1878	Last Indian raid in state
1881	Last cattle drive to Dodge City
1881	Western Kansas homesteaded
1882	Sugar Creek, Linn County drownings (6 died)
1893	Much of town of Leonardville burned to ground
1885	Fear of "Texas Fever", a tick borne disease, ended cattle drives
1887	Large salt deposits discovered in Reno County
1890	Tornado in Sedwick
1892	Dalton gang killed many in Coffeyville
1892	Petroleum found near Neodisha
1903	Topeka flooding (approximately 25 died)
1903	Kansas City Flood (20 thousand homeless)
1905	Tornado in Marquette (34 died)

1915 Oil discovered near El Dorado
1917 Tornado in Sedgewick
1919 Airplane factory opened in Wichita
1932 First major dust storm of the Dust Bowl
1934-35 Dust Bowl drought hit in southwestern part of state
1936-37 Grasshopper infestation plagued farmers

Kentucky
1769 Explored by Daniel Boone
1774 Harrodsburg settled
1775 Daniel Boone set out Wilderness Trail
1775 Boiling Springs, St. Asaph, Fort Boonesborough, Lexington settled
1776 Organized as a county of Virginia
1778 Thirteen-day siege at Boonesborough
1792 Admitted to the Union
1796 Wilderness Road opened to wagons
1800 Louisville had a population of 359
1805 Aaron Burr began plans for a southwestern empire
1815 First New Orleans to Louisville steamboat
1818 Western part of state annexed
1819 Panic of 1819 ruined many banks
1824 Tornados destroyed several towns
1830 Louisville Portland Canal opened
1847 Of 5113 Kentuckians who volunteered for the Mexican War (77 died in battle, 500+ from disease)
1853 Steamboats passengers traveled from New Orleans to Louisville in five days
1861 Declared itself neutral in Civil War
1862 Union forces controlled entire state
1862 Civil War battles at Prestonburg & Perryville
1883 Bellevue flood
1890 Standard Oil Refinery Explosion in Louisville
1890 Blackford Tornado (21 died)
1890 Tornado in Louisville (76 died)
1901 Gas discovered at Menafee Gas Field
1904-09 Black Patch War
1917 Tornado in Jefferson County
1925 Tornado in Tompkinsville (36 died)
1933 Ohio River flooded
1933 Tennessee Valley Authority began building dams in Kentucky
1937 Louisville flooded & nearly 1 million had to be evacuated

Louisiana
1699 French & French Canadian Catholics migrated into area
1718 New Orleans settled by French Acadians
1750 Acadians from Canada arrived
1751 Missionaries introduced sugar cane
1755 French Catholics from Nova Scotia settled in New Orleans
1763 France ceded land to Spain
1763 Acadians began to migrate into Louisiana
1788 Nine hundred houses destroyed by fire in New Orleans

1796 Slave revolt foiled before it began
1800 Spain ceded to France
1803 Part of Louisiana Purchase
1804 Divided into District of Louisiana & Territory of Orleans
1805 Louisiana divided into twelve counties
1807 Orleans Territory divided into nineteen parishes
1808 A black man was found guilty of harboring runaway slaves
1810 Feliciana (east of the Mississippi River) annexed by US
1811 Slave revolt
1812 Admitted to the Union
1814 Battle of New Orleans
1847 Yellow fever epidemic
1850 More Italians resided in Louisiana than any other state
1853 Yellow fever outbreak in New Orleans
1860 Three hurricanes hit the Louisiana area of Gulf of Mexico
1862 Salt mine discovered at Avery Island
1862 New Orleans captured by Union forces
1864 Battles of Mansfield & Pleasant Hill
1873 Colfax Riot between whites & blacks (African-Americans killed)
1878 Yellow fever epidemic (5000+ died)
1891 Eleven Italians "lynched" in New Orleans
1893 Hurricane at Cheniere Caminada Island (2000 died)
1901 Oil discovered near Jenning
1908 Tornado in Gilliam (49 died)
1909 Yellow fever epidemic
1909 Hurricane at Grand Isle (350 died)
1909 Sulphur mining began near Sulphur
1915 Hurricane at New Orleans (275 died)
1918 Southwestern state struck by hurricane
1921 Tornado in Gardner (31 died)
1926 Waterway opened from Gulf of Mexico to Lake Charles
1927 Flooding left 300,000 homeless
1947 Killer hurricane

Maine

1607 Aborted attempt to settle
1623 Saco Bay settled
1624 Kittery settled
1628 Brunswick (Pejepscot) settled
1632 Portland settled
1639 Gorges received grant
1650 Kennebunk settled
1652 Controlled by Massachusetts
1653 York settled
1675-76 King Philips War
1688 Abenaki Indian War on settlers
1690 Indians attacked Falmouth (Portland) & Fort Loyal, killing nearly everyone & few taken prisoner
1690-97 King Williams War
1691 United with Massachusetts
1691 Only Wells, York, Kittery & Appledore were still inhabited
1692 Abenaki Indians raided Wells

1702-13 Queen Anne's War
1708 Settlements destroyed by Indians
1718 Georgetown& Falmouth incorporated
1721-25 Drummers War (Lovewell's War)
1744-48 King George's War
1760 Cumberland & Lincoln Counties formed
1773 British raided Falmouth
1775 Portland demolished by British
1776 Population 47,279 white 488 black
1786 Treaty with Penobscots
1796 Treaty with Penobscots - whites received land
1818 Treaty with Penobscots -- whites received land
1820 Treaty with Penobscots -- whites received land
1820 Admitted to Union
1830 Treaty with Penobscots -- whites received land
1838-39 Maine declared war (Aroostook War) on Canada over Maine-New Brunswick border
1842 Maine-New Brunswick border dispute settled
1866 Fire destroyed downtown Portland
1876 Portland had snowstorm on July 4
1888 Blizzard
1889 Mill workers on the Penobscot River won shorter workdays
1891 Craft unions formed Maine's American Federation of Labor
1896 Weavers at York Mill in Saco shut the plant down
1899 Hydro electric plants brought electricity to Maine towns
1900 West Sullivan, North Jay, & Stonington stone cutters united in strike
1916 Street car workers in Portland walked out
1930's Sixteen thousand from Maine's CCC built 400 miles of roads, Completed Maine's Appalachian Trail & built campgrounds
1936 Disastrous flooding
1938 Hurricane

Maryland
1632 All Christians granted equal rights
1632 Split from Virginia jurisdiction
1632 Lord Baltimore received patent
1634 St. Mary's Colony settled
1638 Swedes settled Delaware River region
1644 English Puritans from Virginia arrived in Anne Arundel Co.
1649 Colony granted rights to anyone affirming belief in the Trinity
1649 Annapolis settled
1651 Catholicism outlawed
1661 Quakers from Massachusetts & Virginia arrived
1671 Slavery encouraged
1689 Protestants overthrew the government
1690 Crown regained control
1692 Protestantism became state religion
1716 Government restored to Lord Baltimore
1729 Baltimore established
1730 Pennsylvania Germans arrived in Baltimore County
1732 Disputed boundary with Delaware determined

1755 French Catholics from Nova Scotia & Irish Catholics arrived in Baltimore
1776 One of original thirteen states
1781 Loyalist & British property confiscated
1781 Baltimore became port of entry
1787 Steamboat launched on Potomac River
1793 French from Santa Domingo arrived in Baltimore
1794 Yellow fever epidemic
1810 Free blacks disenfranchised
1813 First steamboat on Chesapeake Bay
1814 British tried to capture Baltimore
1814 British troops defeated US in Battle of Bladensburg
1829 Chesapeake & Delaware Canal opened
1832 Clipper ship construction began in Baltimore
1834 Federal troops intervened when Irish laborers on Chesapeake Ohio Canal rioted
1864 Confederates held Frederick & Hagerstown for ransom
1866 National Labor Union organized in Maryland
1868 Steamship service between Baltimore & Bremen initiated
1870-1900Immigrants equaled 10% of the population
1872 Garrett County established
1872 Railroad linked Hagerstown & Baltimore
1877 Virginia & Maryland settled Chesapeake Bay boundary dispute
1882 Smallpox epidemic in Baltimore (80+ died)
1887 Blast furnace built at Sparrow Point
1890s Several typhoid outbreaks
1891 Fire in Canton destroyed all of United Oil Company's property
1893 Financial panic & depression
1904 Baltimore fire destroyed 70 blocks of central business district
1904 "Jim Crow Law" enacted concerning public accommodations
1904 Fire in Baltimore destroyed 140 acres of business district
1910 Typhoid epidemic in Cumberland
1910 Nearly 25,000 Russian-born immigrants lived in Baltimore
1918 Edgewood Arsenal established
1922 Ku Klux Klan rallied in Frederick& Baltimore
1926 Tornado at LaPlata (17 died)
1933 Storm cut an inlet at Ocean City
1936 National Guard called out because of flooding
1937 Bethlehem Steel & Glen L. Martin Company received large war contracts
1948 St. John 's College admitted first African-American student

Massachusetts

1620 New Plymouth settled by Puritan immigrants from England & Holland
1620 Puritans received patent
1621 Pilgrims & Wampanoag Indians signed peace treaty
1626 Salem settled by Dorchester colonists from Cape Ann
1628 Salem settled by English
1630 More one thousand Puritans arrived in Massachusetts
1630 Boston settled
1630 Nantucket settled by colonials from Plymouth, England

1632	Duxbury settled by English Protestants
1635	English Baptists arrived in New Town
1636	Hingham was settled
1636-37	Pequot War
1639	Barnstable was colonized
1640	Yarmouth & Marshfield were settled
1653	Major fire in Boston
1657	Measles epidemic
1658	Four Quakers hanged & others mutilated
1661	Quakers left for Maryland
1671	Rehobeth Tornado was first confirmed tornado in the US
1675-76	King Philip's War
1680	Cambridge tornado produced first known tornado fatality in US
1687	Measles epidemic
1689	Insurrection against Royal Governor in Boston
1692	Witchcraft trials & executions
1697	Abenaki Indian raid on Haverhill
1702-13	Queen Anne's War
1704	Deerfield massacre
1713	Disputed boundaries with Connecticut finally established
1713	Measles epidemic
1737	Smallpox on Martha's Vineyard
1739-40	Measles epidemic
1740	Disputed boundaries with New Hampshire settled
1744	Diphtheria outbreak
1746	Colony sent 3,250-man expedition to Canada
1747	Border with New Hampshire settled
1747	Measles outbreak
1755	Three thousand-man expedition against Nova Scotia
1760	Smallpox in Charlestown
1760	Four hundred buildings destroyed in Boston
1765	Stamp Acts caused tumult in Boston
1770	Boston Massacre
1773	Boston Tea Party
1773	Boundary settled between New York & Massachusetts
1775	Battle of Bunker Hill
1776	Became one of original thirteen states
1776	Boston evacuated
1779-80	Severe winter
1780	African-Americans were allowed to hold religious services in Faneuill Hall
1780	"New England Dark Day" occurred & alarmed citizens
1782	Fire destroyed all of North Mills on Mill Pond
1782	First stagecoach from Boston to Hartford on Post Road
1789	Rash of burglaries plagued Boston
1794	Great fire in Boston destroyed homes & businesses
1796	African Society established in Boston promoted end of slavery
1798	School for African-American children established
1808	First racial incident in Boston after slavery ended in state
1820	Maine separated from Massachusetts
1822	Lowell established as factory town
1825	Boston ship carpenter struck for ten-hour work days

1830 Charlestown Naval Yard flooded
1835 Great fire burned forty buildings in Boston
1839 Great December Hurricane (75 vessels lost)
1845 Lawrence founded
1846-47 Major influx of Irish from potato famine
1850 New Bedford fleet employed many Portuguese seamen
1870 Chinese laborers arrived from west to work in factory during North Adams strike
1872 Boston fire (13 died, 800 buildings destroyed, 20,000 jobless)
1890 Tornado in Lawrence (6 killed, 35 injured, 500 homeless)
1894 Two thousand Portuguese lived in Provincetown area
1902 About 250 Chinese arrested in Boston for not carrying their registration certificates with them
1911 First minimum wage law passed
1912 Textile workers walked off on strike in Lawrence
1914 Canal linked Buzzards Bay & Cape Cod
1919 Great Molasses Flood when tank collapsed & released two million gallons of molasses in Boston (21 died)
1920 Largest number of Portuguese in US lived in New Bedford, Fall River, Lowell, Cambridge & Boston
1920 Federal agents raided suspected communist groups near Boston (4000 arrested)
1938 New England Hurricane hit Boston
1942 Nightclub fire in Boston (nearly 500 died)

Michigan

1668 Sault Sainte Marie settled
1701 Antoine de la Mothe Cadillac founded Detroit
1754-63 French & Indian War
1760 French surrendered Fort Pontchartrain (Detroit) to British
1763 Detroit under siege for 135 days
1763 French ceded territory to Great Britain
1803 Became part of the Indiana Territory
1805 Detroit destroyed by fire
1805 Michigan Territory organized
1812 Detroit & Ft. Mackinac surrendered to British
1813 Americans recaptured Detroit
1813 Battle on Raisin River
1818 Public lands attracted New York & New England settlers
1819 Flint established
1819 Six million acres of Indian land ceded to white settlers
1836 Detroit had a population of ten thousand
1837 Admitted to Union
1840s Dutch arrived
1842 Copper mining began on Keweenaw Peninsula
1845 Became first state to have agents recruiting immigrants at New York docks
1845 State's first iron ore mining began in Negaunee in Upper Peninsula
1845 Marquette founded
1846 Iron ore mining began in the Marquette Range
1852 Michigan Central Railroad opened to Chicago

1855 Ship canal at Sault Sainte Marie opened
1856 First Milwaukee to Europe ship passed through Welland Canal
1861-65 More than 90 thousand Michigan men served in Civil War
1871 Federal government constructed canal at St. Clair Flats
1871 Cadillac founded
1875 Iron River settled
1877 Iron ore mining began in Menominee Range
1884 Iron ore mining began in Gogebic Range
1896 Tornadoes in central Michigan (47 died)
1908 First Model T automobile manufactured
1910-20 Detroit's African-American population increased over 600%
1915 Ford Motor Co. produced 1 millionth automobile in Detroit
1927 Bath school dynamited
1930 Detroit-Windsor Tunnel opened
1934 Hotel fire in Lansing (30+ died)
1940 Race riot in Detroit
1941 Auto plants converted for war effort

Minnesota

1659-60 French fur traders explored region
1679 Duluth settled as Indian village
1694 Le Sieur established trading post on Isle Pelee (Prairie) in the Mississippi River between Hastings & Red Wing
1763 Great Britain obtained eastern part in Treaty of Versailles
1770-84 Grand Portage became a fur trading center with British troops Stationed there
1783 US won eastern portion in Revolutionary War
1800 France acquired Louisiana Territory from Spain
1803 US received western part in Louisiana Purchase
1819 St. Paul & Minneapolis settled
1823 First steamboat reached Fort Snelling from St. Louis
1824 Fort. St. Anthony (Snelling) completed
1836 Wisconsin Territory included Minnesota
1841 Chapel of St. Paul built
1849 Minnesota Territory organized
1851 Two treaties with Sioux to turn over their land
1857 Band of Sioux massacred settlers at Spirit Lake
1858 Admitted to Union
1862 Dakota conflict eventually killed 486 white settlers
1862 Following Sioux uprising, many Sioux fled to Missouri
1873 Three day blizzard (70 died)
1881 St. Paul destroyed by fire
1884 Iron mining began in Vermillion Range
1886 Sauk Rapids destroyed by tornado (79 died)
1888 Blizzard (109 died)
1890 Iron ore discovered in Mesabi Range
1892 First iron ore shipped from Mesabi Range
1894 Forest fire destroyed Hinkley & Sandstone (400+ died)
1898 Expedition against Ojibwas
1898 Federal troops put down Chippewa uprising at Leech Lake
1900 Virginia, Minnesota destroyed by fire
1908 Chisholm destroyed by fire

1911 Iron ore mining began in the Cuyuna Range
1916 Large steel mill opened in Duluth
1918 Cloquet & Moose Lake destroyed by high winds & forest fires
1918 Tornado in Tyler (36 died)
1918-24 Rural depression
1919 Tornado in Fergus Falls (57 died)
1930-35 More than 1/2 of all iron ore mined came from Minnesota
1940 Armistice Day Blizzard (49 died)

Mississippi
1699 Ocean Springs founded as French Settlement
1699 Biloxi founded
1716 Natchez settled
1763 French area ceded to Great Britain
1783 Great Britain ceded to United States
1798 Mississippi Territory formed
1811 Additional land acquired
1817 Admitted to the Union
1825 Vicksburg incorporated
by 1830 Columbus settled
1830s Treaties opened Indian land west of the Tombigbee River to white settlers
1840 Tornado killed 317 in Natchez
1851 Springs discovered near Biloxi
1861 Seceded from the Union1861-65, became site of numerous Civil War battles
1870 Re-admitted to the Union
1880 Macon tornado (18 killed 40 wounded)
1898 Gulfport incorporated
1900 Tornados in northwestern portion of state (30 died)
1901 Hurricane
1906 Hurricane hit coast
1907 Boll weevil attacked cotton crop
1908 Tornados in Lamar, Marion, Forrest, Perry & Wayne Counties in Mississippi & into Louisiana (143 died 770 injured)
1917 Payne Field established in West Point to train Army pilots
1920 Tornados in Oktibbeha, Clay, Monroe, & Itawamba Counties in & into Alabama (88 died 700 injured)
1927 Mississippi River flood destroyed $2 million worth of crops
1933 Tornadoes in Jones & Jasper Counties (37 died)
1936 Tornado in Tupelo (216 died)
1940 Dance hall fire in Natchez (200+ died)
1942 Tornado in central Mississippi (63 died)
1947 Hurricane on Gulf of Mexico coast

Missouri
1755 St. Genevieve settled by French
1764 St. Louis founded
1803 Part of the Louisiana Purchase
1803 French & Spanish lived along the Mississippi River
1804-06 Ten thousand settlers entered from Kentucky, Tennessee, Virginia & the Carolinas

1811-12	New Madrid earthquakes
1812	Missouri Territory organized
1820	Kansas City settled
1822	Jefferson City settled
1821	Admitted to the Union
1825	In treaty at St. Louis, Shawnee ceded land in the state
1827	Independence settled
1833	Heavy German immigration
1838	Mormons ordered from state
1843	Ft. Mackenzie burned
1843	American Fur Co. built forts
1849	Steamship fire spread to other ships & 430 buildings in St. Louis (3 died)
1855	First American Bohemian Church established in St. Louis
1860	Pony Express began in St. Joseph
1861	Union forces controlled northern Missouri
1861-65	Civil War battles
1871	Tornado in St. Louis (9 died)
1874	Eads Bridge across Mississippi River at St. Louis opened
1875	Grasshopper plague caused havoc for farmers
1896	Tornado in St. Louis & East St. Louis
1899	Tornado in Kirksville (34 died)
1904	St. Louis hosted World's Fair & first Olympic games
1924-25	Tornados entirely destroyed several towns, including Annapolis & Leadanna
1927	Tornado in St. Louis (79 died)
1938	Tornado in Bakerville (24 died)

Montana

1803	Part of Louisiana Purchase
1807	First trading post established at junction of Big Horn & Yellowstone Rivers
1810	New post at Three Forks was abandoned after massacre
1832	Fort Piegan & Fort Mackenzie established
1832	First steamboat reached Fort Union
1841	St. Mary's Mission founded near present Stevensville
1852	Gold discovered between Butte & Missoula
1853	First large cattle drive on Oregon Trail
1854	Included in Nebraska Territory
1855	Treaty with Indians signed
1858	Gold discovered Benetsee Creek
1862-63	Gold discovered Bannock City
1862	Mullan Wagon Road completed
1862	Roughly 130 Minnesota pioneer arrived at Gold Creek
1864-65	Helena settled
1864	Montana Territory organized
1867	Fort Shaw established to protect Mullan Road
1875	Silver discovered in Butte
1876	Battle of Little Big Horn
1877	Indian Wars ended
1880s	Boom of silver mines
1880	Havre established

1883 Completed Northern Pacific Railway negatively impacted cattle industry
1887 Especially hard winter killed thousands of animals
1888 Coal mining began in Cascade County
1889 Admitted to the Union
1890 Hydroelectric dam at Great Falls built
1892 Great Northern Railway completed through the state
1897 Citizens of Butte waged a boycott of its Chinatown
1903 Amalgamated Copper Company's closing paralyzed state's economy
1909 Chicago, Milwaukee, St. Paul & Pacific Railroad completed to Montana
1910 Western Montana devastated by forest fire
1910-18 Homesteading boom
1917 Mine fire in Butte (160+ died)
1919 Severe agricultural depression
1919 Oil discovered at Cat Creek
1935 Severe earthquake in central part of state
1943 Smith Mine Disaster (70 died)
1950 Great Falls became state's largest city

Nebraska

1763 Treaty of Paris land west of Mississippi River to Spain
1789 Juan Munier received sole trading rights
1800 Spain ceded to France
1803 Became part of Louisiana Purchase
1812 Became part of Missouri Territory
1812 built
1822 Fur trading post established at Bellevue
1848 Fort Kearny established on Oregon Trail
Nebraska Territory organized
1855 Bellevue incorporated
1857 Grand Island settled
1860 Census showed a population of twenty-nine thousand
1862 Homestead Act brought substantial immigration
1865 Union Pacific Railroad began to lay rails across state
1864 Lincoln settled
1867 Admitted to the Union
1870s Grasshoppers ruined crops
1877 Crazy Horse surrendered
1880 Population had grown to 452 thousand
1890s Drought
1900 Economy began to improve
1902 Federal aid earmarked for irrigation
1913 Tornado in Omaha (103 died)
1939 Oil discovered in southeastern part of Nebraska
1944 Pick-Sloan Missouri Basin Project enacted for flood control, dams, reservoirs, hydroelectric plants

Nevada

1825 Peter Ogden discovered Humboldt River
1826-27 Jedediah Smith party crossed Nevada west to east

1828 Humboldt River discovered by Peter S. Ogden
1834 First wagon party crossed Donner Pass
1847 Gold discovered at foot of Mt. Davidson
1848 First settlements
1848 A portion ceded by Mexico
1849 Genoa (Mormon Station) settled by Mormons near present-day Carson City
1849 Placer gold discovered in Carson River
1851 Large influx of Mormon settlers
1851 Eagle Station Trading Post opened at present-day Carson City
1851 Gold discovered at Eureka
1858 Carson City laid out as a town & named
1859 Comstock Lode discovered at Virginia City
1861 Treaty signed with Shoshone
1861 Daily overland mail service established
1863 Virginia City had become a very important western city
1864 Ore strike at Eureka
1864 Admitted to the Union
1866 Virginia City fire caused by arson (400 families homeless)
1867 Virginia City Miner's Union formed
1867 First train entered the state
1869 Ore strike at Hamilton
1873 Mine disasters at Kentuck, Yellow Jacket, Gold Hill, Crown Point
1875 Fires hit Virginia City & destroyed Eureka
1880 Virginia City population had drastically dropped
1889/90 One hundred inches of winter snow killed 80-90% of the livestock
1892 Las Vegas was granted a post office
1902 Much of Wadsworth's business district burned
1903 Gold discovered at Goldfield
1906 Tonopah had become a flourishing mining center
1906 Goldfield population had jumped 20,000 in three years
1909 Flood swept away a squatter town near Rawhide
1913 Miners' homes swept away in storm in Goldfield (5 died)
1923 Fire swept through Goldfield business district
1931 Boulder City founded to house workers of Boulder (Hoover) Dam
1931 Gambling legalized to alleviate hardships of Depression
1936 Boulder Dam completed
1939 Humboldt River stream liner wreck (20 died)
1940 Population reached110 thousand
1946 "Bugsey" Siegel opened the Flamingo resort in Las Vegas

New Hampshire

1621 Gorges & Mason received grant
1623 Portsmouth, Exeter, Rye & Dover settled
1640s Large number of English colonists from Connecticut & Massachusetts arrived
1641 Massachusetts took jurisdiction
1656 Nashua settled
1679 Area separated from Massachusetts
1680 First assembly met in Portsmouth

1689 King William's War
1690 Reunited with Massachusetts
1690 French & Indians decimated Salmon Falls
1692 Separated from Massachusetts
1694 French & Indians attacked Durham
1703 French & Indians ravaged settlements
1719 Irish began to immigrate
1722 Manchester settled
1727 Concord settled
1739-41 Eastern & southern borders with Massachusetts settled
1741 Smallpox epidemic
1744 Diphtheria outbreak
1749 Severe drought
1749 Land grants made in Vermont
1754-61 French & Indian Wars
1764 New Hampshire border with Vermont set along Connecticut River
1764 Vermont separated
1775 Exeter became state capital
1775 Population 80,394 whites, 656 blacks
1776+ Only colony in which no battle occurred during Revolutionary War
1778 Became ninth state to join the Union
1782 Concord became state capital
1812 Large militia raised in anticipation of war
1812 Concern that Portsmouth would be invaded in War of 1812
1838 First railroad opened in state
1888 Blizzard known as the "Great White Hurricane"
1890 Twenty granite quarries employed one thousand
1935 Amoskeag Mills in Manchester closed
1939 USS Squalus submarine disaster
1945 World War II German U-Boat surrendered at Portsmouth
1949 Nashua Manufacturing Corporation mill in Nashua closed

New Jersey
1609 Dutch & Norwegian settlers arrived in Bergen
1612 Swedes arrived in Delaware Valley
1617 Bergen colonized by Dutch
1640 Hoboken settled
1660s Scottish Quaker colony established in East New Jersey
1664 Duke of York received the patent
1664 French settled in West & Scots-Irish in East Jersey
1664 Puritans from Connecticut colonized Newark
1664 Quakers settled along the Delaware River
1667 Became distinct province
1676 Quakers entered from New England
1677 Duke of York claimed West Jersey
1677 Quakers settled Burlington
1680 Scots began to arrive in numbers
1681 Camden settled
1681 Scottish lowlanders settled in the East
1682 More English Quakers settled along the Delaware River

1688 Annexed by Dominion of New England
1702 East Jersey & West Jersey joined to become New Jersey
1710 Dutch Protestants moved from New York to northern New Jersey
1739 Measles epidemic
1758 First Indian reservation established in the United States
1776 Became one of original thirteen states
1800 Quakers migrated to Canada
1807 Women lost the right to vote
1825 Morris Canal opened
1828 Factory strike at Paterson textile plant
1838 Delaware & Raritan Canal completed
1848 Compulsory vital records kept in Trenton
1853 Raritan Bay Union founded near Perth Amboy
1854 First train arrived from Camden to Atlantic City
1859 Wire-rope factory moved from western Pennsylvania to Trenton
1863 Hamburg-American Line established port at Hoboken
1880 Seventy-five Chinese arrived in Jersey City
1882 First amusement pier built in Atlantic City
1890 Streetcar system opened between Newark & Irvington
1902 International Harvester incorporated in New Jersey
1913 Silk workers in Paterson went on strike
1916 Black Tom Island Munitions Plant explosion perhaps set by German saboteurs damaged nearby Ellis Island immigration buildings
1918 German U boat sank six ships off New Jersey coast
1926 Year-long textile workers strike in Passaic
1927 Holland Tunnel opened
1933 Goodyear-Zeppelin airship disaster (73 died)
1934 Fire of *Morro Castle* near Ashbury Park (130 died)
1937 Hindenburg Zeppelin disaster (36 died)

New Mexico

1531 Spanish began colonizing
1598 First capital established twenty-five miles north of present- day Santa Fe
1609-10 Santa Fe settled
1680 Pueblo Indians took back region from Spanish
1692 Spanish re-conquered region
1706 Albuquerque established
1821 Became Mexican province
1822 Santa Fe Trail established
1846 Mexico rejected US offer to purchase area
1846-49 Multiple treaties with the Navajo Indians
1850 New Mexico Territory organized
1854 Gadsden Purchase added Gila Valley
1857 Law prohibited residency of free blacks or mulattos
1862 Re-captured by Union troops
1863 Present boundaries set
1864 Navajos defeated in Canyon de Chilly
1866 Freed blacks allowed to become residents
1866-67 Involuntary servitude made illegal

1878 Railroad arrived
1880 Gallup settled
1886 Apache wars ended
1908 Deadly flood in Folsom
1912 Admitted to Union
1913 Mine disaster in Dawson killed 263
1916 Pancho Villa raided Columbus
1920's Oil & potash discovered
1923 Coal mine fire in Dawson (120-270 died)
1923 Oil discovered on Navajo Reservation
1942-45 Secret atomic lab established at Los Alamos
1945 First atom bomb detonated in southern New Mexico
1950 Uranium discovered near Grants

New York

1609 Hudson River discovered
1610 Dutch settled along Hudson River
1614 First permanent settlement established
1615 Fort built at present-day New York City
1621 Dutch settled into Fort Orange
1623 Fort built at site of Albany
1624 Dutch founded colony of New Netherlands
1625 New Amsterdam founded on Manhattan Island
1626 Manhattan purchased instituted patroon system along Hudson River
1633 Swedes arrived in Mohawk & Schoharie Valleys
1641 Dutch laid claim to Connecticut land
1650 Connecticut boundaries set
1664 New Amsterdam was re-named New York
1664 British took New Amsterdam from Dutch
1680 Claimed jurisdiction over East Jersey & West Jersey
1686 Forbade printing presses
1688 Huguenots settled New Rochelle
1688 United with Dominion of New England
1689-97 King William's War
1690 French & Indians attacked Schenectady
1690 Yellow fever epidemic
1700 Law declared "Popish" priest entering colony could be hanged
1700-1800Pennsylvanians migrated to SW New York, Rhode Islanders to Rensselaer County New York, Connecticut settlers to Delaware County
1706 Palatinate Germans settled in Sullivan County
1710 Palatinate Germans arrived in Columbia County
1718 Scots-Irish moved into Orange & Ulster Counties
1719 Indians destroyed Saratoga
1731 Final boundary with Connecticut established
1738 Londonderry, New Hampshire residents moved to Otsego Co.
1738-42 Scottish Highlanders from Islay arrived
1742 Yellow fever outbreak
1744 Diphtheria outbreak
1744-48 King George's War
1745 Saratoga destroyed by Indians

1746	Yellow fever in Albany
1747	Measles epidemic
1749	French mission established at Ogdensburg
1754-63	French & Indian War
1756	French captured Fort Oswego
1759	Ticonderoga fell to English
1763	Scots received land in Washington County
1769	Boundary between New York & New Jersey settled
1773	Boundary between New York & Massachusetts settled
1773	Scottish Highlanders settled Mohawk Valley
1774	Shakers settled in New Lebanon
1776	Battle of Long Island
1776	Became one of original thirteen states
1781	New York ceded western territory to United States
1786	People from New England, New Jersey & Ireland arrived
1795	Residents of New Hampshire & Vermont poured into Upstate New York
1803	Irish Catholics began arriving
1803	Yellow fever epidemic
1812	Tuberculosis death rate at 700 per 100,000
1825	Norwegians began to arrive in larger numbers
1825	Erie Canal opened
1830s	Chinese sailors & peddlers arrived
1834	Cholera epidemic
1835	Fire destroyed 530 buildings in New York City
1839-46	Anti-rent War in Albany County
1845	Factory fire (30 died)
1856	Chateaugay tornado destroyed hundreds of homes
1851	State militia fired on railroad strikers in Portgage (2 died)
1859	First of the Orphan Trains took children to Michigan
1862	One-quarter of New York City 's population was Irish
1863	Colored Orphan Asylum attacked & blacks killed throughout New York City
1863	New York City Draft riot (1200 killed)
1867	Angola train disaster (approximately 80 died)
1874	Tompkins Square Riot
1876	Theater fire in Brooklyn (280+ died)
1884	East Coast earthquake
1888	Dozens died in blizzard
1889	Floods at Salmanca & Perry
1890	Garment workers unionized after a seven-month strike
1892	Hotel fire in New York City (28 died)
1892	Ellis Island opened
1898	Boroughs combined to form Greater New York City
1899	Hotel fire in New York City
1901	Leary Dye Company fire in Rochester
1904	*General Slocum* fire in New York City (1000+ died)
1911	Factory fire in New York City (145 died)
1912	Deadly office fire in New York City
1916	Marcus Garvey emigrated to US & began "Back to Africa" Movement in Harlem
1916	Nine thousand cases of polio in New York City (2300+ died)

1920 Bombing in Manhattan (30 killed)
1922 State highways received $20 million appropriation
1929 Wall Street Crash in New York City
1935 Riot in Harlem caused $200 million damage (3 died)
1938 New England Hurricane hit New York City
1939 World's Fair held in New York City
1940 Race riot in Harlem
1945 B-25 bomber flew into Empire State Building (13 died)
1945 United Nations established in New York City

North Carolina
1653 Immigration began from Virginia
1653 Roger Greene party settled in the Chowan area north of Albemarle Sound
1660's Influx of Royalists from Barbados
1662 George Durant settled at Perquimans District
1664 Albemarle formed
1664-6 Cape Fear settled by English
1670 Charleston founded
1683 Scottish farmers settled Port Royal
1690 French Huguenots from Virginia settled along Pamlico River
1700 Considered part of Virginia
1700-10 New Bern settled by Germans from the Rhinish Palatinate
1700-10 Huguenots settled Bath
1702-13 Queen Anne's War
1703 Church of England established as state religion
1710 German Palatines settled along the Roanoke & Neuse River
1711 Settlers at Bath & New Bern massacred by Indians
1711 Tuscarora War
1719 Large numbers of Scots Irish arrived
1729 Called as North Carolina & South Carolina although not official
1739 Scottish Highlanders began arriving in Cape Fear Valley
1739 Pennsylvania Germans arrived at Wachovia, Forsythe& Guilford
1745 Germans from Pennsylvania moved to the western region
1745 Germans settled along the Yadkin River
1745 Highlanders from Scotland moved west
1750's Pennsylvania Quakers arrived in Randolph County
1753 German Moravians settled in Betharabia, Wachovia Tract
1756 Cherokee uprising in North Carolina
1766 Wilmington's Sons of Liberty blocked stamps from arriving at port
1771 Fifteen hundred Regulators defeated by militia -- leaders hanged, others fled
1774-75 Scot Highlanders settled Wilmington & the southeast of the state
1776 Became one of the original thirteen states
1799 First gold discovered in United States
1830 Cherokee Indians forced out of their homes
1830 Pennsylvania & Virginia Quakers moved into Rockingham, Guilford & Chatham Counties
1861 Seceded from Union
1866 Tuscarora Indians revolted in Robeson County

1877 Reconstruction ended
1878 Cherokee reservation formed in western North Carolina
1886 Mecklenburg Earthquake
1889 High Point Furniture Manufacturing Co. opened a small factory
1898 Race riot in Wilmington
1903 Orville & Wilber Wright's flight at Kitty Hawk
1906 Greensboro's black sit-in at lunch counter lasted six months
1911 Anti-trust suit divided American Tobacco Company into four companies
1918 Fort Bragg established
1920s Tobacco became important crop
1925 Coal mine explosions in Coal Glenn (between 59 & 71 killed)
1933 Tennessee Valley Authority began relief programs
1940 Two category one hurricanes hit state
1948 Nearly 2500 polio cases

North Dakota

1781 First trading post established
1794 Trading post established near Knife River
1801 Trading post established at Grand Forks
1804 Sacagawea joined Lewis & Clark Expedition
1812 Agriculture commune established by Canadians at Pembina
1818 US acquired eastern North Dakota from England & made it part of the Missouri Territory
1820 Grasshoppers destroyed crops
1823 Boundary between Canada & North Dakota fixed
1837 Smallpox epidemic at Fort Clark
1853 New agriculture community settled at Pembina
1858 Land east of the Missouri River left with no territorial government when Minnesota became a state
1860-80 Troops suppressed Indian uprisings
1861 North Dakota Territory organized
1863 North Dakota opened to homesteading
1863-68 Indian uprisings & military reprisals
1870's Fargo began as outpost
1872 Northern Pacific Railway reached North Dakota
1873 First train arrived in Bismarck
1875 Beginning of enormous wheat farms
1881 Major flood of Missouri River
1881 Sitting Bull surrendered
1889 North Dakota& South Dakota separated
1889 Admitted to Union
1893 Fire destroyed most of Fargo's business district, left many homeless
1894 Fire destroyed four block area of La Moure
1898 Bismarck Business District fire
1903 Fort Lincoln completed south of Bismarck
1905 More than five hundred miles of rail laid in one year
1907 Gas well established south of Westhop
1915 Largest wheat crop to date
1919 Windstorm in Williams County & Divide County (8 killed)
1930 Windstorm (1800+ buildings damaged)

1931 Last lynching in state occurred in Schafer
1933 Violent strike at construction site of new state capitol building
1940 Pick-Sloan Project for development of Missouri River approved
1945 Train wreck in Michigan, North Dakota (30+ died)

Ohio
1701 New York received land grant from Iroquois
1749 Ohio Company received land grant
1772-76 Moravians resided at Schoenbrunn (New Philadelphia)
1780 George Rogers Clark's men destroyed Shawnee Indian villages
1780 New York ceded land to US
1782 At least ninety Indians massacred at Gnadenhutten
1783 Area ceded to Great Britain
1784 Virginia abandoned claims to region
1785 Massachusetts granted Ohio
1786 Connecticut ceded Western Reserve
1787 Ohio became part of the Northwest Territory
1788 Marietta was settled
1789 Cincinnati founded
1789 French settlement at Gallipolis established
1796 Cleveland founded by group from Connecticut
1796 Chillicothe founded
1800 Virginia & Connecticut gave up any claim
1800 Western Reserve became part of the Northwest Territory
1803 Admitted to the Union
1832 Ohio & Erie Canal opened from Waverly to Portsmouth
1833 Delaware & Raritan Railroad began service
1833 Cholera epidemic in Columbus
1834 First freight passed through the Delaware & Raritan Canal
1837 Boundary dispute with Michigan settled
1843 Families arrived in Monmouth County from Albany, New York
1852 Railroad reached Cleveland
1863 Battle of Buffington Island
1876 Ashtabula River rail disaster (90+ died)
1884 Ohio River flooding ($3 million damage)
1884 Riots in Cincinnati
1900 Hungarian influx began
1907 Floods in Athens (7 died, thousands homeless)
1908 School fire in Collinwood (176 died)
1913 Spring flooding (420+ died)
1924 Tornados in Lorain & Sandusky (85 died)
1929 Clinic fire in Cleveland (125 died)
1930 State Penitentiary fire (320 died)
1930 Coal mine fire in Millfield (80+ died)
1930 Fire in Ohio State Penitentiary in Columbus (300+ died)
1942 Circus fire in Cleveland
1944 East Ohio Gas Explosion in Cleveland (130 died)
1944 Large natural gas explosion (100 died)

Oklahoma
1802 First white settlement established at trading post at Salina on east bank of the Grand River

1803	United States acquired territory as part of Louisiana Purchase
1812	Became part of the Missouri Territory
1819	Most of Oklahoma became part of the Arkansas Territory
1821	Beginnings of Santa Fe Trail
1824	Creek & Seminoles received land in middle of Indian Territory
1824	Fort Gibson & Fort Towson established
1830	Indian Territory established by Congress
1834	Land set aside for eastern Indians removed from homes
1835-36	Fort Holmes established by American Fur Co.
1836	Creek, Chickasaws, Choctaws, Cherokees were moved to the Indian Territories of Oklahoma
1844	First newspaper published
1845-48	Seven thousand Choctaws were moved to Oklahoma from Alabama & Mississippi
1850	Texas relinquished claim to the Oklahoma Panhandle
1867	Small grants given to Sauk & Fox Indians
1871-72	Indian raids in southwest renewed under Satana
1871-72	Land grants given to Osage, Pottawatomie & Wichita
1871-73	Missouri, Kansas & Texas Railroad was built across the territory
1875	First cattle ranches established in the western Indian Territory
1876	Land grants given to Pawnee
1878	Land grants given to Punca& Nez Perce
1881	Land granted to Missouri Indians
1883	Land granted to Kickapoo & Iowa Indians
1889	Nearly 2 million acres of central Oklahoma opened for settlement
1891	Indian land began to be opened to white settlement
1892	Coal mine explosion in Krebs (100 died)
1893	Tornado in Moore (31 died)
1901	Red Fork - Tulsa oilfield opened
1905	Tornado in Snyder (97 died)
1907	Counties were established
1907	Oklahoma admitted to the Union
1918	State hospital fire in Oklahoma City (38 died)
1920	Osage County oilfields opened
1920	Tornado in Peggs (71 died)
1920s	Drought covered the state
1921	Tulsa race riot (as many as 300 may have died)
1922	Mine explosion in McCurtain (8 died)
1924	School fire in Hobart (35 died)
1926	Coal mine fire in Wilburton (90+ died)
1928	Oklahoma City oilfield opened
1934-35	Drought brought Dust Bowl -- farmers along Grand River lost their land
1942	Tornados in Pryor (52 died) & Oklahoma City (35 died)
1945	Tornado in Antlers (69 died)
1947	Tornado in Woodward (181 died)

Oregon

1792	Robert Gray discovered Columbia River
1793	Alexander Mackenzie explored for the Northwest Company
1804-05	Lewis & Clark explored region

1811 Astoria area settled
1821 Russians claimed lands along the west coast
1843 Provisional government formed
1843 Eight hundred people established a wagon road to Oregon
1844 Four wagon trains arrived
1844 "Lash Law" required all blacks be whipped twice a year until they left the region (law was soon withdrawn)
1846-48 Part of area disputed with Great Britain
1848 Exclusion law passed
1849 Oregon Territory organized
1851 Gold discovered near Jacksonville
1859 Admitted to the Union
1862 Adopted a law requiring blacks, Chinese, mulattos & Hawaiians pay a $5 a year tax
1862 Gold discovered in eastern Oregon
1866 Oregon did not pass 14th Amendment granting blacks citizenship
1868 Oregon finally passed 14th Amendment
1870-1927Fifteenth Amendment giving African-American suffrage was defeated & the state constitution allowed no black suffrage
1877 Chief Joseph & Nez Perce made peace after 72 years of war
1878 Bannock Indian War
1880 Tornado hit Portland
1883 Transcontinental Railroad completed in Portland
1886 City militias activated to quell Anti-Chinese violence
1891 "Great Fire" in The Delles
1891 Portland annexed Albinia
1894 "Great Flood" in The Delles
1909 Portland to Seattle Railroad completed
1915 Delles-Celilo Canal opened
1936 Los Angeles sent 125 policemen to Arizona & Oregon borders to keep "undesirables" out of California
1936-37 Urban development slowed in Portland
1950 Civil Rights Ordinance defeated in Portland

Pennsylvania

1643 Swedes moved into the uplands
1675 First 25,000 English & Welsh Quakers members arrived
1677 Rhinelanders settled Germantown
1680 Bucks, Philadelphia & settled by Quakers
1681 Penn received a patent
1681 English Quakers settled in Philadelphia
1682 Welsh settled near Philadelphia
1683 Rhinelanders & Palatines settled Germantown
1690 Welsh Quakers settled west of Philadelphia
1692 Governed by New York
1699 Yellow fever epidemic in Philadelphia
1700 German Mennonites moved west of Philadelphia
1710 Large numbers of Palatines arrived but sent to New York
1710 Mennonites settled Lancaster County
1714 Scots-Irish began major influx
1720 Settlers migrated west over the Great Indian War Path

1720	Western Pennsylvania settled
1723	German Protestants from New York settled in Lancaster County
1729	Six thousand arrived from Europe
1731	Schwenkfelders moved into the southeastern part of the colony
1732	Maryland boundary disputed
1737	Pennsylvania purchased Lehigh Valley from Delaware Indians
1740	More Ulster Scots-Irish arrived
1741	Yellow fever epidemic in Philadelphia
1741	Moravians settled Bethlehem & Germantown
1741	Moravians from Georgia arrived
1742	Indians released land on both sides of the Susquehanna River
1746	Diphtheria struck Philadelphia
1747	Measles epidemic
1747	Yellow fever in Philadelphia
1750	Yellow fever in Philadelphia
1754	French built Fort Duquesne (Pittsburgh)
1754-63	French & Indian War (Seven Year War)
1762	Yellow fever epidemic in Philadelphia
1763	Western Pennsylvania settled via the Forbes Road
1767	Mason Dixon Line disputed
1770	Moravians from Effingham, Georgia moved into Bethlehem
1773	Influx of Irish immigrants
1776	Became one of original thirteen states
1784	fled to Canada (mostly New Brunswick & Nova Scotia)
1788	Measles epidemic
1793	Yellow fever outbreak
1794	Yellow fever outbreak
1794	Whiskey Rebellion
1796	Yellow fever outbreak
1798	Yellow ever outbreak
1800	Quakers& Mennonites migrated to Canada
1800	Capital moved from Philadelphia to Washington D.C.
1811	First steamboat to go from Pittsburgh to New Orleans
1826	Schuylkill Canal opened from Philadelphia to Mount Carbon
1827	Union Canal opened
1834	Race riot in Philadelphia
1837	Typhus epidemic
1844	Riots in Philadelphia (16 died, 2 Catholic churches burned)
1852	Pennsylvania Railroad reached Pittsburgh
1859	Oil discovered & production began in Titusville
1860	Smallpox epidemic
1860-77	Molly Maguires worked secretly for miners of descent in anthracite region
1863	Battle of Gettysburg
1869	Coal mine fire in Plymouth (110 died)
1876	Amalgamated Association of Iron & Steel Workers formed
1877	Railroad workers rioted in Reading & Pittsburgh
1885	Typhoid epidemic in Plymouth
1889	Johnstown flood (2209 died)
1891	Strike & violence at Carnegie Steel Mill (60% of workers lost jobs)
1891	Coal mine explosion in Mount Pleasant (100+ died)

1892 Violent strike in Homewood
1894 Miners rioted in Connellsville
1897 Coal miners went on strike
1901 Anthracite miners walked out on strike statewide
1902 Coal mine fire in Johnstown (110+ died)
1902 Anthracite strike
1902-03 Approximately 150 thousand United Mine Workers went on strike
1904 Coal mine fire in Cheswick (nearly 170 died)
1907 Coal mine explosion in Jacobs Creek (230+ died)
1908 Opera house fire in Boyertown (170 died)
1908 Mine explosion at Monongahela (100+ died)
1908 Coal mine fire in Marianna (150+ died)
1913 Coal mine fire in Finleyville (90+ died)
1917-18 More than 300 thousand Pennsylvanians fought in World War I
1919 Anthracite mine fire in Wilkes-Barre (90+ died)
1920's Anthracite strikes
1922 Coal mine fire in Spangler (75+ died)
1927 Industrial fire in Pittsburgh (28 died)
1928 Coal mine fire in Mather (nearly 200 died)
1936 Great Flood in Pittsburgh & western Pennsylvania

Rhode Island

1636 Settled by Roger Williams
1636 English Baptist arrived from Massachusetts
1636 Providence founded
1638 Anne Hutchinson & William Coddington founded Pocasset Portsmouth)
1639 Newport founded
1640 Estimated population of four hundred
1640's Quakers arrived from Massachusetts
1643 Seceders founded Warwick
1643 Roger Williams obtained a charter
1652 Passed first anti-slavery bill in North America
1657 Colony gave protection to Quakers
1658 Colony granted protection to Dutch Jews
1660's More Quakers arrived from England
1661 Quakers held first annual meeting
1665 Quakerism outlawed
1686 Part of Dominion of New England under Royal Governor Andros
1709-1807Nearly one thousand ships left Rhode Island to import more than one hundred thousand slaves from Africa
1729 Ship captains had to pay £50 for each immigrant not from England, Ireland, or the Channel Islands
1737 Smallpox
1740 Estimated population 25,250
1747 Rhode Island gained Bristol, Tiverton, Little Compton, Warren & other towns in Bristol County from Massachusetts
1763 Synagogue opened in Newport
1765 Mob in Newport destroyed a British warship
1769 Citizens burned a crown revenue ship at Newport
1774 Slave importation outlawed

1776 Became one of original thirteen states
1780-81 French troops were stationed in state
1784 Gradual abolition of slavery became law
1786 Farm strike led to farmers burning grain, dumping milk & leaving crops to rot when merchants refused to take depreciated paper money
1790 Became the last of the original 13 states to ratify the constitution
1824 Female weavers went on strike over wages & hours in Pawtucket
1842 Dorr's Rebellion
1847 Pennsylvania Railroad completed from Harrisburg to Pittsburgh
1853 Rail service extended to Chicago
1860s-90 French Canadians arrived in large numbers
1863 Battle of Gettysburg (43 thousand Union and Confederates died)
1900-17 Jewish immigration peaked
1905 More than 50% of population was Roman Catholic
1907 Steamer *Larchmont* sunk in Block Island Sound (111 died)
1911 Fabre Line of Marseilles, France chose Providence as main terminus
1913 Town of West Warwick was founded
1938 Hurricane caused $100 million damage (310+ died)
1942 Large Portuguese population in Providence
1945 Walsh-Kaiser shipyard nearly deserted

South Carolina

1562 Huguenots built a fort at Port Royal
1660s Influx of English Royalists from Barbados
1670 Barbadian colonists settled on islands
1671 Kussoe Tribe uprising
1671 Dutch from New York arrived in Charleston
1675-1750New England trading ships wintered along the coast
1678 Quakers settled along coast
1680 French settled in Charleston
1683 Baptists from Somerset, England arrived in Charleston
1683 Scots-Irish settled along Ashley River & Scots at Fort Royal
1685 Huguenots from Wurttemberg, Germany arrived in Beaufort
1696 Huguenots were given full rights
1702 Five hundred Carolinians pillaged St. Augustine
1711 Tuscarora War
1715 Yemassee War came about when Native Americans rebelled against British abuse (approximately 100 settlers died)
1736 Welsh Baptists from Pennsylvania settled along the Great Pee Dee River
1738 Measles epidemic
1739 Angolan slaves attacked white planters in St. Paul 's Parish
1730 Major migration from Virginia began
1747 Measles epidemic
1751 Diphtheria outbreak
1752 Seaboard colonists feared French attacks
1753 Influx of settlers from Antigua
1754 First cotton exported

1754-63	French & Indian War (Seven Years War)
1756	Cherokee uprising
1762	New Jersey & Pennsylvania Quakers moved to Newberry County
1767	Regulators became active in back country
1776	Became one of original thirteen states
1790	Migrations into East Tennessee began
1798	Divided into judicial districts
1800	Migrations into Central Tennessee began
1804	Hurricane hit Georgia & the Carolinas
1820-35	As many as half the population moved west
1822	Denmark Vesey's Slave Conspiracy put down in Charlestown
1830	Locomotive service between Charleston & Hamburg launched
1838	Ansonborough destroyed by fire
1860	Seceded from Union
1861	Confederates fired on Ft. Sumter
1865	Columbia burned by Union forces
1876	Racial tensions high
1886	Earthquake in Charleston (92 killed)
1886	Low Country Earthquake (83 died)
1893	Hurricane went ashore at Myrtle Beach (28 died)
1919	Boll Weevil began crop devastation
1923	School fire in Beulah (77 died)
1924	Tornadoes in rural parts of state (53 died)
1934	United Textile Workers strike
1938	Charleston tornado (32 died)
1940	Hurricane hit near Georgia & South Carolina border (100 died)

South Dakota

1804	Lewis & Clark passed through
1812	Became part of the Missouri Territory
1831	Steamboat service began on the Upper Missouri River
1832	Fort Pierre settled
1834	Eastern part became part of Michigan Territory
1836	Eastern part became part of Wisconsin Territory
1838	Eastern part became part of Iowa Territory
1849	Became part of Minnesota Territory
1856	First settlement at Sioux Falls lasted six years
1857	First farm settlements started
1858	Yankton Sioux ceded southeastern portion to the United States
1859	Dakota Territory organized
1863-65	Indian uprisings
1868	Red Cloud Indian War ended
1872	Railroad built from Sioux City to Yankton
1873	Russian Mennonites settled
1874	Gold Rush in Black Hills began
1876	War broke out between gold prospectors & Sioux Indians
1886	Railroad across the state completed
1889	North & South Dakota separated & admitted to the Union
1889	Yankton, Chamberlain & Douglas County prairie fires
1890	Eleven million acres of Indian reservation was opened to white settlement

1890	Battle of Wounded Knee
1895	Over 160,000 acres of Yankton Sioux lands opened to settlement
1899	Bijou Hills tornado (7 died)
1900	Aberdeen Gas Plant fire completely destroyed plant
1904	Over 400,000 acres of Rosebud Reservation opened to settlers
1926	Passenger train derailed near McIntosh
1932	Many farmers faced foreclosure

Tennessee

1768	Eastern Tennessee settlers arrived
1771	Watauga settled
1776	Battle of Island Flats between settlers & Cherokees
1779	Jonesborough settled
1784	State of Franklin organized
1786	Thousands of settlers arrived in the State of Franklin
1787	Franklin legislature met for last time
1789	Franklin reunited with North Carolina
1790	Population of 35,691
1795	Walton Road linked Knoxville to Nashville over the Cumberland Plateau
1796	Admitted to the Union
1800	Population of 105,602
1810	Population of 261,727
1818	Gen. Andrew negotiated treaty with Chickasaws to purchase western Tennessee
1819	First steamboat reached Nashville
1835	Treaty of Removal led to resettlement of Indians
1838	Cherokees forced to leave
1857	Memphis Charleston Railroad opened route from Atlantic Ocean to the Mississippi River
1861	Tennessee joined the Confederacy
1861-65	Numerous Civil War battles fought in the state
1865	Ku Klux Klan organized in Pulaski
1865	*Sultana* exploded in Mississippi River near Memphis
1866	Memphis massacre (46 African-Americans killed, more than 100 houses, schools & churches burned)
1878	Yellow fever epidemic (1/4+ of Memphis' residents died)
1881	Tennessee segregated railroad cars
1889	Enormous damage from tornado in Liberty, DeKalb County
1890	Phosphate deposits explored near Columbia
1902	Coal mine fire in Coal Creek (180+ died)
1911	Coal mine fire in Briceville (80+ died)
1917	Tornados in Lawrence, Trousdale, Gibson, Carroll, Henry, Benton, Stewart, McNairy, Chester, Henderson Decatur, Perry; Davidson, Wilson, Hickman, Dickson, Montgomery counties
1918	Train wreck in Nashville (101 died)
1925	Scopes "Monkey Trial"
1933	Tennessee Valley Authority (TVA) established
1933	Tornados in downtown Nashville (44 died)
1942	Construction of Atomic Energy plant at Oak Ridge began

Texas

1519	Spanish explored region around Rio Grande
1720	Spanish forces attempted to occupy Texas
1821	Became Mexican state
1825	First Americans allowed in Coahuilla (Mexican state of Texas)
1826	Anglo-Americans attempted to establish Republic of Fredonia
1830	Mexico increased taxes, established military outposts & prohibited further colonization to discourage American settlers
1835	Texans defeated Mexican troops at San Antonio
1836	Texas declared independence from Mexico & became a republic
1836	Battle of San Jacinto between Texans & Mexican forces led by General Santa Anna
1845	Admitted to the Union
1846-48	Mexican-American War
1848	Rio Grande established as southern border
1850	Construction of first railroad in Texas begun
1854	Reservations established for Comanches in Throckmorton County & for the Tawakonis, Wacos & Tonkas in Young County.
1859	Indians on west-central Texas reservations moved to Indian Territory in Oklahoma
1861	Texas seceded from Union
1863	Federal troops occupied Galveston
1865	Last Civil War battle fought at Palmito Ranch in South Texas
1866	Cattle drives began to northern markets
1874	Red River War between US Army & Southern Plains Indians
1896	Tornado in Sherman (70+ died)
1900	Hurricane at Galveston (6000+ died)
1901	Oil discovered near Beaumont
1902	Tornado in Goliad (114 died)
1906	Oil discovered at Petrolia
1909	Tornado in Zepher
1909	Hurricane at Velasco (41 died)
1911	Oil discovered at Electra
1915	Hurricane at Galveston (275 died)
1919	Hurricane at Corpus Christi
1919	Tornado moved across Henderson, Van Zandt, Wood, Camp & Red River Counties (42 died 150 injured)
1921	Oil discovered at Mexia
1921	Multiple tornadoes
1921	Oil discovered at Amarillo
1927	Rock Springs Tornado (74 died)
1930	Tornado in Frost (41 died)
1930	Oil discovered in East Texas
1932	Hurricane at Freeport (40 died)
1933	South Texas Hurricane (40 died)
1937	School fire in New London (300+ died)
1943	Hotel fire in Houston (50+ died)
1946	Hotel fire in Dallas (10 died)
1947	Ship packed with ammonium nitrate exploded in Texas City (500+ died)
1947	Tornados in White Deer (42 died 201 injured)

Utah

1776	Franciscan friars explored region
1843-5	Region explored & mapped by John Charles Fremont
1847	Mormon pioneers arrived
1848	Grasshopper plague stopped by seagulls
1849	Mormons adopted a constitution for State of Deseret
1850	Utah Territory organized & boundaries established
1854	Grasshoppers endanger crops
1857	Johnston's Army arrived
1857	Mountain Meadows Massacre of 120 emigrants headed for California
1860	Pony Express crossed the territory
1861	Telegraph line completed
1862	US Congress made polygamy illegal
1863	Silver & lead discovered in Bingham Canyon
1865-67	Indian was led by Blackhawk
1869	Transcontinental railroad connected Utah with east & west
1890	Polygamy banned by Mormon Church
1896	Admitted to the Union
1900	Mine explosion & fire at Scofield (200 died)
1906	Open pit copper mining in Bingham Canyon
1911	Strawberry Reservoir completed
1924	Coal mine fire in Castle Gate (170+ died)
1942-45	Japanese interment camp near Delta
1943	Geneva Steel Plant opened in Utah County
1946	Train accident near Ogden (48 died)

Vermont

1609	Champlain discovered lake named for him
1690	British fort built at Chimney Point
1721-25	Drummers War (Lovewell's War)
1724	Outpost at Brattleboro settled
1749	Severe drought
1749-64	New Hampshire & New York both claimed the area
1754-61	French & Indian Wars
1761	Bennington settled
1764	Border with New Hampshire settled along Connecticut River
1770	Green Mountain Boys formed to drive out New Yorkers
1771	Approximately 7,000 Vermonters lived in more than 55 towns
1775	Ft. Ticonderoga captured from British
1775	Declared its independence from New York & New Hampshire
1775	Westminster Massacre came from one of the earliest acts of resistance to British authority
1777	Claimed its independence from Great Britain
1777-81	Loyalists fled to Canada
1780	Last major Indian raid
1781	Approximately 30,000 Vermonters lived in more than 95 towns
1786	One hundred Shay supporters ordered to leave Shaftbury
1787	Montpelier settled
1791	Admitted to Union
1793	Influenza epidemic

1795 Vermonters began to flood into Upstate New York
1808 First lake steamship on Lake Champlain
1810 Spotted Fever epidemic
1812 War of 1812
1823 Champlain Canal opened
1843 Chambly Canal opened, bypassing rapids between Montreal & Quebec
1846 Two hundred railroad workers went on strike in Burlington
1855 Association organized in Rutland to move Vermonters to western states
1864 St. Albans Raid became northern-most Civil War engagement when rebels robbed businesses & set fire to a bridge
1864 Battle of the Wilderness in Virginia (191 Vermonters killed & 96 missing)
1867-71 Roughly 1400 Fenians dedicated to overthrowing the British rule of Ireland continuously raided Canada from St. Albans
1883 Ely War during which National Guard was called out when 200 miners seized the Ely Mining Company
1888 Great Blizzard, also known as the "Great White Hurricane"
1892 Growing discord with Canadian immigrants
1894 First polio epidemic
1922 Barre Granite Strike broken by poor French-Canadian laborers
1930 More cattle in state then people
1936 Vermont Marble Workers Strike
1950 Population 377+ thousand

Virginia

1587 First English child born in America named Virginia Dare
1591 Roanoke Island colonists disappeared
1606 Patent granted
1607 Twenty-one Jamestown settlers died within one month
1607 Jamestown settled
1608 Jamestown plagued by disease & starvation (66 died)
1612 Slaves introduced at Jamestown
1622 Jamestown Massacre (500 settlers killed)
1630s English Anglicans spread out along the Eastern Shore
1632 Maryland removed from Virginia jurisdiction
1640s English Quakers arrived
1644-46 Indian War
1649 Cavaliers (supporters of dethroned English king) sought refuge
1661 Mass migration of Quakers into Maryland
1662 Church of England law established
1667 Hurricane killed most livestock & grain
1675-77 Threats of Indian uprising
1676 Bacon's Rebellion (Virginia Civil War)
1677 Arrival of British fleet
1680 All settlers who took oath of allegiance were naturalized
1683 Printing presses banned
1685 French Huguenots began arriving, mostly settling in Henrico Co.
1700 Hundreds of Huguenots settled on the James River
1712 Divided into two parishes
1714 Col. Spottswood passed into the Ohio Valley

1714	Lutherans from Nassau-Siegen, Germany settled in Essex Co.
1716	Spottswood led planters over Blue Ridge Mountains to Shenandoah Valley
1717	Lutherans from Wurttemberg, Germany settled in Essex County
1726	Pennsylvanian Germans settled in the Shenandoah Valley
1730	Protestants from Maryland, Delaware, & New Jersey moved into the Shenandoah Valley
1730-36	Scots-Irish moved into the Shenandoah Valley
1737	Yellow fever epidemic
1740	More Ulster Scots arrived, many moving from Pennsylvania to Frederick County
1748-49	Ohio Company formed
1749	Britain granted 200,000 acres in upper Ohio to Virginia
1755	Washington made commander in chief in preparation of French invasion of Ohio Valley
1769	Virginia settlers migrated into Watauga Valley, Tennessee
1771	"Great Fresh" flood on Rappahannock & James Rivers destroyed area's tobacco crop
1776	Became one of original thirteen states
1776	British fleet bombarded Norfolk, setting it on fire
1779	British fleet entered Hampton Roads & destroyed continental supply depot
1780	State capital transferred from Williamsburg to Richmond
1781	British invaded Virginia & captured Richmond
1782	Population had reached in excess of 567,000
1784	Ceded western territory to US
1785	Dispute with Maryland over Potomac River
1790	Gave Arlington & Alexandria to federal government for the District of Columbia
1793	Influenza epidemic
1811	Theater fire in Richmond (160 died)
1831	Nat Turner's slave uprising (60 whites & 100 slaves died)
1845	Appomattox County established
1846	Congress returned Alexandria & Arlington area to Virginia
1847	Arlington County created out of Alexandria County
1847	Highland County established
1861	Battle of Bull Run
1861	Seceded from the Union
1862	Richmond captured by Union soldiers
1863	West Virginia broke off from Virginia
1865	Richmond evacuated
1865	Battle at Appomattox
1867	Coal mine fire in Winterpock (nearly 70 died)
1870	Virginia reentered the Union
1876	Coal discovered in southwestern portion of the state
1877	Richmond flooded
1877	Reconstruction ended
1884	Coal mine explosion in Pocahontas (100+ died)
1885	Rural unrest
1901	"Jim Crow " Laws created legal segregation
1910	Major black migration into Norfolk

1915 Major black migration into southwestern, Virginia
1929 Rye Cove tornado (44 died)
1936 Richmond flooded
1938 Mine disaster at Keen Mountain (50+ died)
1941-43 Pentagon built in Arlington
1950 School desegregation began at University of Virginia Law School

Washington

1775 Land claimed by Spain
1787 Boston merchants sent ships to explore likelihood of establishing trading posts
1792 Spain established first non-Indian settlement
1805 Lewis & Clark reached Pacific Ocean
1811 John Jacob Astor established Fort Astoria at mouth of Columbia River
1819 Spain relinquished claim to region
1825 Fort Vancouver founded
1845 First permanent American settlement north of Columbia River settled
1848 Oregon Territory created with Washington as part of it
1851 Seattle area settled
1853 Washington Territory created
1853 Separated from Oregon Territory
1855 Gold discovered in eastern Washington
1855-59 Yakima Indians wage war on settlers
1858 Gold discovered near Fort Colville
1859 Gold discovered along the Similkameen River
1860's Silver discovered in the Okanogan
1863 Canyon flood washed away building in Port Angeles
1883 Northern Pacific Railroad completed to Tacoma
1885 Anti-Chinese riots led to martial law
1886 Roslyn found as coal mining town
1886 Tacoma & Seattle ejected all Chinese
1887 Northern Pacific Railroad reached Tacoma
1889 Admitted to the Union
1889 Seattle destroyed by fire
1893 Great Northern Railroad completed to Seattle
1897-99 Alaskan gold rush increased Seattle population
1899 Mining wars at Coeur d'Alene
1900 Weyerhauser began logging business
1910 Seattle International District became only place on the mainland where Japanese, Chinese, Filipino, African-Americans & Vietnamese built a neighborhood together
1917 Lake Washington Ship Canal completed from Puget Sound to Lake Washington
1917 Fort Lewis established
1920-21 Coal Wars over efforts to unionize
1928 Filipino farm workers driven from Yakima Valley
1932 Unemployed marched on Olympia
1933 Unemployed built a cardboard & scrap lumber city in Seattle
1937 Bonneville Dam completed on Columbia River

1941	Grand Coulee Dam completed

West Virginia

1722	Virginia let families to live on state land for ten years, rent-free
1727	New Mecklenburg (Shepherdstown) established by Pennsylvania Germans
1731	First permanent settlement
1732	Scots-Irish, Welsh, & Germans began to settle
1744	Indians ceded land between Allegheny & Ohio Rivers to England
1744	Scots-Irish from Pennsylvania moved into Brooke County
1755	Scots-Irish from Pennsylvania moved into Lewisburg
1758	Morgantown settled
1766	Morgantown destroyed by Indian raids
1767	Morgantown founded
1768	Williamstown founded
1769	Large influx of settlers
1772	Fort Morgan built & Morgantown settled nearby
1776	Fort Fincastle (Henry) built at Wheeling
1782	British & Indian sieges at Ft. Henry
1810	Oil discovered
1818	Cumberland Road completed
1833	Cholera epidemic in Wheeling
1834	First commercial coal mining occurred in Kanawha Valley
1859	John Brown led a raid on Harpers Ferry
1861	Forty counties broke from Virginia
1863	Admitted to the Union
1870	Charleston incorporated
1870	Huntington founded at western end of C & O Railroad
1873	C & O Railroad crossed the state
1877	Governor sent state militia to Martinsburg where railway workers were interfering with train movement
1879	First oil pipeline from Volcano to Parkersburg
1879	Mail Pouch Tobacco began production in Wheeling
1880	Militia sent to break up coal strike at Hawk's Nest
1884	Ohio River flooded at Huntington
1886	Mountain Brook mine disaster (39 killed)
1889	Oil drilling commenced near Mannington
1897	Coal miners strike
1905	Morgantown incorporated
1906	Mine disasters in Mercer, Kanawha, Fayette & Barbour counties (86 died)
1907	Mine disaster in Monongah (360+ died)
1907	Mine fire in Stuart (80+ died)
1907	Asian Americans driven from Bellingham
1909	Earthquake in Charles Town & Martinsburg area
1910	Mount Hope destroyed by fire
1912	Paint Creek Miners walked out on strike
1912	Mine disaster at Jed (83 died)
1912-13	West Virginia Mine War
1913	Ohio River flooding left thousands homeless in Huntington & Parkersburg

1914 Mine disaster in Eccles (180+ died)
1915 Coal mine fire at Layland (100+ died)
1920-21 Coal miner strikes statewide
1924 Three year strike against northern coal operations
1924 Mine disaster at Benwood (119 died)
1927 Mine disaster at Everettville (97 died)
1940 Coal mine fire at Bartley, McDowell County (90+died)
1944 Tornadoes in central part of state (100 died)

Wisconsin

1666 Fur trade opened
1701-38 Fox Indian Wars
1763 Became British Territory
1764 Green Bay settled
1774 Quebec Act annexed region to Quebec Province
1783 United States took possession
1788 Added to Northwest Territory
1795 Trading posts opened at Sheyboygan, Kewaunee & Mantowoc
1800 Added to Indiana Territory
1809 Added to Illinois Territory
1818 Added to Michigan Territory
1820's Influx of settlers to southern Wisconsin lead mining region
1822 New York Indians were moved into the region
1830's Heavy influx of settlers to Lake Michigan shoreline
1832 Black Hawk War
1835 First steamboat at Milwaukee
1836 Wisconsin Territory organized
1837 Madison survey & mapped
1840's Dutch settlers began to arrive
1844 Utopian colony established at Ceresco (Ripon)
1845 Dutch settled in Fond du Lac County
1845 Mormons settled at Voree (Burlington)
1845 Swiss colony arrived at New Glarus
1848 Admitted to Union
1848 Large influx of Germans began
1860 *Lady Elgin* sank in Lake Michigan on a Milwaukee to Chicago run (approximately 400 died)
1861 Bank riot in Milwaukee
1871 Forest fire near Peshtigo (nearly 1200 died)
1883 Hotel fire in Milwaukee (71 died)
1884 Iron ore mining began in state
1887 Marshfield nearly destroyed by fire
1886 Militia called in to confront 2000 strikers in Milwaukee
1894 Forest fires in northern & central parts of state
1899 Tornado at New Richmond (117 died)
1905 State civil service established
1911 First income tax law & teacher's pension act established
1921 Equal rights act enacted
1932 State passed 1st unemployment insurance
1933 Dairy farmers went on strike

Wyoming

1803 Became part of Louisiana Purchase
1807 Yellowstone region explored
1812 South Pass discovered, opening the Oregon Trail
1826 Wagons for a fur company from St. Louis arrived at Wind River
1834 Fort William (Fort Laramie) built as first white settlement in Wyoming Territory
1843 Fort Bridger established on Oregon Trail
1847 Major Mormon migration passed through
1848 Fort Kearny erected
1849 Fort Laramie purchased by federal government
1851 Treaty with Arapaho, Sioux & Cheyenne
1853 Fifty-five Mormons settled at Fort Bridger & renamed it Fort Supply
1857 Mormons abandoned Fort Supply
1860 Census taken with Nebraska
1867 First Union Pacific train arrived at East Cheyenne
1868 Northeastern Wyoming Territory reserved for Sioux Indians
1868 Wyoming Territory organized with women allowed to vote
1874 Gold discovered in Black Hills brought influx of prospectors
1883 First oil well drilled near Lander
1885 Rock Springs Massacre when miners attacked 400 Chinese brought to work the mine (28 killed, 15 wounded)
1885 Widespread anti-Chinese violence, especially in Rock Springs
1890 Admitted to Union with women given the right to vote
1892 Johnson County Cattle War
1901 Seventy-mile rail line laid to Cody
1903 Union Pacific Coal Company mine explosion in Hanna (17 killed)
1908 Explosion & cave-in at UPC mine in Hanna (60 killed)
1910 Buffalo Bill Dam completed on the Shoshone
1912 Oil discovered near Casper
1918 Uranium discovered near Lusk
1922 Salt Creek Oil Field opened
1923 Coal mine fire in Kemmerer (nearly 100 died)
1927 Guernsey Dam completed
1939 Mineral trona discovered in Sweetwater County
1949 Severe blizzard paralyzed state
1950 Kortes Dam completed

Although this chapter provides timelines of events occurring within each state which might have affected ancestors, the far-reaching repercussions of some disasters cannot be denied. The *SS Central America* left Colón, Panama bound for New York City on September 3, 1857 carrying thirteen to fifteen tons of gold from the gold fields of California. Off the coast of the Carolinas, the *Central America* found herself caught in the strong winds and surf of a hurricane. Of the 578 passengers and crew on board, only 153 managed to get into life boats. In addition to the 425 from various countries and states who went to the bottom with the ship, the loss of gold led directly to the financial panic of 1857.

A severe drought in the Midwest and southern plains in the 1930's was another event with far reaching consequences. Initially, poor land management practices led to farmers losing their land. Combined with the crash of the stock market, by the time Roosevelt took office, the country was in serious trouble. Meanwhile, the drought spread, covering 75% of the country. Erosion became a major enemy. An estimated 850 million tons of topsoil blew off millions of acres of the Southern plains. However, even Roosevelt admitted that more that 30% of the nation was "ill-housed, ill-clad, ill-nourished." Scores of refugees of the Dust Bowl fled to the San Joaquin Valley of California in hopes of finding work, any work. Instead, tempers exploded, unions formed, strikes called and hundreds injured. Under Roosevelt, farmers who still owned land were paid to use soil-conservation techniques. However, real relief, in the form of rain, did not come until 1939.

The destruction of the steamboat *Sultana* near Memphis, Tennessee on April 27, 1865 became America's largest maritime disaster. But adding to the tragedy, the disaster received little press coverage since it came just thirteen days after the assassination of President Lincoln and just nineteen days after the end of the Civil War.

The *Sultana* was only approved to carry 376 persons. So the 2400 passengers were packed into every nook and deck, making the steamboat top heavy when a leaky steam boiler exploded. In addition, most of the 2400 passengers were Union soldiers who had just been released from Confederate prison camps and were heading to their homes in the North - many weak from imprisonment or illness.

While some died in the explosion, others succumbed to drowning, hypothermia or burning to death. The "1700" that supposedly died was only an estimate. In reality, the number could have been anywhere from 1300 to 1900, since bodies were found as far away as the mouth of the Mississippi River, while others were never recovered. Many of those found remained unidentified. Loved ones never knew what happened to them while survivors were burned horribly and left scarred for the rest of their lives.

10

And Region By Region

History teaches us that men and nations behave wisely once they have exhausted all other alternatives.

-Abba Eben

Everyone thinks they are and always have been tied to certain groups. They forget how nomadic humans are and how other groups could have affected their own history.

The Melding of Nationalities

When asked, I reply I am of Scottish ancestry. But really what I am doing is claiming an ancestry strictly because of my maiden name and because one of my grandfathers was Scottish. If I look at my grandparents and do the math, I discover that I appear to be 25% Scottish (Mathieson), 50% English (Taylor and Landon) and 25% Irish (Reynolds). But if I really go farther back I realize that

- For all I know, the Scottish Mathiesons may have originated as Norwegian Vikings
- I have only been able to trace the Taylors and their wives back to their arrivals in Canada
- Although they married descendants of early English emigrants, the Landons only spent one generation in England after leaving France and Anglicizing their name. Also on that side, ancestor John Askin married a French Canadian and ancestor William Cassidy was from Ireland.
- On the Reynolds side, John Reynolds may have emigrated from Ireland, but he was a Scots-Irishman who married a French woman living in Buffalo, New York. On the same branch, Mary Ann Balch's mother was descended from Dutch.

Although more likely interconnections of nationalities do not just occur in the Americas and they have continued throughout history. One cannot assume that because their family was not French that they could not have been affected by a French War. Eggenberger[54] demonstrated the interconnections perfectly. In 1798, Napoleon drove the AUSTRIAN

---

54 Eggenberger, David. An Encyclopedia of Battles. New York: Dover Publications, Inc., 1985.

armies out of northern ITALY before crossing the Mediterranean to EGYPT from where he intended to lead his armies across the TURKISH Empire to hit the BRITISH in INDIA. With 36,000 men, he stopped first at MALTA. After seizing that island, Bonaparte went on to EGYPT. On July, 2, 1798, his army seized Alexandria. Although the invasion of EGYPT seemed successful, a BRITISH attack at the mouth of the Nile cut the French off from Europe by sea. Instead, Napoleon turned east to attack the OTTOMANS in SYRIA.

In another demonstration of the effect one country's history has on another, Papp[55] maintained that, at the turn of the century, the Industrial Revolution in ENGLAND, FRANCE and GERMANY slowed immigration to the UNITED STATES. On the other hand, that same revolution in AMERICA, demanded manpower which came from ITALY, AUSTRIA, HUNGARY and POLAND.

Just One City

A complete time line of genealogically important data for any one country in the world could be a book in itself. Take just Danzig, also known as Gdansk, the Free City of Danzig, or the Republic of Danzig. Because of the city's location on the southern coast of the Baltic and the value of Danzig as a commercial center fighting over it by Prussia, Germany, Poland and the Soviets has continued since the Middle Ages.

1320-30	Fights over Danzig led to wars and legal suits in the papal court
1440	Danzig joined newly founded Prussian Union
1454-66	Thirteen year war ended with Prussia becoming part of Poland
1522	As part of Hanseatic Cities, Danzig joined fight against Denmark
1523	Mob destroyed interior of St. Mary's Church
1526	Polish King and eight thousand troops handed Danzig churches to the Catholic Church and Lutherans were given two weeks in which to leave.
1529	"English Sweat" epidemic killed three thousand in three days
1530	Prussia forbade Jews to settle in Danzig
1618-48	Thirty Years War
1655-60	Northern Wars
1709	Bubonic Plague epidemic
1734	Russians laid siege to the city
1772	Gdansk / Danzig workers went on strike

55 Papp, Susan M. Hungarian Americans and Their Communities. Cleveland: Cleveland State University, 1981.

1772	Poland was partitioned but Danzig managed to remain in Poland while being surrounded by Prussian territories
1793	Prussia annexed Danzig as part of province of West Prussia
1807	Napoleon created the semi-independent state of Danzig out of land taken from Prussia
1813	State of Danzig ended
1814	After Napoleon, Danzig reverted to Prussia
1815	Danzig was annexed by the Kingdom of Prussia and make capital of the province of West Prussia
1824-78	East and West Prussia were united into a single province
1830s	Cholera outbreaks
1871	Danzig became part of the German Empire
1920	Following World War I, Danzig regained Free City status under League of Nations and Polish oversight. Larger than Napoleon's state of Danzig, the Free City was really a combination of more than 300 cities and villages over more than 750 sq. miles. Poles poured into the region
1923	The Free City of Danzig had a population of nearly 367,000
1925-34	Polish -German trade war allowed Danzig to profit
1933	Nazi Party won the local election
1934	Anti-German military interest in Gdansk
1939	Germans annexed after defeating Polish resistance within city
1939	Most of Danzig's Jewish population had fled
1939-45	Danzig was nearly destroyed & 90% of her population died or fled (5 to 7 thousand died when a German ship carrying refugees sank)
1945	Germans attempted to evacuate Danzig
1945	Red Army conquered, looted & returned Danzig to Poland
1945	Typhus epidemic
1946	Pneumonia epidemic
1946	Returning German Danzigers were viewed as enemy aliens

International Time Lines

There is no way to do justice to each town and city; every province, state or shire; a country. Nor can there be a complete list of every outbreak of disease, every skirmish, every vehicle crash that might have occurred over hundreds of years.

The following are genealogy-related, general time lines for regions of the world. But researchers are urged to go to books containing the histories where ancestors originated. There should also be the caution here to remember groups, such as the Kurds, Slavs, and Indians resided in various countries and boundaries and ownership of areas, such as Alsace Lorraine, changed time and again. In most cases, when numbers of deaths are given, they are estimates as sources seldom agree.

Dates given range from 1500 to 1950 for the New World and from 1300 to 1950 for Europe, Asia and Africa. When using the times lines, remember that since record keeping was sporadic and crude, early dates may not be exact. In addition, the Gregorian Calendar replaced the Julian Calendar at different times in different countries.

Even within the same, present-day countries, there can be discrepancies. Between 1582 and 1585, the Catholic German kingdoms, duchies and states adopted the Gregorian Calendar, it was not until the 1600's that Germany's Protestant ones did. Despite the fact that Scotland changed in 1600, England kept the Julian Calendar until 1752. Though Spain changed in 1582, its colony Mexico did not change until 1583 and Peru in 1584.

Timing and definitions must also be considered using the following time lines. Did a war begin on the day of the first skirmish or when war was formally declared? Did an epidemic begin when the first person in the area became ill or when a certain percentage of the population was ill? Was a town "settled" when the first person built a cabin, the first family arrived, the town was formally established or the first local government was elected?

The Rest of North America

1520	Spanish seized Neuva Espana
1520s	English & French fished off Newfoundland & Labrador
1521	Ciudad de México became oldest capital in continental Americas
1521	Cortez conquered the Aztecs in Mexico
1526	Mexico became part of the viceroyalty of New Spain
1526	Montejo conquered the Mayans
1530	Silver discovered in Mexico
1531	Measles outbreak in Mexico
1531	Guadalajara founded by Spanish
1540s	Basques established whaling station on Labrador
1541	Cartier attempted to colonize Quebec, Canada
1579	Monterrey, Mexico founded
1581	Canadian fur trading expeditions began
1583	English claimed Labrador
1605	Acadia settled
1608	Quebec City founded by fur traders
1610	Henry Hudson discovered Hudson Bay, Canada
1613	Port Royal, Acadia was destroyed by English
1625	Jesuits received land grant at Notre-Dame-des-Agnes
1629	English occupied French Quebec City

1632 English king granted control over New France (Quebec) & Acadia (Nova Scotia & New Brunswick) to France
1634 Trois Rivières & Montreal established
1662 French established colony at Placentia, Newfoundland
1663 New France was named a French royal colony
1670 Newfoundland had thirty English settlements along its coast
1670 English established trading posts on & Hudson Bay
1676 Fort Niagara built
1687 Scots settled Port Royal, Acadia (Nova Scotia)
1690 Americans attacked Quebec
1690 Americans seized Port Royal
1691 French regained Port Royal
1692 French destroyed Saint John's, Newfoundland
1713 Peace of Utrecht gave Britain Newfoundland & mainland Acadia
1717 French families began moving from Newfoundland to Cape Breton Island
1719 Port la Joie (Charlottetown) was settled on Prince Edward Island
1720 Prince Edward Island colonized by French
1720 France founded Louisbourg, Cape Breton Island
1738 Winnipeg, Canada developed as French fur-trading post
1739 French built a fort on Lake Winnipeg
1744 French captured Canso, Nova Scotia
1745 British & colonials captured Fort Louisbourg Cape Breton Island
1748 British founded Halifax, Nova Scotia
1751 Scottish immigrants settled in Canada
1754 France forced to relinquish St. Lawrence & Quebec
1755 French Acadians expelled by British
1755 Smallpox epidemic in Canada
1756-63 After Seven Years War Britain received France's North American possessions, except for islands of Saint Pierre & Miquelon
1758 British assumed permanent possession of Prince Edward Island
1758 British captured Louisbourg on Cape Breton Island & Fort Frontenac on Lake Ontario
1759 British seized Quebec
1771 Moravians founded missions on Labrador
1772 Highland Scots immigrated to Prince Edward Island
1774 Act of Quebec recognized Catholic religion & French language
1775-83 Canada experienced influx of English loyalist fleeing US
1784 Nearly 1000 Loyalists sought refuge on Prince Edward Island
1791 Canada Act divided Canada into English-speaking & French-speaking territories
1791-1841 Canada was divided into Upper Canada (Ontario) & Lower Canada (Quebec)
1793 Mackenzie crossed Canada east to west'
1810 Mexico began its struggle for independence from Spain
1821 Mexico obtained its independence from Spain
1821 Russians extended influence through Pacific Canada south to Oregon
1822 California became part of Mexico
1823 Santa Anna's uprising forced abdication of emperor in Mexico

1824 Mexico became a republic
1826 Rideau Canal completed in Canada
1828 Mexico declared itself a federal republic
1830-60 Canada served as a northern stop on the Underground Railroad
1836 Texas won independence from Mexico
1837 First Canadian Railroad
1840 Upper & Lower Canada were united
1841-67 Upper & Lower Canada became known as Canada West (Ontario) & Canada East (Quebec), respectively
1846 Exiled dictator Santa Anna returned to Mexico
1846 Zachary Taylor captured Monterrey, Mexico after 4-day siege
1846 Territorial war between Mexico & US
1846-48 US defeated Mexico
1847 Zachary Taylor defeated Santa Anna at Battle of Buena Vista
1849 US war with Mexico ended
1857 Civil War between liberals & conservatives in Mexico
1858 Gold discovered in northwest Canada
1863 French occupied Mexico City
1864 St. Hilaire tram disaster (nearly 100 died)
1865-73 Mexican Kickapoo uprising in Southwest
1867 Juarez regained control of Mexico
1867 Establishment of Federation of Canada
1867 France withdrew from Mexico
1867 Unification of Dominion of Canada
1868 French captured Mexico City
1869 First Riel Rebellion of Red River Metis in Canada
1869-70 Smallpox epidemic among Canadian Plains Indians
1873 Prince Edward Island became a province of Canada
1876-1911Mexico governed by dictatorship
1879 Tornado at Buctouche, New Brunswick, Canada
1882 Monterrey, Mexico connected by rail with Laredo, Texas
1885 Completion of Canadian Pacific Railroad spanning the continent
1887 Mine explosion in Nanaimo, British Columbia, Canada (150 died)
1891 Canada signed compromise agreement with US gave both countries right to police Bering Sea
1895 Canadian portion of Sault Sainte Marie Canals completed
1896 Tornado outbreak in Ontario, Canada
1896-98 Over 100 thousand went to the Yukon during the gold rush
1897 Beginning of Klondike Gold Rush
1899 Northern Mexico tornado (20+ died)
1902 Mine disaster in Coahuila, Mexico (130+ died)
1904 Punjabi Sikhs began to enter British Columbia
1905 Provinces of Alberta & Saskatchewan formed in Canada
1906 Northwest Passage navigated
1906 Anti-Asian riot in Vancouver
1907 Bridge collapsed in Quebec Canada
1908 Canada curbed Asian Indian immigration
1908 Two mine disasters in Coahuila, Mexico (200 & 100 died)
1910-11 Mexican Revolution
1912 Typhoid epidemic in Mexican Federal Army
1912 Regina, Saskatchewan, Canada cyclone

1914 Mine disaster in Hillcrest, Alberta, Canada (180+ died)
1914 Asian Indian immigrants were barred from landing in Vancouver
1914 Canadian *RMS Empress of Ireland* sank in St. Lawrence River (1000+ died)
1914-18 Canada supported Allies in World War I
1916 Quebec, Canada bridge collapsed
1916 Matheson forest fire in Ontario
1917 Halifax explosion in Nova Scotia (1600 died)
1929 Burin Peninsula Canada tsunami
1929 North Atlantic tsunami at Placentia Bay, Newfoundland
1930 Construction of Inter-American Highway began
1931 Commonwealth of Canada given autonomy
1936 Military dictatorship established in Mexico
1939-45 Canada supported Allies in World War II
1949 Newfoundland joined Canadian Federation

Central America and the Caribbean
1501 Balboa began a farm on Haiti
1502 Santo Domingo rebuilt after being destroyed by a hurricane
1502 Spain transported slaves to Caribbean
1507 First sugar cane cultivated in Hispaniola
1508 Spanish settled Puerto Rico & enslaved the inhabitants
1509 Spanish settled Jamaica
1509 Terra Firme (Panama) colony established
1510 Darien, Panama founded by Spain
1511 Spanish conquered Baracoa, Cuba
1513 Balboa crossed the Isthmus of Panama
1514 Santiago de Cuba founded
1518-19 Smallpox attacked Indians in Hispaniola
1519 Havana, Cuba founded
1521 African slaves taken to gold mines on Hispaniola
1523 Honduras conquered by Spain
1524 Spanish arrived in the area of El Salvador
1525 Germans built silver factory on Hispaniola
1532-34 Trinidad's first government was formed by Spain
1536 Spanish had wiped-out Indian population on Barbados
1541 Guatemala City devastated by earthquake
1553 French attacked coastal settlements in Hispaniola & Puerto Rico
1562 English began trading in West Indies
1562-67 British John Hawkins introduced 1st black slaves to Spanish West Indies
1576 Smallpox epidemic throughout Central America
1585 Yellow fever in West Indies
1592 San José de Oruña (St. Joseph) became Trinidad's first permanent settlement
1609 Bermuda settled by shipwreck survivors bound for Virginia
1612 Bermuda founded
1616 First African slaves taken to Bermuda
1625 St. Kitts established by French Huguenots, English & Dutch
1626 Tobago settled by English from Barbados
1627 French from Normandy settled on St. Kitts

1627	English & their slaves settled Barbados
1628	Nevis settled
1629	English & their slaves settled in Barbados
1632	Spain & Indians burned Dutch & English settlements on Tobago
1646	Tobago resettled by Dutch & French
1649	Royalists escaping Cromwell's rule took refuge in Barbados
1662	French colonists on Tobago forced out by Dutch
1698	Darien Expedition launched unsuccessful Scottish settlement in Panama
1707	Hurricane arrived at Nevis
1712	Hurricane went ashore in Jamaica
1713-14	Hurricanes hit Guadeloupe
1717	Danish settled St. John
1721	Smallpox epidemic hit West Indies
1722	Hurricane went ashore in Jamaica
1726	Hurricane at Jamaica
1728	Hurricane hit at Antigua
1733	Slave revolt in Danish West Indies (Virgin Islands)
1733	Hurricane in Danish West Indies (Virgin Islands
1733	France sold Saint Croix to Denmark the West Indies & Guinea
1734	Hurricane rolled ashore in Jamaica
1735	Diphtheria broke out on St. Kitts
1737	Hurricane hit Santo Domingo
1738	Hurricane went ashore Guadeloupe
1741	Smallpox epidemic broke out in Trinidad
1748	Coffee plant introduced in Cuba
1754	Moravians settled Antigua
1755	Denmark designated Saint Croix a crown colony
1756	Bridgetown, Barbados fire (160+ buildings burned)
1758	Bridgetown, Barbados fire (90+ buildings burned)
1759	British occupied Guadeloupe
1761	British took Dominica from French
1761	Smallpox outbreak on Bermuda
1762	British captured Havana, & French islands of Martinique, Saint Lucia, Saint Vincent & Grenada
1762	Yellow Fever epidemic in Havana, Cuba
1763	France controlled Martinique, Saint Lucia & Guadeloupe
1763	British returned Havana to Spain
1763	Dominica & Tobago ceded to Great Britain
1763	British captured Cuba
1763	France ceded claims to Saint Vincent, Dominica & Tobago to Britain
1766	Bridgetown, Barbados fire (1100+ buildings burned)
1768	Slave rebellion took place on Montserrat
1772	Hurricane ravaged Virgin Islands
1777	French from Saint Lucia arrived in Trinidad
1778	French controlled Saint Vincent
1779	French regained Grenada
1779	British seized Trinidad
1780	Hurricanes raged across the Caribbean (22 thousand died)
1780	Grenada sugar industry wiped-out
1784	Spain ceded Saint Lucia & Dominica to British

1785 Devastating hurricane went ashore in Virgin Islands
1789 Slave revolts in Martinique
1791 Slave uprising in Haiti
1794-1802British occupied Martinique
1795 Maroon Rebellion on Jamaica
1797 Trinidad was returned to British
1800-03 British occupied Curacao
1801-02 British occupied Danish West Indies (Virgin Islands
1802 Tobago became part of British Windward Islands
1802 Guadeloupe restored slavery
1804 Slaves overthrew French in Haiti
1807-15 British occupied Danish West Indies (Virgin Islands
1813 Hurricanes hit Barbados, Puerto Rico, Bahamas, Bermuda, Leeward Islands, Jamaica, Dominica, Martinique, St. Christopher (thousands died)
1816 Sugar Rebellion of slaves in Barbados
1816 Dutch controlled Curacao
1821 San Salvador was incorporated into the Mexican Empire
1821 Nicaragua declared independence from Spain
1821 Panama declared its independence from Spain
1821 Costa Rica declared independence from Spain
1821 Major fire burned Bridgetown, Barbados
1821 El Salvador declared independent
1823 Nicaragua, Honduras, Costa Rica, Guatemala & El Salvador became the United Provinces of Central America
1823 Cuban independence movement quashed by Spain
1823 Sonsonate & San Salvador united to form the new state of El Salvador within the United Provinces of Central America .
1826 More than160 homes burned in Bridgetown fire
1828-45 Dutch West Indies governed by Surinam
1830 Puerto Rico began to develop a plantation economy
1831 Slaves revolted in Jamaica
1833 Jamaica emancipated slaves
1834-48 Thousands of immigrants from other islands arrived in Trinidad
1837 Cuban slave uprising
1838 Slaves freed on Barbados
1838 Costa Rica, Honduras & Nicaragua ceded from United Provinces of Central America
1840 Portuguese settlers arrived in Saint Vincent
1840-48 European & free West Africans to work in Trinidad's cane fields
1841 A cargo of slaves mutinied on board the US Brig *Creole* out of Hampton Roads, Virginia & made their way to the Bahamas.
1841 Americans from Baltimore & Pennsylvania arrived to work on Trinidad
1844 East Indian laborers arrived on Trinidad
1845 More than180 building burned in fire in Bridgetown
1848 Slave rebellion on Saint Croix
1849 Indentured Chinese arrived on Trinidad
1851 Cuban rebellion against Spanish
1853 Malaria & cholera epidemics on Saint Thomas Virgin Islands (1800+ died)
1861-65 Bahamas became base for blockade runners during American

	Civil War
1866	Cholera epidemic on Saint Thomas (1200+ died)
1867	Hurricane & tidal wave hit Virgin Islands
1868-78	Spanish at war with Cuba
1870s	French laborers on other islands migrated to Saint Thomas
1871	Two hurricanes hit Virgin Islands
1880	Spanish troops arrived in Cuba to suppress uprising
1895	Cuban uprising against Spanish
1897	Cuba became autonomous, but not independent from Spain
1898	US warship blown up in Havana
1898	US occupied Cuba in Spanish-American War
1898	Spain ceded Puerto Rico to the US following the Spanish-American War
1902	US Congress authorized construction of the Panama Canal
1902	Mount Pelée erupted, destroying Saint Pierre, Martinique (30,000+ died)
1902	La Soufriere Volcano erupted on Saint Vincent
1903	Panama declared republic after US-backed rebels seized control
1906	War pitting Guatemala against El Salvador & Honduras ended
1906-09	US troops occupied Cuba after liberal revolt
1909	US ousted Nicaraguan president after his government killed 500
1912	Plague outbreak in Cuba & Puerto Rico
1914	Panama Canal opened
1917	Puerto Ricans were granted U.S. citizenship
1919	Theater fire in San Juan, Puerto Rico (approximately 150 died)
1920	US occupied Nicaragua
1926-33	US occupied Nicaragua
1928	Deadly hurricane came ashore at Puerto Rico
1932	Devastating hurricane hit US Virgin Islands & Puerto Rico
1935-38	Strikes & riots in West Indies

South America

1500	Portuguese landed in Brazil
1520	Venezuela was colonized
1521	Smallpox introduced in Mexico
1525	German miners arrived in Venezuela
1527	Smallpox arrived in Peru
1529	Germans established settlement in Maracaibo, Venezuela
1530-31	Measles epidemic in Peru
1530s	Portuguese first settled Brazil
1532	Spanish conquered Incas in Peru
1533	Santa Marta, Columbia founded
1535	Lima, Peru & Asunci6n, Paraguay founded
1536	Spanish invaded & colonized Bolivia & Chile
1537-38	Spanish conquered northwestern South America
1540	Spanish founded Santiago, Chile & Quito, Ecuador
1541	First permanent white settlement in Argentina
1545	Silver discovered in Bolivia
1549	Jesuits arrived in Bahia, Brazil
1552	1000 Spanish settlers arrived in Chile
1552	Gold discovered in Chile

1555	French settled near present-day Rio de Janeiro, Brazil
1560	French expelled from Brazil
1565	Portuguese founded Rio de Janeiro, Brazil
1567	Typhoid fever outbreak across South America (2 million died)
1580	Asunción, Santa Fe, & Buenos Aires had already been settled
c1580	Dutch settled Surinam (Dutch Guiana)
1585	English sacked Cartagena, Columbia
1590	Gold discovered in Brazil
1654	Dutch colony of Recife, Brazil fell to Portuguese causing Jews to flee to North America
1680	Portuguese established Colonia, Uruguay
1700s	Basques arrived in Chile
1726	Spanish settled Montevideo
1740	New Granada (Columbia, Ecuador, Panama & Venezuela) broke off from the Viceroyalty of Peru
1741	Three thousand Americans attacked Cartagena, Columbia, at the instigation of the British
1764	French founded settlement on East Falkland Island
1765	British founded settlement on West Falkland Island
1776	Argentina, Bolivia, Paraguay & Uruguay separated from Viceroyalty of Peru & became Viceroyalty of Rio de la Plata
1778	Free trade opened the Atlantic coast, chiefly near Buenos Aires
1780-83	Indians revolted against Spain in Peru
1782	Peruvians unsuccessfully revolted against Spanish
1808	South American colonies began to revolt
1808-21	Brazil served as refuge for Portuguese government during Napoleon's invasion
1810	Argentina won independence
1810	Chile revolted against Spanish rule
1811	New Granada (Venezuela, Columbia & Ecuador) rebelled against Spain
1811	Paraguay became independent
1811	Uruguay became independent
1815	Spanish troops arrived in Columbia & began a reign of terror
1818	Chile declared independence
1819	Republic of Gran Columbia (Ecuador, Columbia, Panama & Venezuela) formed in opposition to Spain
1820	Argentina declared sovereignty over the Falkland Islands
1821	Peru declared its independence from Spain
1821	Bolivia won Venezuelan independence
1821	Portuguese reclaimed Uruguay
1822	Brazil received independence
1822	Gran Columbia won independence from Spain
1822	Venezuelan generals invaded Peru
1822	Du Sucre gained the independence of Quito, Ecuador
1823	US officially recognized South America countries
1824	First Germans arrived in Brazil
1824	Peru secured its independence while Spanish troops withdrew
1825	Bolivia gained its independence from Peru
1826	Uruguay revolted against Brazilian rule
1827	Peru declared independence
1828	Uruguay became independent

1829-30	Venezuela & Ecuador seceded from Gran Columbia
1833	British reclaimed Falkland Islands
1864-70	War of the Triple Alliance fought between Paraguay & combined troops from Argentina, Brazil & Uruguay
1870	Large migration of Europeans to Argentina
1870	Paraguay cut tin half due to War of the Triple Alliance
1879	Chilean army conquered Lima, Peru
1879-83	Chile, Peru & Bolivia fought over mineral rich Atacama desert
1880	Chile took territory to its north
1881	First Germans arrived in Paraguay
1891	Civil War in Chile
1896	Brazil recorded a rubber boom
1899	Yellow Fever epidemic in Santiago, Chile
1899	Columbian revolt / War of a Thousand Days (100,000 died)
1899	Japanese immigration began in Peru
1900	Brazil was world's major coffee producer
1900	Italians immigrated to Argentina in larger number
1902	British, Italian & German navies blockaded Venezuela
1903	Brazil & British Guiana were embroiled in border disputes
1912	Plague in Ecuador
1930	Military revolt began in Brazil
1932	Democracy returned to Argentina
1932	Chaco War caused by Bolivia's claim of northern Paraguay
1934	Vargas gained control of Brazil in military revolution
1939	Earthquake in Chile
1940s	Chile entered World War II on the side of the Axis
1943	Chile severed ties with the Axis countries

British Isles

1315-17	Great Famine (5 thousand+ died)
1337	Hundred Years War started
1347-49	Bubonic Plague or Black Death devastated England
1351	After the plague, government attempted to regulate wages & prices at 1340 levels following labor shortages
1361	Second severe outbreak of the Black Death
1366	Statutes of Kilkenny outlawed intermarriage of English & Irish in unsuccessful attempt to suppress Gaelic culture
1375	Truce in Hundred Years War truce cost England most of her French possessions
1381	Peasants' Revolt in protest of poll tax
1382	Earthquake in Kent
1386	Treaty of Windsor between Britain & Portugal
1388	Battle of Otterburn, Northumberland
1400	Rebellion of Glendower of Wales against Henry IV
1403	Battle of Shrewsbury
1415	Battle of Agincourt
1432–38	Britain snowbound for six of seven winters
1437	Assassination of King James I of Scotland at Perth
1453	End of Hundred Years War
1454	Stamford Bridge became site of Wars of the Roses first battle
1455	Fall of the Black Douglases in Scotland
1465	Irish near English settlements forced to take English surnames

1468 Orkney & Shetland Islands acquired by Scotland from Norway
1485 Epidemic of Sweating Sickness (2 thousand died)
1507 Epidemic of Sweating Sickness
1512 Treaty with France made all Scots citizens & vice versa
1513 Battle of Flodden brought defeat of Scottish Army
1517 Epidemic of Sweating Sickness
1528 Epidemic of Sweating Sickness
1533-34 English Reformation of the Catholic Church ordered by Henry VIII
1536 Dissolution of monasteries commenced in England
1541 Henry VIII proclaimed king of Ireland
1544-45 Henry's VIII's "Rough Wooing" of the Scottish Borders
1547 Battle of Pinkie
1544 Vagrants Act allowed the use of able-bodied tramps as slaves
1548 Priests in England allowed to marry
1549 First Act of Uniformity in England made Catholic mass illegal
1549 English Parliament declared enclosures legal
1550 Walloon Protestants arrive as refugees from the Low Countries
1550-1700 The "Little Ice Age" with frequent severe gales
1551 Epidemic of Sweating Sickness
1554-58 Brief Catholic restoration under Queen Mary Tudor forced married priests to live at least thirty miles from their wives
1555 Approximately 300 Protestant burned at stake
1557 Influenza epidemic
1557 Scotland's first Covenant signed becoming foundation of the Presbyterian Church
1558 French took Calais, England's last holdings in France
1558 Policy of Plantation began
1558-1603 Protestantism restored in England
1559 Scottish Reform
1559 Acts of Supremacy ended papal power over England & Wales & established the Church of England
1560 Protestantism established in Scotland
1562 African slave trade starts
1563 Papal recusants heavily fined for non-attendance at Church
1563 Plague (20 thousand died)
1563 Test Act excluded Roman Catholics from governmental office
1568 Battle of Langside
1571 Laws penalizing Catholics in England were passed
1571-72 Presbyterianism introduced into England
1579 Act of Uniformity in matters of religion enforced
1580 Colonization of Ireland
1588 Defeat of Spanish Armada off Gravelines
1592 Congregational (or Independent) Church formed in London
1592 Plague outbreak
1592 Presbyterian Church formally established in Scotland
1594 Earl of Tyrone, leads Irish rebellion against English rule
1597 Poor Law Act brought erection of parish workhouses for the poor
1599 Irish rebels defeated Earl of Essex
1600 Scotland adopted New Year beginning January 1, instead of March 25

1601 Great English Poor Law Act passed
1601 East India Company founded
1603 Death of Elizabeth I led to union of Scottish & English crowns under James VI of Scotland & I of England
1603 Plague in England
1605 Gunpowder plot at Westminster
1607 Prominent Ulster families fled into exile
1607 Bristol Channel storm surge & flood (2 thousand died)
1607 Flooding in Devon
1608 English & Scottish settled in Ulster, Northern Ireland
1610 James VI & I established the Episcopal Church in Scotland& began persecution of Presbyterians
1611 Plantation of Ulster established with English & Scottish colonists
1638 Great thunderstorm in Widecombe-in-the-Moor, Devon
1638 A "Covenant" (swearing to resist changes to the death) was signed in Greyfriars Church, Edinburgh & accepted by hundreds of thousands of Scots bringing a revival of Presbyterian Church
1639 Act of Toleration in England established religious toleration
1641 Up to fifty thousand Protestants killed during Ulster Insurrection
1641 England recognized Presbyterianism as the Church in Scotland
1642 English Civil War broke out between Royalist and Parliamentarians
1642 Discord spilled into Scotland
1644 Battle of Marston Moor
1645 At Battle of Naseby, Parliament's Army crushed Royalist forces
1645 Battle of Philiphaugh in Scotland
1645 Plague made its last appearance in Scotland
1646 Royalists surrendered at Oxford
1648 Society of Friends (Quakers) founded
1649 King Charles I executed
1649 Commonwealth declared
1649 Theaters & Christmas banned by Cromwell
1649 Cromwell's Irish campaign commenced
1649 King Charles II proclaimed King of Scots & England in Scotland
1651 Dutch Wars
1651 Scottish prisoners transported to English settlements in America
1651-52 Second English Civil War
1652 Quakers organized
1653 Act of Settlement stripped Cromwell's opponents of land
1657 A few Jews permitted to settle in England
1658-60 Richard Cromwell became Lord Protector after his father's death
1659-60 Restoration of British monarchy
1660 Ten Regicides are executed at Charing Cross & Tyburn
1660 Clarendon code restricted Puritans' religious freedom
1660 Scotland adopted Gregorian Calendar
1661 Persecution of Non-Conformists in England
1661 Restoration of Episcopacy in Scotland
1661 Corporation Act prevented non-Anglicans from holding municipal office
1662-89 Hearth Tax enacted

1662 Act of Uniformity produced persecution of all non-conformists (i.e. Presbyterians & Independents)
1665 Great Plague of London (more than 60 thousand died)
1666 Great Fire destroyed most of London & ended plague epidemic
1666-89 Religious unrest on Scotland included Covenanters uprising at St. John's town of Dalry
1672 War with Holland
1673 First Test Act kept Catholics & Non-Conformists from holding civil & military office
1675 Malaria epidemic in England
1678 Test Act extended to include peers
1679 Battle of Bothwell Bridge in Scotland
1681 Second Test Act against Non-Conformists
1685 Earl of Argyll's Invasion of Scotland
1685 Monmouth rebellion & Battle of Sedgemoor
1685 Bloody Assizes trials led to 200 executed & 800 transported for rebelling against James II
1685 Revocation of the Edict of Nantes brought thousands of Protestants (Huguenots) from France to England
1686 Release of all prisoners held for their religious beliefs
1688 During "The Glorious Revolution," James II was overthrown by King William of Orange & Queen Mary II, daughter of James II
1688 Hearth Tax abolished
1689 Deposed James II fled to Ireland
1689 Toleration Act for Protestant non-conformists
1689 Battle of Killiecrankie in Scotland
1689 Devonport naval dockyard established
1690 Great Synagogue founded
1690 Presbyterianism finally established in Scotland
1690 Battle of the Boyne
1692 The massacre of Glencoe
1692 Land Tax introduced
1693-1700 Repeated oat harvest failure in Scotland led to widespread starvation
1694 National Debt came into effect in England
1694 Stamp Duties introduced into Britain from Holland
1694-99 Poll Tax imposed in Scotland for everyone over sixteen, exceptions made for the destitute & insane
1696 Act of Parliament established workhouses
1696 Window Tax replaced Hearth Tax
1700 Dramatic increase in tuberculosis deaths
1700 Property rights denied to Irish Catholics
1701 Act of Settlement insured Protestant rule on the British throne
1702 War of Spanish Succession (1702-1713)
1703 Great storm in the English Channel (8 thousand died, 1/3 of Britain's merchant fleet lost, & Eddystone lighthouse destroyed)
1704 British take Gibraltar
1704 Battle of Blenheim
1704 Penal Code barred Catholics from education, the military, & voting
1707 Union with Scotland
1707 The Kingdom of Great Britain established

1708 First Jacobite uprising in Scotland
1709 Bread riots in Britain
1710 Tax on apprentice indentures enacted
1711 Incorporation of South Sea Company, in London
1712 Imposition of Soap Tax (abolished 1853)
1712 Last trial for witchcraft in England
1712 Toleration Act passed – first relief to non-Anglicans
1714 English Schism Act, prevented Dissenters from being schoolmasters
1714 Landholders forced to take the Oath of Allegiance & renounce Roman Catholicism.
1714 Quarter Sessions Records began to mention Protestant dissenters & Roman Catholic recusants.
1715 Riot Act passed
1715 Second Jacobite uprising in Scotland
1716 Thames frozen so solid that a spring tide lifted the ice bodily 13ft without interrupting the frost fair
1719 Third abortive Jacobite uprising
1720 South Sea Bubble, a stock-market crash on Exchange Alley – government assumed control of National Debt
1720 Manufacturing towns began increase in population -- rise of new wealth
1722 Last trial for witchcraft in Scotland
1722 Knatchbull's Act (poor laws)
1723 Excise tax levied for coffee, tea, & chocolate
1723 The Waltham Black Acts allowed death sentence for theft & poaching
1725-26 Treaty of Hanover (France, Prussia & England with Spain & Austria)
1740 Irish famine began (100 thousand died)
1741 Benjamin Ingham founded the Moravian Methodists (Inghamites)
1742 England's war with Spain was incited by William Pitt the Elder (Earl of Chatham) for the sake of trade
1744 Church of Scotland split over taking of Burgess' Oath
1745 Jacobite uprising in Scotland
1745 Bonnie Prince Charlie landed in the western Highlands to raise support among Episcopalian & Catholic clans
1745 Army of Bonnie Prince Charlie invaded Perth, Edinburgh, & reached as far as Derby in England
1746 Battle of Culloden became the last battle fought in Britain
1747 Heritable Jurisdictions abolished in Scotland
1747 Act for Pacification of the Highlands enacted
1750 Typhus epidemic in London
1752 England dropped Julian Calendar & adopted Gregorian Calendar
1755 Period of canal construction began in Britain (till 1827)
1756 Seven Years War with France began
1760 Usually accepted start of the "First Industrial Revolution"
1760 Beginning of intense Inclosure Acts in England
1770s First French religious refugees arrived in Wales
1772 Judge ruled that there is no legal basis for slavery in England

1775-83 Irish unrest
1779 Naval battle between Britain & USA off Flamborough Head
1780 Gordon Riots in London -- widespread destruction
1780 Great hurricane of Caribbean & North America sank three British ships (1000 died)
1782 Life of the poor began to alter due to industrialization & new factories in growing towns required a workforce
1782 Atlantic hurricane destroyed six British ships
1783 July was hottest month in Britain until 1983
1784 Wesley broke with the Church of England
1788 First British convicts & free settlers left for New South Wales
1790 Forth & Clyde Canal opened in Scotland
1790 Protestant uprising in Ireland (50 thousand died)
1792 Repression in Britain included restrictions on the press
1793 England declared war on France (1793-1802)
1795 A famine year
1795 Speenhamland Act proclaimed the parish was responsible for increasing laborers' wages to subsistence level
1795 Seditious Meetings & Political Speech Practices Bills outlawed mass meetings & political lecture
1796 Pitt's "Reign of Terror" & treason trials forced radicals to emigrate
1796 Lynmouth flooding in Devon
1797 French invasion of Fishguard, Wales, became the last time UK was invaded
1797 With England in financial crisis, the Bank of England suspended cash payments
1797 Mutinies in the British Navy at Spithead & Nore
1798 English suppressed Irish Rebellion (roughly 25 thousand died)
1800 Parliamentary union of Great Britain & Ireland
1801 Britain abolished Irish Parliament, formed the United Kingdom & established Anglican Church as the Church of Ireland
1802 Treaty of Amiens signed by Britain, France, Spain, & the Netherlands brought fourteen months of peace during the Napoleonic Wars, allowing for travel & correspondence across the English Channel again
1803-15 Resumption of the Napoleonic Wars with France
1804 Spain declared war on Britain
1805 London docks opened
1806 Dartmoor Prison was built by French prisoners
1807 Slave trade ended by Parliament
1810 Tornado in Fernhill, Hampshire, England
1810 Tornado in Plymouth, England
1810 Pleasure boat capsized in Paisley Canal (80+ died)
1811 Shipwrecks in North Sea storm caused many deaths
1811-15 Anti- Luddite uprisings in the Midlands occurred when groups of workmen rebelled against the increased mechanization of textile production & destroyed the new machinery
1814 "Year of the Burning" in Sutherland & Ross
1815 Corn Bill passed with enormous benefit to landlords
1816 Economic depression & rise in wheat prices
1816 "Year without a summer"

1818	Manchester cotton spinners' strike
1819	Acts passed against radical political unions prohibited assemblies & imposed press censorship
1819	Peterloo Massacre at Manchester
1822	Caledonian Canal opened
1828	Repeal of Test & Corporation Acts which had kept Catholics & Dissenters from holding public office & along with other rights
1829	Catholic Emancipation Act restored civil liberties to Roman Catholics
1830	Agricultural "Swing" Riots in southern England
1832	Cholera epidemic
1833	Factory Act made it illegal to employ children under nine
1834	"Tolpuddle Martyrs" shipped off to Australia because of Trades Union activities in Dorset
1834	New Poor Law
1836	First potato famine in Ireland
1836	Avalanche in Lewes, England
1836-42	Economic down turn
1838	Publication of the Chartists demanding involvement in politics drew demonstrations of 100-300 thousand in Glasgow, Birmingham, & West Yorkshire
1838	Smallpox epidemic in England
1838-49	Chartist Movement called for universal suffrage, secret ballot, annual elections, no property qualification for members of Parliament & equal electoral districts
1839	"Night of the Big Wind" in Ireland (250+ died)
1840-70	Irish Potato Famine & uprisings (about 2.5 million Irish emigrated)
1842	Second Chartist Petition presented to Parliament
1842	British massacred in Khyber Pass
1842	British Mines Act outlawed women & girls working in the mines, & required supervision of boy labor
1842	Depression & high unemployment among cotton mill workers& ironworkers in Bolton
1842	Civil Registration in Channel Islands started
1843	Disruption of the Church of Scotland when 470+ ministers signed the Deed of Demission & formed the Free Church of Scotland
1845	Temporary repeal of the Corn Laws
1848	Third Chartist Petition led to mass arrests & movement failure
1850s	Welsh began moving to cities, attracted by Industrial Revolution
1853	Smallpox epidemic in England
1854	*RMS Tayler* sank off Lambry Ireland (380 died)
1854-55	Cholera epidemic in England
1857	European financial crisis
1858-65	Pertussis outbreak in England (120 thousand died)
1862	Mine disaster in Northumberland, England (200+ died)
1863-65	Smallpox epidemic in England (20 thousand died)
1864	Great Sheffield flood in England (270 died)
1865	Welsh began to immigrate to South America
1866	Oaks Colliery explosion disaster (350+ died)
1867	Reform Act gave right to vote to workingmen

1868 Last convicts sent to Australia
1869 Imprisonment for debt abolished in Britain
1869 Disestablishment of Irish Church
1870 Smallpox epidemic in England (nearly 45 thousand died)
1871 Trades Unions legalized in Britain, but picketing made illegal
1871-74 Smallpox in Birmingham, England (7 thousand+ died)
1872 Italians & Jews increasingly settled in Wales
1875 Plimsoll Line established for loading of ships
1877 Blantyre mine disaster (200+ died)
1879 First Tay Bridge completed
1879 Tay Bridge collapsed in storm taking train with it
1880s Somalians began to settle in Cardiff, Wales
1881 First Boer War
1881 Evemouth Disaster, Scotland
1882 Phoenix Park murders in Dublin
1883 Married Women's Property Act became law
1884 Colchester Earthquake, Essex, England
1885 First train ran through the Severn Tunnel
1886 Crofters Act
1887 Theater fire in Exeter, England (200 died)
1889 Dock Strike
1891 Great Blizzard (220 died)
1892 Shop Hours Act limited work week to 74 hours for minors
1892 London smog deteriorated (approximately 1 thousand died)
1894 Manchester Ship Canal opened
1899-1902 Second Boer War
1902 Political unrest in Dublin led to state of emergency
1905 British Aliens Act gave the Home Office control over immigration
1908 British Coal Mines Regulation Act limited men to an eight hour day
1909 Burns Pit Disaster in Stanley, County Durham, England (160+ died)
1910 Railway & coal strikes in Britain
1911 Anti-immigrant riots in southern Wales
1911-12 Strikes by seamen, dock & transport workers
1912 Irish Home Rule crisis increased in Britain
1912 *Titanic* sank (thousands died)
1913 Tornado in Wales
1913 Coal mine disaster in Cardiff, Wales (430 died)
1913 Third Irish Home Rule Bill rejected by House of Lords led to threat of civil war in Ireland & formation of Ulster Volunteers to oppose
Home Rule
1914 British ship cut all German undersea telegraph links to outside world
1914 First Zeppelin air raid on England
1914 Irish Home Rule Act provided for a separate Parliament in Ireland & decreed the position of Ulster to be decided after the War
1915 German submarine blockade of Britain started
1915 Quintinshill rail crash, Dumfries & Galloway, Scotland (225+ died)

1915 RMS Lusitania sunk by German submarine off coast of Ireland
1916 Easter Uprising in Ireland
1916 Britain forced to initiate the draft
1918 Mail ship torpedoed in Irish Sea outside Dublin (500+ died)
1918 Armistice signed
1918 War of Independence in Ireland
1918 World-wide Influenza epidemic
1919 Ship sank in Scotland (200+ died)
1919 Treaty of Versailles
1919 Irish Republican Army (IRA) began war for Irish independence
1921 Irish Free State & Northern Ireland formed
1921 Hull Air Disaster (44 died)
1921 Irish Regiments of British Army disbanded
1922 Law of Property Act effectively ended the manorial system
1922-23 Ireland was partitioned following the civil war
1923 General strike
1923 Adoption of children was legalized in Britain
1926 British workers launched a general strike
1929 Abolition of Poor Law system in Britain
1931 National Government attempted to deal with economic crisis
1931 Earthquake in England
1932 Great Hunger March of unemployed to London
1933 Twenty-five percent unemployment in Britain
1934 Mine disaster in Wrexham (260+ died)
1935 Unemployment in Jarrow in Northeast England reached nearly 75%
1936 Two hundred Jarrow ship workers marched to London to petition
Parliament for help with unemployment
1939 British fleet mobilized while civilians began to evacuate London
1939 Two hundred thousand English children sent to safety in Wales
1939 Nearly two million mothers & children were removed from metropolitan areas in just four days
1940 Rationing began in Britain
1940 Most of island of Alderney evacuated to Weymouth, England
1940 Germans bombed Scapa Flow Naval Base near Scotland
1940 Battle of Britain began with German bombing of English airfields & factories, air battles & daylight raids all over Britain
1940 Hitler declared a blockade of the British Isles
1941 Heavy German bombing of London continued
1942 First American forces arrived in Great Britain
1942 Germans led air raids against the cathedral cities of Britain
1945 Residents of islands in English Channel began to return home
1948 Large numbers of Polish refugees arrived in Britain

The Rest of Europe

1347 Bubonic Plague spread throughout Europe
1348 Jews were accused of poisoning wells during plague outbreak
1371 Ottomans took Macedonia
1380 Norway shared a king with Denmark
1380 Iceland united with Denmark
1397 Kalmar Agreement united Denmark, Norway & Sweden

1410 Battle of Tannenberg (in northeast Poland) with Poland & Lithuania versus Knights of Teutonic Order (Teutonic Knights)
1415 Portugal encouraged exploration
1421 Dike disaster in Holland
1429 Joan of Arc brought relief to Orleans, France
1442 Hungary defended itself against the Ottomans
1444 Albanian regional leaders united
1453 Fall of Constantinople
1453 English withdrew from France
1458 Hungarian Renaissance
1459 Serbia fell to the Ottomans
1463 Bosnia (Hum) became a Turkish
1466 Poland defeated Teutonic Knights
1478 Beginning Spanish Inquisition (2 thousand burned at the stake)
1482 Holland passed to Habsburg rule
1489 Venetians took Cyprus
1492 Jews expelled from Spain
1492 Moors lost the province of Granada in southern Spain
1494 France invaded Italy
1514 Hungarian Peasant Revolt
1516-1700 Hapsburgs ruled Spain & its colonies
1517 Martin Luther postulated his theories in Germany
1524 German Peasant's War crushed
1524-1641 Monaco was under Spanish protection
1526 Turks took Croatia
1530 Dike breach in Holland (400 thousand died)
1531 German Protestants formed League of Schmalkalden to resist the emperor
1534 Protestant Christian III overthrew Catholic supporters of his brother John in Denmark
1541-64 John Calvin established Puritan state in Geneva, Switzerland
1555 Peace of Augsburg decreed that no member of the Holy Roman Empire would make war against another over religion
1557 Influenza epidemic throughout Europe
1558 French took Calais (last English possession in France)
1562-1918 Hapsburgs ruled Hungary & Bohemia
1563 Plague throughout Europe
1568 Forty thousand died of unidentified disease in Lisbon, Spain
1571 Naval Battle of Lepanto Greece between united forces of Venice, Spain & the Pope vs. the Ottoman Turks ended with thousands taken prisoner
1572 French Huguenots attacked on St. Bartholomew's Day (20 thousand massacred)
1572 Holland revolted against Spain
1573 Venice surrendered Cyprus to the Turks
1576 French outlawed Protestantism
1580 Spain conquered Portugal
1581 Dutch provinces united to declare independence from Spain
1585-89 French War of the Three Henrys between Catholics & Huguenots
1588 Major storm and English sank Spanish Armada (approximately 20 thousand sailors died)

1598 Edict of Nantes ended French Civil War
1599 Plague outbreak in Spain
1601 Plague throughout Europe
1608 Protestant Union formed in Germany
1609 Catholic Union formed in Germany
1610-20 Leiden / Leyden, Holland became home for English Pilgrims prior to sailing to the New World
1617 Catholic officials closed Protestant churches in Bohemia
1618-48 Defenestration of Prague led to Bohemian Revolt & Thirty Years War which centered in Germany but included, the Holy Roman Empire, France & others
1634 Imperial forces defeated Swedes
1640 Catalans of northeast Spain revolted
1643-45 Denmark at war with Sweden
1644 Peace of Westphalia brought peace to Spain, Holland, Germany, France & Sweden & gave Sweden control of Baltic Sea
1651 Outbreak of Anglo-Dutch Wars
1656 Venetians removed Turks from the Dardanelles
1669 Venice surrendered Crete to Turkey
1669 Tornado in LaRochelle & Paris, France
1670 Measles epidemics
1672-76 Poland at war with Turkey over Ukraine
1672-78 France at war with the Netherlands
1673 Hungarian constitution suspended & absolute rule imposed
1674 Utrecht, Netherlands tornado
1683 Earthquake centered in Sicily, Italy (60 thousand died)
1683 Ottomans defeated at Vienna, Austria
1683-99 Repeated hostilities between Ottoman Empire & Holy Roman Empire (Austria, Poland, Venice, Russia)
1685 Edict of Nantes revoked & thousands of Huguenots fled France
1688 French invaded Holy Roman Empire 's Rhenish or Lower Palatinate along the Rhine River in Germany
1689 England & Netherlands joined in alliance against France's invasion of the Rhenish Palatinate
1690 Turks finally routed from Hungary
1695 Pertussis (Whooping Cough) epidemics in Rome & Paris
1699 Treaty of Karlowitz ended hostilities between Ottoman Empire & Holy Roman Empire
1700-21 Great Northern War pitted Sweden against her Baltic neighbors
1702-13 Spanish Succession War pitted France & Spain against England, Netherlands, Denmark, & Austria
1703-11 Hungary revolted against Austria
1704 British fleet captured Gibraltar
1709 Poor harvests throughout Europe
1709-10 Plague in Scandinavia & Germany
1711 Montenegro allied itself with Russia
1712 Religious warfare in Switzerland
1713 Treaty of Utrecht included France, Britain, Holland, Prussia, Portugal, Spain & Savoy. France ceded colonies, including Canada, Spain ceded Gibraltar
1719-20 Plague in Marseilles, France

1733-35	War of Polish Succession
1737	Austria joined Russia in war against the Ottomans
1739	Treaty of Belgrade ceded northern Serbia & Little Walachia to Ottomans
1740	Smallpox in Berlin
1740-48	War of Austrian Succession
1750-65	Pertussis killed forty-five thousand in Scandinavia
1755	Lisbon, Portugal devastated by earthquake(70+ thousand died)
1763	Smallpox epidemic killed large numbers in France
1763	Famine in Sicily (30 thousand died)
1768	Italians & Greeks immigrated to Florida
1770	Famine (150,000 from Saxony & 80,000 from Bohemia died)
1772	Poland was partitioned
1774	Moldavia came under Russian control
1783	Earthquake centered in Calabria, Italy (50 thousand died)
1789	French Revolution
1790	Hungarian Revolt
1791	Principality of Liechtenstein founded as part of the Holy Roman Empire
1792	Denmark abolished slave trade
1792	In the Franco-Prussian War, France took the Netherlands, Switzerland, the Rhineland & Italy.
1793	Russia claimed more Polish land inside the Ukraine
1793	France annexed Monaco
1795	Russia took Kurland, Lithuania & Wolhynia from Poland while Austria took Poland Minor & Prussia annexed Masowia
1796-97	French conquered most of Italy
1797	France annexed land west of the Rhine River
1798	French organized Switzerland as the Helvetic Republic
1799	Napoleon rose to power in France via a coup
1800	French defeated Austrians
1801	France overran Belgium
1801-15	Aachen, Germany was taken over by France
1803	Napoleon replaced a republic with the Swiss Confederation
1804	Serbia revolted against Turks
1809-13	France occupied Serbia
1813	Battle of Leipzig (Battle of the Nations) was decisive defeat for Napoleon & demolished French power over German & Poland
1814	Congress of Vienna reduced France to its 1789 borders; created Polish kingdom under Russian oversight; gave Belgium to the Netherlands, Rhine River to Prussia & Genoa to Italy
1814	French Bourbon King restored
1814	Denmark ceded Norway to Sweden
1814	Battle of Waterloo
1815	Belgium united with Holland to become the Netherlands
1815	France returned land west of the Rhine to Germany
1815	German Confederation organized
1815	Monaco placed under protection of Sardinia
1815	Congress of Vienna recognized Swiss independence
1815-66	Liechtenstein & Luxembourg joined German Confederation
1820	Neapolitan (Naples) Revolution
1820	Revolutions in Spain & Portugal

1821	Nationalist Greeks revolted against the Ottomans
1822	Greek rebels declared Greece independent
1822	Ottomans massacred thousands of Greeks
1822	Spanish rebels took their king prisoner
1823	French defeated Spanish Rebels
1824	Pasha of Egypt captured Crete
1830	Revolution in France
1830	Polish Rebellion
1830	Belgium revolted & claimed independence from the Netherlands
1831	Smallpox in Wurttemberg, Germany & Marseilles, France
1831	Cholera epidemic in Central Europe
1834-39	Carlist Wars in Spain
1842	One-quarter of downtown, Germany destroyed by fire
1848	Paris Revolution
1848	Austrians captured Milan
1848	Hungarian Revolution
1848	Italian Revolution
1848	Civil war in Switzerland led to the formation of a new federal state
1848	Prussian Revolution
1848	Revolution in Vienna
1848	Swiss formed a confederation
1851	Tornado in Sicily, Italy (approximately 500 died)
1859	Austria at war with France & Piedmont in present-day Italy
1860	Garibaldi conquered Sicily & Naples
1860	Piedmont united with Parma, Modena, Tuscany & Romagna
1861	Except for the Papal States, Rome & Venice, Italy was united
1861	Monaco became independent
1861	Italy proclaimed a kingdom
1862	Garibaldi led unsuccessful drive into the Papal States
1863	Greece unified
1866	Northern German Confederation established
1867	Garibaldi led unsuccessful drive into the Papal States
1867	Croatia became part of Austro-Hungarian Empire
1868	Spanish Revolution
1870	Italian forces took Rome
1870	Franco-Prussian War
1871	French forces crushed Paris Commune (20 thousand killed, 38 thousand arrested & 7 thousand deported)
1871	Smallpox outbreak in Bavaria, Germany (30+ thousand died)
1871	German States united into German Empire
1873	First republic in Spain
1873	Tornado in Vienna, Austria
1874	Spanish monarchy restored
1876	Coal mine disaster in Walbrzych, Poland (nearly 20 died)
1876	Bulgarian Massacres, ("Bulgaria") committed when Ottomans brutalized the populace to subdue rebellious Bulgaria
1877	Russia at war with Turkey in the Balkans
1877	Romania declared its independence
1878	Serbia became independent
1878	Bismarck declared anti-socialist laws in Germany
1879	Germany allied with Austria

1880 German Chancellor ended anti-Catholic policies
1880-1920Two hundred thousand Portuguese immigrated to New York
1880s Greeks began emigrating to US in large numbers
1881 Theater fire in Vienna, Austria (620 died)
1881 Two-thirds of Naples, Italy's population was out of work
1887 Opera house fire in Paris, France (200 killed) 1890 Greek economic problems
1891 French forces killed nine striking miners at Fourmies
1892 Cholera epidemic in Hamburg, Germany
1893 Greeks defeated Ottomans
1893 Germany increased the size of its military
1895 Kiel Canal opened connecting Baltic & North Seas
1896 Christians rebelled against Ottomans on Crete
1897 Christian insurgents on Crete blew up a Turkish fort
1900 Italian king assassinated
1902 Russian Czar abolished Finland's autonomy & appointed Russian governor general
1902 Spanish legislature was suspended due to increasing unrest
1903 Underground subway station fire in Paris (100 died)
1903 King & Queen of Serbia were assassinated
1903 Ottomans massacred Bulgarians following rebellions
1905 Norway declared independence from Sweden
1905 Earthquake in provinces of Basilicata & Calabria, Italy
1906 Mine disaster in Courriere, France (1000+ died)
1906 Mount Vesuvius erupted burying entire towns in Italy
1908 Bulgaria declared independence from Ottomans
1908 Crete declared independence from Ottomans
1908 Earthquake in Messina, Italy (70-110 thousand died)
1908 Portuguese rebellion included assassination of the King & Crown Prince
1908 Austria annexed Bosnia-Herzegovina
1909 Ottoman Empire sold Bosnia-Herzegovina to Austria
1909 Spain put down anti-government uprising in Catalonia
1909-15 Cholera outbreaks in Hungary
1910 Mount Etna erupted in Sicily
1910 Montenegro declared independence from Ottomans
1910 Cholera epidemic in Madeira, Portugal
1910 Portugal overthrew the monarchy & declared itself a republic
1911 Polio outbreak in Sweden
1912 Montenegro fought against Turkey during the Balkan Wars
1912-13 Balkan Wars
1913 Serbia annexed much of Macedonia
1913 Greece acquired lands lost by the Ottomans
1914 World War I
1917 Frejus rail tunnel disaster (500+ died)
1917 Finland gained its independence
1918 Influenza Pandemic (21 thousand died)
1918 Iceland became an independent state of Denmark
1918 Influenza pandemic
1918 Slovaks & Czechs united to form Czechoslovakia
1919 Germany lost the Polish Corridor to Poland, the Rhineland & to France & its colonies following World War I

1921	Explosion in Oppau, Germany (500+ died)
1921	Department store fire in Paris (150 died)
1922	Fascists rose to power in Italy under Mussolini
1923-25	France & Belgium occupied Germany's coal rich Ruhr Valley
1924	Cyprus became a British Crown Colony
1925	Tornado in Borculo, Netherlands
1926	Italy became one-party state headed by Mussolini
1926	Military coup in Poland
1926	Coup in Latvia
1926	Dictatorship established in Portugal
1929	Royal dictatorship established in Yugoslavia
1929	German banking system collapse (30 thousand banks closed)
1929	More than five million Germans unemployed
1929	Europe-wide depression following stock market crash in America
1929	Vatican City was set-up in Rome but independent of Italy
1930	Tornado in Po-Udine, Italy
1930	Allied forces withdrew from Rhineland, Germany
1930	Germans elected Nazis into 10% of their offices
1931	Central European banks failed
1931	King fled as Spain declared itself a socialist republic
1932	Six million Germans were unemployed
1933	Adolf Hitler becomes Chancellor of Germany
1933	Germans opened concentration camp at Oranienburg near Berlin
1933	German Nazis boycotted Jewish owned businesses
1933	Nazis open Dachau concentration camp
1934	Hundreds of Hitler's perceived opponents were killed by SS ("Night of the Long Knives")
1934	Australia established authoritarian rule
1934	Stavisky Riots in France
1934	Sweden was first nation to recover from the Great Depression
1935	Nuremberg Race Laws stripped German Jews of rights
1935	Saarland annexed by Germany
1935	Greece established a military dictatorship
1936	Germany became the second nation to recover from Great Depression through deficit spending to prepare for war
1936	Mussolini's Italian forces invaded Ethiopia
1936	Military dictatorship took over in Bulgaria
1936	Election of Republican Popular Front prompted a military coup & civil war in Spain (600 thousand died)
1936	Germany pushed into the Rhineland
1937	Massive bombing of Basque town of Guernica during Spanish Civil War
1937	League of Nations imposed sanctions on Italy
1938	Romania instituted a royal dictatorship
1938	Germany announced a union with Austria
1938	Fire destroyed much of central Marseilles, France (70+ died)
1938	German troops invaded the Sudetenland part of Czechoslovakia
1939	Nazis embarked on the killing of the sick & disabled in Germany
1939	Soviets attacked Finland
1939	Nazis & Soviets divided up Poland

1939 Britain, France, Australia & New Zealand declared war on Germany
1939 Britain signed treaty with Poland
1939 Nazis signed pact with Soviets
1939 Warsaw, Poland surrendered to Germany
1939 Soviets moved into Poland
1939 Germany overran western Czechoslovakia & renamed the region Bohemia & Moravia
1939 Spanish Civil War ended with General Franco capturing Madrid
1939 Gypsies were exterminated in German death camps
1939 German troops invaded Poland
1939 Genthin, Germany rail disaster (270+ died)
1939 Nazis signed pact with Italy
1939-45 Slovakia was considered independent, but under German control
1940 German troops marched into Romania, Denmark & Norway
1940 Hungary joined the Axis
1940 Romania joined the Axis
1940 German U-boats attacked Atlantic merchant ships
1940 Soviets invaded the Baltic States
1940 Axis Pact signed by Germany, Italy & Japan
1940 Italians occupied Egypt & Greece
1940 Nazis swarmed into Belgium, Luxembourg, France & the Netherlands
1940 Allied troops evacuated Dunkirk
1940 Italy declared war on Britain & France
1940 Germans & then moved into Paris & France fell
1940 French resistance began against German occupation
1940 Belgium & Holland surrendered to the Nazis
1940 British began air raids on Berlin
1941 Greece & Yugoslavia surrendered to Germany
1941 Nazis ordered Jews to wear yellow stars
1941 Nazi SS began committing mass murders
1941 British bombarded Hamburg, Germany
1941 British forces moved into Greece
1941 Yugoslavian coup overthrew pro-Axis government
1941 Gas chambers at Auschwitz were first tested
1942 Germans & Italians marched into unoccupied portions of France
1942 Deportations began from Warsaw Ghetto to concentration camps
1942 Mass gassing of Jews was initiated at Auschwitz
1942 British began air raids against Cologne, Germany
1942 Treblinka extermination camp opened
1943 Allies shelled Rome
1943 In Battle of the Atlantic, German U-boats sank 27 merchant ships
1943 German SS besieged Jewish resistance in the Warsaw ghetto
1943 Nazis arrested White Rose (a non-violent German resistant group) leaders in Munich
1943 British shelled the Ruhr Valley of Germany
1943 Allies landed in Sicily
1943 Himmler ordered elimination of all Jewish ghettos in Poland

1943 Allies penetrated to Naples, Italy

1943 Allied landed at Salerno & Taranto in southern Italy

1943 Italian surrender is announced

1943 Americans initiated daylight air raids on Regensburg & Schweinfurt, Germany

1943 Germans evacuated Sicily as allies arrived in Messina

1943 Italy declared war on Germany

1943 Allies increased air raids on Hamburg

1943 Americans took Palermo, Sicily

1943 Germans took Rome

1944 Allies freed Athens

1944 Warsaw Uprising ended with Polish Home Army's surrender to the German

1944 Allies bombarded Holland from the air

1944 Finland & the Soviet Union signed a cease-fire

1944 Allies liberated Verdun, Dieppe, Artois, Rouen, Abbeville, Antwerp & Brussels in the north

1944 Soviet troops marched into Poland

1944 Iceland became fully independent

1944 Allies attacked Cassino, Italy

1944 German forces surrendered in mass at Aachen, Germany

1944 Allies landed at Anzio, Italy & marched into Rome

1944 British continued to bombard Berlin from the air

1944 Allied daylight bombing raids on Berlin began

1944 British dropped 3000 tons of bombs in one air raid on Hamburg, Germany

1944 Allies landed in France (D-Day)

1944 Soviets began an offensive along Finnish front

1944 Nazis destroyed the town of Oradour-sur-Glane, France

1944 Open Slovak rebellion against Germany began

1944 Paris liberated

1944 French resistance rebelled in Paris

1944 Allies liberated Southern France

1944 Americans liberated Coutances in Normandy, France

1944 Soviet troops found their first concentration camp at Majdanek

1944 US troops reached Saint Lo in Northern France

1944 British & Canadian troops captured Caen, France

1944 US troops freed Cherbourg, France

1944 Gas chambers at Auschwitz were used for the last time

1944 French captured Strasbourg (French) / Strassburg (German)

1944 German SS murdered 81 American POWs at Malmedy

1944 Soviet troops lay siege to Budapest, Hungary

1944 Soviet troops occupied Romania

1944 Lavano, Italy rail disaster (500+ died)

1944 Leon, Spain rail disaster (500+ died)

1944 Soviets initiated attack on the Balkans with assault on Romania

1944 Civil War broke out in Greece

1945 Americans reached Nuremberg,

1945 German military in the Ruhr Region surrendered

1945 Soviets secured Berlin

1945 Allies liberated Venice, Italy

1945 Americans liberated Dachau

1945 Unconditional surrender of all German forces
1945 Allies partitioned Germany & Berlin & took control of government
1945 US, British, & French troops moved into Berlin
1945 Soviet forces took Warsaw, Poland
1945 Soviet troops liberated Auschwitz Concentration Camp
1945 Dresden was destroyed by Allied bombing raids
1945 Last German offensive of the war began to defend Hungarian oil
1945 Allies took Cologne, Germany
1945 Soviet troops captured Danzig
1945 Germans withdraw from the Ardennes Forest of Belgium, Luxembourg & France
1945 Allies lodged an assault in Northern Italy
1945 Allies liberated Buchenwald & Belsen Concentration Camps
1947 Marshall Plan for recovery in Europe announced
1948 Danzig became a fully independent democratic republic
1948-49 USSR blockaded Berlin
1948-89 Romania was under communist rule
1949 Two Germanys, East & West, were created
1949 Dwor, Poland Rail disaster (200+ died)
1950 Italy experienced an economic boom

Africa
1612 Portuguese exported 10,000 slaves a year from Angola
1621 Maravi Empire, which then stretched from Zambezi to Mozambique, conquered Mutapa of the lower Zambezi Valley
1634 French established settlement in Senegal
1635 Muslim sultanate established in Chad
1637 Dutch took Portuguese fort of Elmina
1637 French slavers established in Senegal
1639 Dutch seized Congo Kingdom from Portuguese
1641 Dutch captured Angola from Portuguese
1645 Portuguese took slaves from Mozambique to Brazil
1650 Berber tribes vied for supremacy
1650 Portuguese recaptured Angola from Dutch
1650 Portuguese evicted from East Africa of Oman
1651 Swedes captured slave fort on Gold Coast
1652 Dutch landed at Cape of Good Hope to build a supply station
1654 Portuguese forced the Dutch out of Angola
1655 Moroccan dynasty was overthrown
1659 Dutch East India Company allowed Boer farmers to settle in South Africa
1660 Approximate collapse of Mali Empire
1662 Portugal ceded Tangiers to England
1664 England took Guinea
1665 Civil war in the Congo
1670 Omani Arabs raided East African coast
1674 French expelled from Madagascar
1684 English abandoned Tangiers
1684 French annexed Madagascar
1687 French Huguenots settled at Cape Colony
1697 French conquered Dutch in Senegal

1698 Omani Arabs captured Mombassa
1699 Omani Arabs captured Zanzibar
1700 Bantu kingdom began rise in power
1713 Smallpox epidemic attacked Khoisan people of the Cape
1744 Mombassa declared itself independent of Oman
1756 Algerians occupied Tunisia
1769 Egypt declared independence from Ottoman Turkey
1773 Egyptian revolt against Ottomans repressed
1776 Muslim holy war along Senegal River
1777 Egypt unsuccessfully revolted against Ottomans
1779 Wars between Dutch settlers & Nguni began
1779 Boers & Bantu War in South Africa
1780 Masai expanded into East Africa
1781 Massacre of Xhosa by Boer Settlers
1795 British took Cape of Good Hope from Dutch
1798 French invaded Egypt
1811 British attempted to take control of Madagascar
1815 British subdued rebellion of Boer farmers
1815 Mfecane Tribal Wars of South Africa began
1818 Zulu nation united & drove enemies north
1820 Egypt captured Sudan
1822 Liberia established as home of freed American slaves
1830 French captured Algiers
1834 Boers moved north after British abolished slavery
1842 British moved into Natal
1844 French bombarded Morocco
1846-47 Bantu-British War in South Africa
1847 France established control over Algeria
1864 Lozi's Revolt against the Kololo
1865 War between Orange Free State & the Basuto
1867 Diamonds discovered in Cape Colony Province of South Africa
1870 Diamonds discovered in Kimberly, South Africa
1873 Anglo-Ashanti War
1876 Egypt was declared bankrupt
1876 Ethiopians forced Egyptians to relinquish claim on Nile Basin
1877 British annexed South Africa (Transvaal)
1877 British war with Xhosa
1879 Zulus defeated by British in first Zulu War
1879 Missionaries arrived in Uganda
1879 France controlled of Algeria
1880 Boers declared war on the British & drove them out of Transvaal
1880s At least one hundred thousand British poured into mining towns in Thodesia, Transvaal & Bechuanaland
1882 British fleet bombarded Alexandria, Egypt
1882 British occupied Egypt
1884 Germany declared Cameroon (Kamerun) a protectorate
1884 Egyptian garrisons besieged in Sudan
1891 Belgian attacked copper-rich province of Katanga, Zaire
1891 British claimed region north of the Zambezi to the Congo Basin
1892 Railroad from Cape Colony to Johannesburg completed
1893 British South Africa Company invaded Matabeleland
1893 British occupied Bulawayo

1893 France destroyed the Tukulor Empire
1894 British occupied Uganda & Buganda
1894 French conquered Dahomey
1895 French captured capital of Madagascar
1895 Sleeping Sickness epidemic in the Congo
1896 Ethiopians defeated the Italians at Adowa
1896 Madagascar was declared a French colony
1896 British invaded Ashanti kingdom
1896 Ethiopia recognized as an independent nation
1896 Sultan of Zanzibar surrendered to the British
1898 Anglo-French tensions led to a standoff when France occupied Fashoda on the Nile before British forced them out
1898 British defeated Sudanese
1899 Germany took control of Rwanda
1899-1902Boer War pitted British against Afrikaner Republic of Transvaal & Orange Free State
1900 Nigeria became a British protectorate
1900 Copper mining began in Katanga, Zaire
1901 Mozambique to Lake Victoria railroad completed
1901 British annexed Ashanti kingdom to the Gold Coast (Ghana)
1902 Boers surrendered to British
1902 Bulawayo to Salisbury, Zimbabwe railroad completed
1903 British-led West African Frontier force took over Sokoto, Nigeria
1904 Hottentot uprising in Southwest Africa
1905 German soldiers massacred Herero rebels in Southwest Africa
1906 Britain forced Turkey to surrender the Sinai peninsula to Egypt
1906 Zulus & British troops clashed over poll tax (60 Zulus died)
1906 Transvaal & Orange Free State became self-governing
1906 British forces ended protests of Tiv against Muslim Hausa rule in Nigeria
1907 French navy bombarded Casablanca, Morocco
1907 South African white miners went on strike
1908 Belgium assumed control of government of Congo Free State
1909 South Africa put apartheid into effect
1909 Lake Victoria region affected by Sleeping Sickness
1909 Plague outbreak in Morocco
1910 France took Agadir, Morocco
1910 France renamed the French Congo to French Equatorial Africa
1910 Pneumonia epidemic in black miners in Transvaal (South Africa)
1911 Italy conquered Libya
1911 Plague outbreak in southern Morocco
1911 Cholera outbreak in Tripoli & Tunisia
1912 Plague in Nairobi & Kilimanjaro region
1912-40 Sleeping Sickness in southern Chad (1/3 of population died)
1912 Morocco became French & Spanish protectorate
1913 Gandhi was arrested in South Africa for leading miners
1914 Egypt became a British protectorate
1914 South Africa joined the Allies for World War I
1916 French & British deposed German governor of Cameroon
1919 Plague epidemic in Morocco
1922 League of Nations gave 80% of Cameroon to France, 20% to Britain

1922 Egypt regained independence from Britain & France
1926 Italy signed friendship agreement with Abyssinia
1926 Moroccans revolted against French
1926 South Africa became Autonomous Dominion of the British Empire
1928 Muslim Brotherhood was founded in Egypt
1934 Italy put down revolt in Libya
1935-36 Italy conquered Ethiopia
1937 Tunisian uprising against French
1940 Italians occupied British Somaliland in East Africa
1940 Italians occupied Egypt
1940 British initiated western desert offensive against Italians in North Africa
1941 Tobruk in North Africa fell to the British & Australians
1941 British forces moved into Italian Somaliland in East Africa
1941 German General Rommel & German 'Afrika Korps arrived in North Africa
1941 Rommel retreated to El Agheila in North Africa& began a counter-offensive
1942 Rommel captured Tobruk
1942 Rommel reached El Alamein near Cairo, Egypt
1942 Americans invaded North Africa
1942 Rommel withdrew from El Agheila
1943 British liberated Tripoli
1943 Germans withdrew from Tunisia as Britain's 8th Army advanced
1943 Allies captured Tunisia
1943 German & Italian troops surrendered in North Africa

Russia and the Rest of the Former Soviet Union Countries

1345 Ottomans invaded the Balkans
1480 Destruction of the Golden Horde (Mongols) who had expanded into European Russia
1547 Ivan the Terrible took the title of "Tsar of all the Russias"
1571 Invading Tartars set Moscow, Russia afire (200 thousand died)
1579 Ottoman Turks captured Armenia
1613 First Romanov became Czar of Russia
1629 Poland lost Livonia (southern Estonia & Latvia) to Sweden
1648-54 Ukrainians destroyed hundreds of Jewish communities & committed other atrocities
1667 Russian Peasant Revolt
1669 Earthquake in Caucasus (80 thousand died)
1689 Peter the Great instituted reforms
1709-10 Plague outbreaks in Turkey
1721 Russia acquired Livonia & Estonia
1773 Peasant uprising
1774 Moldavia was annexed by Russia
1783 Georgia sought Russian protection
1791 Russia's Elizabeth II established "Pale Settlement " in effort to keep Jews out
1795 Russia annexed Lithuania
1800 Ukraine fell under Russian domination
1801 Georgia was annexed by Russia

1810 Russia expanded into Central Asia & Siberia
1812 Napoleon entered Moscow to find it burning & empty of people & firefighting equipment
1812 France invaded Russia
1815 Russia received Grand Duchy of Warsaw
1823 Cholera outbreak
1825 Decembrist uprising against Romanovs crushed
1828 Russians captured Teheran
1828 Russia declared war on Turkey in an effort to protect Greece
1830 Polish Revolt
1830-31 Cholera epidemics (250+ thousand died)
1831 Molokans received 50-year exemption from military service if they left central Russia & moved to Transcaucasus
1836 Lithuania joined a Polish Revolt
1853-56 Crimean War
1859 Moldavia & Walachia united to form Romania
1860s Russia annexed most of Tajikistan
1861 Emancipation of Russian serfs
1877 Russians capture Ottoman's Kars fortress in Caucasus
1877 Russians declared war on Ottomans
1877-89 Plague outbreaks in region of Ural Mountains & Caspian Sea
1878 Ottomans ceded Armenia to Russians
1880 Nearly five million Jews lived in Russia's "Pale Settlement "
1880s Russians conquered Turkmenistan
1881 Non-Jewish revolutionary assassination of Czar Alexander II led to wide-spread attacks on Russian Jews
1891 Thousands of Jews forced into Russian ghettoes
1891 Russia began construction of Trans-Siberian Railroad
1892 Russia hit by severe famine
1894 Ottomans controlled Armenian revolutionary movement by massacring population
1894 Thousands of Armenians killed by Ottomans following protests
1895 British intervened in Armenian massacres
1895 Treaty with China allowed Russia to build Trans-Siberian Railroad through Manchuria
1896 Armenians killed by mobs of Turks & Kurds (50 thousand+ died)
1900 Azerbaijan produced ½ the world's oil
1901-11 Molokans left Russia
1902 Russia agreed to withdraw troops from Manchuria in treaty with China
1902 Thirty thousand Russian students struck against government
1903 Russian-Chinese negotiations over Manchuria collapsed
1903 Czar Nicholas issued manifesto granting reforms
1903 Lenin split from Russian socialists to lead Bolsheviks
1903-06 Mob violence (pogroms) against Jews in Russia
1904 Russo-Japanese War fought
1904 Russian fleet at Port Arthur demolished
1904 Tornados in Moscow, Russia (approximately 30 died)
1905 Violent crushing of workers demonstrating in St. Petersburg, Russia (Bloody Sunday)
1905 Russia established a representative assembly
1905 One thousand Jews killed in Odessa

1905 Trans-Siberian Railroad opened
1905 Crew of battleship Potemkin mutinied & hoisted Red flag
1905 Russian fleet destroyed by Japanese in Straits of Tsushima
1905 Strikes across Russia
1905 Czar's troops attacked strikers (500 killed)
1906 Russia declared martial law & representative assembly dissolved
1906 Massacre of Russian army officers who mutinied in Sebastopol, Crimea
1907 British & Russians agreed to share influence in Afghanistan, Tibet & Persia
1907 Twenty million Russians starved
1908 Comet exploded in Siberia
1910 Cholera epidemic in Donets Basin, Russia
1910-22 Cholera epidemic in Balkan States
1915 Turkey deported Armenians to Syria & Mesopotamia (600 thousand starved or were killed)
1917 Workers seized St. Petersburg
1917 Ukraine & other states seized by Russia fought for independence
1917 Azerbaijan declared independence from Russia
1917 Bolshevik Revolution in Russia gave Jews full civil rights
1918 Germany occupied Lithuania
1918 Baltic States (Latvia, Lithuania & Estonia) declared independence from Russia
1918 Russian Revolution continued
1919 Soviet Republic established
1919-39 Poland held most of northwestern Ukraine while Soviets held rest
1920 Soviets retook Azerbaijan
1921 Soviet regime was installed in Georgia
1921 Lenin released a new economic policy
1924 Moldavia became a Soviet Republic
1925 Port Arthur fell to Japanese
1927 Stalin headed the Union of Soviets Socialist Republics (USSR)
1929 Stalin mounted 5-year plan of industrialization & collective agriculture
1930 Great Blood Purge
1930 Soviets began rearmament program
1932-33 Approximately five million died of famine in Ukraine
1933 Stalin began significant purge of communists
1934 Purge trials began
1934 Dictatorship installed in Latvia & Estonia
1936 Armenia became a republic within the USSR
1936-38 Stalin initiated more purges & trials (the Great Terror) in an effort to solidify his dictatorship
1937 Stalin began a purge of Red Army generals
1939 Russia & Japan signed a neutrality pack
1939 Russo-Finnish War
1940 Soviet Union recaptured the Baltic States
1940 Soviets conquered Lithuania, Latvia & Estonia
1941 Germany invaded Baltic States & Russia

1941 Stalin called for a "scorched earth" policy
1941 German attack on Moscow was abandoned while Soviet Army launched a major counter-offensive around Moscow
1941 Germans captured Odessa
1941 Germany attacked the Soviet Union
1941 Germans took Rostov temporarily
1941 Nazis captured Kiev (33,700+ Jews slaughtered)
1941 Germans captured Minsk, Kharkov , crossed into the Ukraine
1941 Nazi lay siege to Leningrad & advanced on Moscow
1941 Agreement signed between British & Soviets
1941 Germans reached Sevastopol
1942 The Battle of Stalingrad began after massive German air raid
1942 Soviets began counter-offensive at Stalingrad
1942 Soviets overcame Italian troops on the River Don in the USSR
1942 German initiated summer offensive in the Crimea, & eventually resistance collapsed
1942 Germans lay siege to Sevastopol before finally taking the city
1943 Soviets begin an offensive against the Germans in Stalingrad
1943 Russians retook Kiev, Ukraine, Kursk & Kharkov
1943 Germans initiated a withdrawal from the Caucasus
1943 Germans surrendered at Stalingrad making it Hitler's first big defeat
1943 Soviets began assaults on the Ukrainian front
1943 Germans re-captured Kharkov
1944 Soviet troops captured Riga, Latvia & Estonia
1944 Soviets liberated Minsk
1944 Soviet troops recaptured Sevastopol
1944 Soviet troops initiated an offensive to liberated Crimea
1944 Soviet troops launched an offensive on the Byelorussian front;
1944 Soviets moved the 400 thousand citizens of Chechnya & 200 thousand others from Caucasus region to central Asia
1944 Leningrad relieved after 900-day siege
1945 Soviets declared war on Japan & Manchuria
1948 Earthquake in Ashgabat, Turkmenistan (110 thousand died)

Middle East

1300s Turkish Sultan invited Jews fleeing Spanish Inquisition to settle in Turkish Empire
1300s Spanish & other Mediterranean Jews settled in Jerusalem
1453 Ottomans destroyed Byzantine Empire & captured Constantinople (Istanbul)
1500s Ottomans defeated Syria & Egypt
1502 Safavid dynasty captured Azerbaijan
1502-1736Safavid dynasty ruled Iran
1516 Ottoman Empire took control of Syria & Lebanon
1517 Ottomans gained control of Arabian Peninsula
1517 Palestine became part of Ottoman Empire
1521-1602 occupied Bahrain
1570-1650Portuguese controlled Oman
1602-18 War between Turkey & Persia
1616 British East India Co. began trading with Persia from India
1630 Ottoman Turks took Hamadan (Persia)

1638 Ottoman Turks took Baghdad
1669 Venice surrendered Crete to Turkey
1683-99 Open hostilities between Ottoman Empire & Holy Roman Empire
1700-1800Bahrain controlled Qatar as part of the Ottoman Empire
1700-1800sOman expanded into Africa & Zanzibar became its capital
1709-10 Plague outbreak in Turkey
1709-11 Afghans rebelled against Persia
1710 Kuwait City was established
1716 Ottomans lost control of Qatar, which became a British protectorate
1724 Russians & Turks agreed to divide Persia
1726 Persia defeated Turks
1727 Earthquake centered in Tabriz, Persia (77 thousand died)
1735 Russians returned conquest to Persia
1736-39 Turkey at war with Austria & Russia
1738 Persia invaded Kandahar
1747-50 Anarchy in Persia
1779 Iran became economically controlled by Russia & Britain
1780 Sauds took over the rule in the area of Saudi Arabia
1798 Napoleon entered Palestine
1799 France invaded Syria
1812 Egyptians took Mecca & Medina
1820 British obtained treaty with leaders of the "Pirate" or Trucial Coast (United Arab Emirates or UAE)
1820 Britain took on the responsibility for Bahrain's defenses
1828 Russia declared war on Turkey in an effort to protect Greece
1828 Russians captured Teheran, Persia (Iran)
1843 British began to administer, but not govern the states within the modern United Arab Emirates
1854 Suez Canal built
1856 Persia invaded Afghanistan
1856 British declared was on Persia
1860 Religious warring led to a massacre of Maronites by Druze
1875 Britain took more than a 40% share of Suez Canal
1878 Britain invaded Afghanistan
1880 Of Palestine's 400 thousand citizens, 24 thousand were Jews
1891 Exiled Al Saud family fled to Kuwait as Rashids took over control in Saudi Arabia
1892 United Arab Emirates agreed to limit foreign relations to Britain
1895 Turks attempted to exterminate Christian Armenians
1896 Armenian revolutionaries seized Ottoman bank in Istanbul
1897 Ottomans at war with Greece
1898 Ottomans evacuated Crete
1899 German & Ottoman pressure forced Kuwait to seek British control of its foreign affairs
1902 Ibn Saud recaptured Riyadh
1904 Saudis regained control of their territory
1905 Jewish National Fund formed to purchase land in Palestine
1906 British forced Turkey to cede the Sinai Peninsula
1906 Rebellion in Teheran
1907 Britain & Russia defined their influence in Persia

1909 Fear of famine led to widespread unrest across Persia (Iran)
1909 Rioters in Teheran, Persia
1909 British forces landed in Tabriz, Persia
1909 Anglo-Persian Oil (BP) founded in Persia (Iran)
1909 Turks toppled Ottoman sultan & despot Abdul Hamid
1910 Britain & Russia continued to intervene during Persian unrest
1911-12 Serious cholera outbreaks in Persia
1914 Turkish military governor of Palestine ordered deportation or internment of all foreign nationals, most of whom were Jewish
1914 Britain established Kuwait as a protectorate
1914-18 Ottoman Empire allied with Germany & Austria in World War I
1914-18 Palestine experienced numerous outbreaks of cholera & typhus
1915 Turkey attempted to capture Suez
1915 In an effort to capture Istanbul, the British attacked Gallipoli & after laying siege, were forced to withdraw (250 thousand died)
1915-27 Britain held Saudi Arabia region as a protectorate
1916 Sykes Picot Agreement gave Syria & Lebanon to France& placed Palestine under British control
1917 Ottomans lost control of Iraq
1917 British government promised Jews a homeland in Palestine
1918 Ottomans lost control of Yemen
1919 Iraq & Syria agreed to creation of Jewish State in Palestine
1920 Transjordan (Jordan) was established under British mandate
1920 Plans were made for Kurdish state which never came to be
1920-22 Ibn Saud led nomadic tribesmen against the Rashids to regain control of Saudi Arabia
1920s Many Kurds became farmers rather than continue nomadic life
1921 R. Shah Pahlavi seized control of Iran in a coup
1921 British created a kingdom in Iraq
1922 League of Nations mandated Britain create a Jewish homeland in Palestine
1923 Turkey was declared a republic
1926 Ibn Saud declared himself King of Hejaz & Sultan of Nejd
1927 Jordan became independent
1927 Oil discovered in Iraq
1929 Hundreds died in Arab-Jewish skirmishes in Palestine
1931 Jewish terrorists organized themselves in Palestine
1932 Palestinians revolted against British
1932 British granted Iraqi independence
1932 Ibn Saud united Hejaz & Nejd into Saudi Arabia
1934 Boundary agreement reached between Northern Yemen& the Southeastern, British-controlled Yemen
1935 Persia changed its name to Iran
1936 Arabs in Palestine revolted against Jewish immigration
1936 Anglo-Egyptian alliance began guarding Suez Canal Zone
1938 Oil discovered in Saudi Arabia
1938 Saudi Arabia granted oil concession to Standard Oil of California
1939 Massive earthquake in Turkey
1940 Jewish terrorists bombed ship in Haifa (200 Jewish immigrants killed)
1941 Pro-Allied government installed in Iraq

1941 British occupied Syria
1941 Pro-Axis regime set up in Iraq
1941 Allies invaded Syria & Lebanon
1944 Syria received its independence
1945 Turkey sided with the Allies during World War II
1946 Jewish terrorist bombed Jerusalem's King David Hotel (91 died)
1946 Lebanon became fully independent
1947 United Nations partitioned Palestine into a Palestinian State & a Jewish State & declared Jerusalem an international zone
1947 Hundreds killed by Jewish Haganah terrorists in Baldat-al-Shaikh, Palestine
1947 Up to 200 thousand Palestinians flooded into Southern Lebanon
1948 Israel was created
1948 Israeli troops occupied numerous Palestinian Arab cities
1948- Israeli & Palestinian attacks on each other continued
1948-49 Israeli war for independence
1949 Israel won control over West Jerusalem
1950 Jordan annexed West Bank of Palestine
1950s Molokans left Iran & Syria for US

Asia
1505 Earthquake in southern Tibet & Mustang Region of Nepal
1556 Earthquake in Shansi, China (estimated 830 thousand died)
1641 Dutch maintained trading post on island in Nagasaki Harbor, Japan
1657 Great fire destroyed Edo (Tokyo), Japan
1660 First English arrived in Japan
1660s English acquired Bombay
1661 Chinese took Formosa (Taiwan)
1661 English took Bombay
1666-68 Muslim monarch Aurangzeb at war with Muhammadans in central & northeast India
1669 Aurangzeb persecuted Hindus in India
1683 Formosa surrendered to Manchus
1707 Mt. Fuji erupted in Japan
1720 China established garrisons in Tibet
1721 Revolt in Formosa
1721 Edo (Tokyo), Japan was world's largest city with 800 thousand
1723-35 China at war with Mongols
1730 Earthquake in Japan (estimated 140 thousand died)
1732-33 Famine in western Japan
1737 Earthquake in Calcutta, India (estimated 300 thousand died)
1757 Battle of Plassy when Bengals attempted to oust British
1757 Nearly 150 British imprisoned in Black Hole of Calcutta
1758 British began to dominate India politically
1761 Afghans occupied Delhi
1766 First Mysore War in India
1773 Civil War in Vietnam
1773-1858East India Company governed Hindustan (northern India)
1775 First Anglo-Maratha War in India
1777 Christian missionaries arrived in Korea

1780 Second Mysore War in India
1786-87 Chinese suppressed revolt on Formosa
1787 Rice Riots in Edo (Tokyo) during a famine
1792 China closed Tibet to visitors
1792 China invaded Nepal
1796 White Lotus Rebellion in central China
1799 Mysore became a principality in southern India
1803 Second Anglo-Maratha War in India. British took Delhi
1815 British extended control into Himalayas in Anglo-Gurka War
1821 British began recruiting Gurka soldiers from Nepal
1823 Third Anglo-Maratha War waged in western India
1825 Dutch annexed West New Guinea
1826 Cholera epidemic in India
1831 British claimed Mysore in southern India
1833 Earthquake centered in Kathmandu Valley, Nepal (500 died)
1838 Tornado in Calcutta
1839 Cyclone in India (300 thousand died)
1839-42 First Opium War
1839-42 British took control of Hong Kong
1840 France, Britain, Russia & Ottoman occupied Syria & Palestine
1841 British occupied Kabul, Afghanistan
1841 British occupied Hong Kong
1842 British massacred in Khyber Pass
1845 Theater fire in Guangzhou, China (1600+ died)
1852 Cholera in India
1853 Commodore Perry landed in Japan
1856 Persia invaded Afghanistan
1856-60 Anglo-Chinese War
1857 Indian mutiny
1858-59 France captured Saigon, Vietnam
1860 British & French occupied Peking, China
1862 Japan expelled foreigners
1863 French established protectorate over Cambodia
1864 British, American, Dutch & French forces bombarded Shimonoseki, Japan
1864 Cyclone near Calcutta (approximately 70 thousand died)
1871 Theater fire in Shanghai (900 died)
1871 Japanese feudal domains abolished
1872 Miao rebellion in southwestern China
1872-92 Smallpox epidemics in Japan
1873 Russians captured Uzbekistan
1873 Famine in Bengal
1876 Queen Victoria declared Empress of India
1876 Three year drought in China (9 million died)
1876 Japan recognized Korean independence & set up trade with it
1876 Cyclone in India, now Bangladesh Region (215 thousand died)
1877 Rebellion in Japanese feudal domain Satsuma
1877 Chinese attempted to retake Chinese Turkistan
1877-79 Famine in northern China (10 million died)
1878 Chinese conquered Chinese Turkistan
1878-79 Second Afghan War began when British invaded
1879 Afghanistan gave territory to Britain

1879	Japan invaded Ryukyu Islands
1880	British were besieged at Kandahar
1880	Pro-British king crowned in Afghan
1881	Typhoon hit China (300 thousand died)
1885	France established protectorate over Annam & Tonkin, Indochina
1885-86	Third Burmese War
1887	Flooding of Yellow River in China (up to 1 million died)
1887	Chinese banned from emigrating to US
1889	Border settled between India & Afghanistan
1891	British forces sent to northern India
1891	Chinese put down uprising of Golden Elixir sect
1892	Violence at Japanese election polls
1893	Siam (Thailand) gave territory east of the Mekong to France & recognized Laos as a French protectorate
1894	Chinese & Japanese troops crushed rebellion in Korea
1894	Japanese & Chinese declared war
1894	Japanese sank Chinese ships & British steamer carrying Chinese troops
1895	Japan defeated China and gained control over Formosa
1895	China recognized Korean independence
1895	Europe forced Japan to return Liaodong Peninsula to China
1895	China allowed Russians to begin building the Trans-Siberian Railroad through Manchuria
1895	Anti-Christian riots in China
1896	Britain & France promised independence to Siam (Thailand)
1896	Catholic homes raided by Big Sword Society in China
1897	Earthquake centered in Bengal / Assam, India (1500+ died)
1897	Uprising against British in northwestern India
1898	Empress led coup against Emperor of China
1898	Britain secured 99 year lease of New Territories of Hong Kong
1898	Germany "leased" territory from China
1900	Cholera in India (800 thousand died)
1900	Boxer Rebellion against western institutions in China
1900	Western allies took Beijing, China
1900-05	Russia occupied Manchuria
1901	Boxer Rebellion ended in China
1901	Viceroy of India created the Northwest Frontier between Punjab & Afghanistan
1902	Russia agreed to withdraw troops from Manchuria
1902	Anglo-Japanese alliance recognized Britain's interest in China & Japan's interest in Korea
1903	Russia & China negotiated over Manchurian collapse
1903	Japan sent marines to Mok-Phot to deal with Korean labor riots
1904	Bengal was partitioned
1904	British signed treaty with Tibet
1904	Russo-Japanese War over Japanese attempts to gain control of Manchuria
1904	Japanese attacked Russian fleet at Port Arthur
1904	Tibet tried to halt British operation (300 Tibetans killed)
1905	Earthquake centered in Kangra, India (20 thousand died)
1905	Port Arthur fell to Japan

1905	Japanese decimated Russian fleet in Straits of Tsushima
1907	Famine in China (4 million died)
1907	Nationalist riots in India
1907	Japan returned Manchuria to China
1908	Reforms gave Indians participation in their government
1910	Dalai Lama fled to India ahead of Chinese invasion
1910	China granted Britain control over Tibet
1910	China abolished slavery
1910	Plague in Manchuria, China
1910	Japan annexed Korea
1911	Chinese Revolution led by Sun Yat-sen ousted Qing Dynasty
1911	Chang Jiang flood (100 thousand killed)
1912	Plague in Mekong Delta of Vietnam
1914	Germany relinquished colonies in Asia & the Pacific to Japan
1915	Japan claimed Chinese territory
1915	East Indies uprisings against Dutch
1919	British massacred demonstrators at Amritsar in northern India
1920	Gansu, China earthquake (200 thousand died)
1920	Major earthquake in Northern China
1922	British imprisoned Gandhi in India
1923	Earthquakes, fires & tsunamis near Kanto Japan (100 thousand died)
1926	Communists defied Dutch in Java & Sumatra, Indonesia
1926-28	Much of China united under Chiang Kai-shek
1927	Communist Chinese purged
1927	Civil War between Chinese Communists & Nationalists
1927	Jiangxi / Qinghai, China earthquake (200 thousand died)
1928	Drought in China (nearly 3 million died)
1928	Nehru demanded independence for India
1930	Japan took Canton, China
1930	Indians protested Salt Tax
1931	Yellow River flood (nearly 4 million died)
1931	Japan invaded Manchuria
1932	Siam (Thailand) abolished its absolute monarchy
1932	Gansu, China earthquake (70 thousand died)
1933	Japan occupied China's northeastern Jehol (Rehe) Province & declared Manchuria a protectorate
1934	Mao led Chinese communists & began "Long March"
1934	Earthquake in Bihar, Nepal (10,000+ died))
1935	India-Pakistan earthquake (60 thousand died)
1936	Japan signed pack with Germany
1936	Famine in China
1937	Movie theater fire in Antoung, China (650+ died)
1937	Japanese invaded Peking & Shanghai
1937	Sino-Japanese War united Chinese communists & nationalists
1937	Burma was separated from India & made a British Crown Colony
1937	Japanese massacred the population at Nanking
1939	Russia & Japan signed neutrality treaty
1939-41	Severe droughts in China
1940	Japan joined Germany & Italy as an Axis power
1941	US & British declared war on Japan

1941-44 Miao in southwest China revolted against war lords
1942 Coal mine fire in Manchuria (1500+ died)
1942 British interned leaders of Indian Congress, including Gandhi
1945 US dropped atomic bombs on Hiroshima & Nagasaki, Japan
1945 Soviets declared war on Japan & invade Manchuria
1945 Dynamite explosion in Thailand (150+ died)
1945 Korea freed from Japan
1945 Japanese surrendered
1946 Start of Civil war between French & Ho Chi Minh's Vietnamese Nationalists
1946 Independence negotiations begun for Pakistan & India
1947 Pakistan established
1947 Rioting & sectarian violence in India & Pakistan (500 thousand died)
1947 Independence granted to India
1947-49 First Indo-Pakistan War
1949 China's Nationalist government escaped to Formosa (Taiwan)
1949 France recognized Vietnam & Cambodia as independent nations
1949 Communists established throughout China
1950 Korean War
1950 Earthquake centered in Assam, India

Oceania - Australia and Island Nations

1511 Spanish visited the Solomon Islands
1511 Approximate Portuguese exploration of the Pacific
1521 Philippines discovered by Magellan
1525 Portuguese visited Caroline Islands
1526 Portuguese landed at Papua, New Guinea
1567-69 Spaniards reached Ellice Island, Solomon Islands & New Guinea
1595 Spanish reached Marquesas Islands
1616 Dutch visited west coast of Australia
1627 Dutch visited Australia's south coast
1642 New Zealand sighted by Dutch
1642 Tasmania explored for first time
1668 Spain colonized the Northern Mariana Islands
1722 Dutch reached Samoa & Easter Islands
1744 Capt. James Cook explored (Vanuatu) New Hebrides
1767 Pitcairn Island discovered by British
1767 British arrived at Tahiti
1768 Bougainville claimed Tahiti for France
1769 Capt. James Cook charted New Zealand
1770 Spanish reached Easter Islands
1772 Capt. James Cook discovered Botany Bay, Australia
1788 First British settled at Botany Bay, Australia
1788 Britain established penal colony at Port Jackson (Sidney), Australia
1789 Smallpox outbreak in New South Wales, Australia
1790 Pitcairn Island settled by mutineers from the *Bounty*
1792 British settled New Zealand
1793 First free British settled in Australia

1797 English missionaries arrived in Tahiti
1799 Civil war in Tonga
1803 Hobart, Tasmania established as whaling port
1808 Rum Rebellion in Australia
1813 Route across the Blue Mountains discovered in Australia
1814 Protestant missionaries from Britain arrived in New Zealand
1815 Volcano on Tambora, Indonesia
1821 Protestant missionaries arrived in Cook Islands
1824 Brisbane founded as a penal colony
1824 British built Fort Dundas on Melville Island, Northern Territory Australia
1825 Dutch annexed western New Guinea
by 1825 Whaling & sealing stations established on New Zealand's east coast
1829 First non-convict settlement established in Western Australia
1829 New South Wales became a crown colony
1830 Port Arthur penal colony in Tasmania established
1835 Traders & missionaries arrived at Fiji
1835 Melbourne & Adelaide, Australia founded
1840 New Zealand named British Crown Colony
1841 Whaling stations established in Tasmania
1841 New Zealand became a British Crown Colony
1842 France annexed Marquesas Islands & made Tahiti a protectorate
1843-45 Australia's first Jewish synagogue was built
1850-56 Four Australian colonies became self governing
1851 Gold discovered in South Australia
1853 France annexed New Caledonia
1856 Britain annexed Pitcairn Island
1856 Spain claimed Guam
1859 Brisbane became capital of Queensland
1860 Macdonnell Range 1st explored in Northern Territory of Australia
1860-70 Maori War in New Zealand
1861 Gold discovered in New Zealand
1864 French convicts sent to New Caledonia
1865 Capital of New Zealand moved from Auckland to Wellington
1868 Last convicts arrived in Western Australia
1869 Germany acquired Caroline Islands
1870 Germans began to purchase land in Western Samoa
1870's Alice Springs started as station on the Overland Telegraph Line
1870s Gold Rush in New Caledonia
1874 Fiji proclaimed British Crown Colony
1874 Britain annexed Fiji
1876 Probable last full-blooded Tasmanian aborigine died
1878 New Caledonians rebelled against French
1880 Tahiti became a French Colony
1883 Volcano Krakatau / Krakatoa in Sundra Strait erupted
1885-86 Gold Rush in Papua, New Guinea
1890 Gold discovered at Coolgardie, Australia
1891 Gold discovered near Murchison River, Australia
1892 Britain declared Gilberts & Ellice Islands as protectorates
1892 Gilbert, Ellice, Line & Phoenix Islands became British

Protectorates

1893 New Zealand became first country to give women right to vote

1893-1900 Solomon Islands under British protection

1895 More than 50 thousand Milanesians were indentured in Australia's cane fields

1896 Mine disaster in Brunner, New Zealand (60+ died)

1897 Fremantle Harbor opened

1898 US seized Guam from Spain

1898 Spain ceded Guam to US

1898 Philippines ceded by Spain to US

1899 US & Germany divided Pacific Samoa between them

1899 Spain sold the Northern Mariana Islands to Germany

1899 Samoa divided between Germany & US

1900 New Zealand annexed Cook Islands

1900 Colonies were federated into the Commonwealth of Australia

1901 Australia proclaimed a self-governing commonwealth of Britain

1902 Philippine Government Act mandated a US presidential commission rule Filipinos

1905 British New Guinea became possession of Australia

1906 Typhoon in Tahiti (10 thousand+ killed)

1911 Measles epidemic in Fiji

1913 Wallis Islands became French Protectorate

1914 Japan occupied the Northern Mariana Islands

1914 Japan took German colonies in the Pacific

1914 New Zealand occupied Western Samoa

1914 Australia occupied Bismarck Archipelago

1918 Influenza Pandemic (1/5 of Western Samoans died)

1918 Tornado in Brighton, Victoria, Australia

1919-62 Samoa administered by New Zealand

1920-40 Australian government established reserves for the Aborigines

1926 Dominion status given to Australia & New Zealand

1926 Communists revolted against Dutch in Java & Sumatra, Indonesia

1927 Volcano on Krakatoa erupted

1929 Maus of Samoa rebelled against New Zealand government

1940s Australia's immigration of non-English Europeans erupted

1940s Philippines invaded by Japan

1941-44 Japan occupied Guam

1942 Japan invaded the Solomon Islands

1945 Philippines liberated by US

1946 Philippines declared itself a republic

1947 US received Northern Mariana Islands as a UN Trust Territory

1947 Nauru made UN Trust Territory under Australia

1950 Guam became US territory

Timeline Bibliography

Adams, John W. and Alice B. Kasakoff. "Anthropology, Genealogy and History: A Research Log.". *Generations and Change: Genealogical Perspectives in Social History*. Robert M. Taylor, Jr. And Ralph J. Crandall (eds). 53-78. Macon, Georgia: Mercer University Press, 1986.

Adams, Charles Francis. *Massachusetts: Its Historians and Its History: An Object Lesson*. New York: Houghton, Mifflin and Company, 1894.

"African American Perspectives: Pamphlets from the Daniel A. P. Murry Collection: 1818-1907". Library of Congress Rare Book and Special Collections Division. 10/19/1998. <memory.loc.gov/ammenem/aap. aaphome.html> Printout dated 04/12/2008.

Alanen, Arnold R. "Companies as Caretakers in the Lake Superior Mining Region." *A Century of European Migrations, 1830-1930*. Rudolph J. Vecoli and Suzanne M. Sinke (eds). Urbana: University of Illinois Press,1991.

Anderson, Robert Charles. "The Place of Genealogy in the Curriculum of the Social Sciences." *Generations and Change: Genealogical Perspectives in Social History*. Robert M. Taylor, Jr. And Ralph J. Crandall (eds). 79-88. Macon, Georgia: Mercer University Press, 1986.

Anderson, Robert Charles. The *Great Migration Begins: Immigrants to New England: 1620-1633*. vol.1. Boston: New England Historic Genealogical Society, 1995.

Armentrout, L. Eve. "Conflict and Contact Between the Chinese and Indigenous Communities in San Francisco 1900-1911." *The Life; Influence and the Role of the Chinese in the United States, 1776-1960: Proceedings/ Papers of the National Conferences held at The University of San Francisco. July 10, 11, 12, 1975*. San Francisco: The Chinese Historical Society of America, 1977.

Arnold, Guy. *Book of Dates: A Chronology of World History*. New York: Warwick Press, 1989.

Barry, John M. "The 1927 Mississippi River Flood and its Impact on U.S. Society and Flood Management Strategy" Geological Society of America Session No 225. Flood Hazard on Dynamic Rivers: Human Modification, Climate Charge, and the Challenge of Non-Stationary Hydrology. (October 30, 2000) <gsa.conflexc.com/gsa> Printout dated 04/27/2008.

Bockstruck, Lloyd. "Family Tree: All the king's descendants." *Dallas Morning News*. December 14, 2002. 8C.

Bollet, Alfred Jay. *Plagues & Poxes: The Rise and Fall of Epidemic Disease*. New York: Demos Publications, 1987.

Bonomi, Patricia. *The Middle Colonies as the Birthplace of American Religious Pluralism.* National Humanities Center. <www.nhc.rtp.nc.us. 8080/tserve/eighteen/ekeyingo/midcol.htm> Printout dated. 05/19/2006.

"Born in Slavery: Slave Narratives from the Federal Writer's Project, 1936-1938." Library of Congress Manuscript Division. WPA Federal Writers Project Collection. <memory.loc.gov>

Bosworth, Timothy W. *Those Who Moved: Internal Migrants in America Before 1840.* Madison: University of Wisconsin (Thesis), 1980.

Brewster, William. The *Fourteenth Commonwealth: Vermont and the State That Failed.* Philadelphia: George S., MacManus Company, 1960.

Brooks, Harold E. and Charles A. Doswell III. *Normalized Damage from Major Tornadoes in the United States: 1890-1999.* NOAA National Severe Storms Laboratory. <www.nssl.noaa.gov/users/brooks/public_html/ damage/tdam1.html> Printout dated. 05/12/2006.

Brown, Richard Maxwell. "A Selective Listing of American Colonial Riots: 1641-1759." American Colonial Riots <www.adena.com/adena/usa/rv/ rv005.htm> Printout dated 02/26/2008

Browne, Ray B. and Lawrence A. Kreiser, Jr. The Civil War and Reconstruction. Westport, Connecticut: Greenwood Press, 2003.

Burnham, Will. *Chronology of Church History.* Kenya: Evangel Publishing House, 1975.

Campbell, Alan. *The Lanarkshire Miners: A Social History of their Trade Unions, 1775-1874.* Edinburgh: John Donald, 1979.

Clark, Robert L. "Some Sources in the National Archives for Studies of Afro-American Population: Growth and Movement." *Pattern and Process: Research in Historical Geography.* Ralph E. Ehrenberg (ed.) Washington, D.C: Howard University Press, 1975.

Colletta, John Philip. *Only a Few Bones: A True Account of the Rolling Fork Tragedy and Its Aftermath.* Washington, D.C: Direct Descent, 2000.

Conzen, Kathleen Neils. "Community Studies, Urban History, and American Local History." *The Past Before Us.* Michael Kammen (ed.) Ithaca: Cornell University Press, 1980.

Cush, Cathie. *Disasters That Shook the World.* Austin: Raintree Steck-Vaughn, 1994.

Dadrian, Vahakn. "German Responsibility in the Armenian Genocide: The Role of Protective Alliances." *Genocide Perspectives II: Essays on Holocaust and Genocide.* Colin Tatz, Peter Arnold and Sandra Tatz (eds). Sidney: Brandl & Schlesinger, 2003.

Davidson, James West and Mark Hamilton Lytle. *After the Fact: The Art of Historical Detection*. New York: Alfred A. Knopf, 1982.

"The Deadliest Hurricanes in the United States 1900-1996." Taken from *NOAA Technical Memorandum NWS TPC-1*, last updated 07/20/1999. NCEP. <www.nhc.noaa.gov/pastdead.html> Printout dated 05/12/2006.

Derks, Scott, (ed). *The Value of a Dollar: Prices and Incomes in the United States: 1860-1999*. Lakeville, Connecticut: Grey House Publishing, 1999.

DeVille, Winston. *Rapides Post - 1799: A Brief Study in Genealogy and Local History.* Baltimore: Genealogical Publishing Company, 1968.

Dinnerstein, Leonard and David M. Reimers. *Ethnic Americans: A History of Immigration*. New York: Columbia University Press, 1999.

Eggenberger, David. *An Encyclopedia of Battles.* New York: Dover Publications, Inc., 1985.

Eldridge, Carrie. *An Atlas of Southern Trails to the Mississippi*. Huntington, West Virginia: CDM Printing, 1999.

Encyclopedia Britannica 2003 Ready Reference. CD-ROM. Pub by Britannica. Copyright 1994-2003. Encyclopedia Britannic, Inc. Patent # 5241671.

Epstein, Ellen Robinson and Rona Mendelsohn. *Record and Remember: Tracing Your Roots Through Oral History*. New York: Monarch, 1978.

Everton, George B. Sr. (ed) *The Handy Book for Genealogist*. Logan, Utah: Everton Publishers Inc., 1971.

Faron, Fay. *Missing Persons: A Writers Guide to Finding the Lost, the Abducted and the Escaped.* Cincinnati: Digest Books, 1997.

Fires. Los Angeles: Emergency & Disasters Management, Inc. 1997-2005. <www.emergency-management.net> Printout dated 08/01/2006

Fletcher, William. *Recording Your Family History*. New York: Dodd, Mead & Company, 1986.

Genealogical Society (The). "Boundary Changes of the Former German Empire and the Effects Upon Genealogical Research." Research Pamphlet Series C. No. 4 Salt Lake City: The Genealogical Society of the Church of Jesus Christ of Latter-Day Saints, Inc., rev. 1979.

Gordon, Ann D. "Using the Nation's Documentary Heritage: The Report of the Historical Documents Study." National Archives. Washington, D.C.: National Publications and Records Commission, 1992.

Green, Betsey J. Discovering *the History of Your House and Your Neighborhood.* Santa Monica, California: Santa Monica Press LLC, 2002.

Gyory, Andrew. Closing *the Gate: Race Politics and the Chinese Exclusion Act*. Chapel Hill: University of North Carolina Press. 1998.

Hardwick, Susan Wiley. *Russian Refuge: Religion, Migration and Settlement on the North American Pacific Rim*. Chicago: University of Chicago Press, 1993.

Harland, Derek. "A Basic Course in Genealogy". vol 2 *Research Procedure and Evaluation of Evidence*. Salt Lake City: Bookcraft, Inc. 1958.

Harley, Sharon. *The Timetables of African-American History: A Chronology of the Most Important People and Events in African-American History*. New York: Simon & Schuster, 1995.

Hatcher, Patricia Law. "Developing a Colonial Mindset" Lecture. Presented at Second Conference on Early American Genealogical Research. National Society Daughters of the American Revolution. Washington, D.C., October 2006.

Hathorn, John Cooper. *Early Settlers of Lafayette Co., Mississippi*. Columbia, Tennessee: P-Vine Press, 1980.

Hays, Samuel P. "History and Genealogy: Patterns of Change and Prospects for Cooperation" *Generations and Change: Genealogical Perspectives in Social History*. Robert M. Taylor, Jr. And Ralph J. Crandall (eds). 29-52. Macon, Georgia: Mercer University Press, 1986.

Hirschmann, Kris. *Plagues*. San Diego: Lucent Book, Inc., 2002.

Hoffer, Peter Charles (ed) *The Peopling of a World: Selected Articles on Immigration and Settlement Patterns in British North America*. New York: Garland Publishing Inc., 1988.

"How to Make a Timeline." *Do History*. maintained by Film Study Center, Harvard University and Center for History and New Media, George Mason University. <dohistory.org> Printout dated 03/06/2006.

Howell, Martha and Walter Prevenier. *From Reliable Sources: An Introduction to Historical Methods*. Ithaca, New York: Cornell University Press, 2001.

Jacobson, Judy. *Southold Connections: Historical and Biographical Sketches of Northeastern Long Island*. Baltimore, Maryland: Clearfield Company, 1991.

Kessler-Harris, Alice. *Social History*. Temple University: American Historical Association, 1990.

Kirkham, E. Kay. *Research in American Genealogy: A Practical Approach to Genealogical Research.* Washington, D.C.: 5th Institute of Genealogical Research, 1954.

Kolhoff, Michael. "Fugitive Nation: Secret History." *Anarchy: A Journal of Desire Armed.* no. 52. (Fall/Winter 2001/2002) Infoshop News. <www. infoshop.org/pipermail/inforshop-news/2002-January/000420.html> Printout dated 08/30/2006.

Krieger, Leonard Ranke. *The Meaning of History.* Chicago: University of Chicago Press. 1977.

Lewis, Earl. "Expectations, Economic Opportunities and Life in the Industrial Age: Black Migration to Norfolk, Virginia 1910-1945." *The Great Migration in Historical Perspective: New Dimensions of Race, Class, and Gender.* Joe William Trotter, Jr. (ed.) Indianapolis: Indiana University Press, 1991.

"List of natural disasters in the United Kingdom." Wikimedia Foundation, Inc. GNU Free Documentation License. <en.wikipedia.org/wiki/List_of_ natural_disasters_in_the_United_Kingdom> Printout dated 08/07/2006.

Lottinville, Savoie. *The Retoric of History.* Norman, Oklahoma: University of Oklahoma Press, 1976.

Luttmer, Frank. "Why Study History?" Department of History. Hanover College. Hanover Indiana. <history.hanover.edu/why.html> Printout dated 12/18/2002.

Marinbach, Bernard. *Galveston: Ellis Island of the West.* Albany: State University of New York Press, 1983.

Matthäus, Jurgen. "A Case of Myth-Making: The "Führer Order" During the Einsatzgruppen Trial, 1947-8." *Genocide Perspectives II: Essays on Holocaust and Genocide.* Colin Tatz, Peter Arnold and Sandra Tatz (eds). 32-47. Sidney: Brandl & Schlesinger, 2003.

McCormick, Anita Louise. *The Industrial Revolution in American History.* Springfield, NJ: Enslow Publishers, Inc. 1998.

Merriam Webster Collegiate Dictionary. 10th ed. Merriam Webster, Inc., 2002.

Mills, Elizabeth Shown. "Ethnicity and the Southern Genealogist: Myths and Misconceptions, Resources and Opportunities." *Generations and Change: Genealogical Perspectives in Social History.* Robert M. Taylor, Jr. and Ralph J. Crandall (eds). Macon, Georgia: Mercer University Press, 1986.

Muller, Herbert J. *The Uses of the Past: Profiles of Former Societies.* New York: Oxford University Press, 1957.

Myers, Lois and Elinor Maze. "Oral History Workshop." Henderson County Historical Commission and Baylor University Institute of Oral History. Athens, Texas. May 2008.

Nicola, Patricia Hackett. "Chinese Exclusion Act Record: A Neglected Genealogical Source." *Association of Professional Genealogists Quarterly.* vol. 21: 1. (March 2006).

Nikiforuk, Andrew. *The Fourth Horseman: A Short History of Epidemics, Plagues, Famine and Other Scourges.* New York: M. Evans & Company, Inc., 1991.

Nips, Gladys Nadler. *Coming to America: Immigrants from Southern Europe.* New York: Delacorte Press, 1981.

Noll, Mark A. *A History of Christianity in the United States and Canada.* Grand Rapids, Michigan: William B. Eerdmans Publishing Company, 2000.

"Other Infamous and Devastating Fires." Eric Morgan, webmaster. <www. olafire.com/otherFires.asp> Printout dated 03/08/2006.

Papp, Susan M. *Hungarian Americans and Their Communities.* Cleveland: Cleveland State University, 1981.

Parrott, Susan. "Corsicana dealt economic blow." *Dallas Morning News* January 19, 2003. 48A.

Plecker, W.A. "The New Virginia Law to Preserve Racial Integrity." *Virginia Health Bulletin* vol. 16: 2 (1924). <www.eugenicsarchives.org> Printout dated 05/04/2006.

Powell, Kimberly. "What You Need to Know About: Genealogy Tip of the Day: Using Timelines in Your Genealogy Research." The New York Times Company. copyright 2002 by Kimberly Powell and About.com <genealogy. About.com/library/tips/bltimeline.htm> Printout dated 11/17/2002.

Price, Joy. "Timelines." *UGA's How To's : News of the Utah Genealogical Association.* vol. 32: 1. (January-February 2003.) 7-8. Salt Lake City: Utah Genealogical Association, 2003.

Price, Joy. "Telling It As It Was - Oral Histories" UGS How To's: News of the Utah Genealogical Association.. vol 31: 6. (November-December 2002) 7-8. Salt Lake City: Utah Genealogical Association, 2002.

Quaife, Milo E. (ed.) *The John Askins Papers. Volume I: 1747-1795.* Detroit: Detroit Library Commission, 1928.

Ramirez, Bruno. "Quebec and International Migrations." *A Century of European Migrations, 1830-1930*. Rudolph J. Vecoli and Suzanne M. Sinke (eds). Urbana: University of Illinois Press, 1991.

Rawley. James A. *The Trans-Atlantic Slave Trade: A History*. NY: W.W. Norton & Company, Inc, 1981.

Rips, Gladys Nadler. *Coming to America: Immigrant from Southern Europe*. New York: Delacorte Press, 1981.

Ritter, Harry. *Dictionary of Concepts in History*. New York: Greenwood Press, 1986.

Rose, Albert C. *Historic American Roads: From Frontier Trails to Superhighways*. New York: Crown Publishers, Inc., 1976.

Rubel, David. The United States in the 19th Century. New York: Agincourt Press, 1996.

Rubincam, Milton. Pitfalls in Genealogical Research. Salt Lake City: Ancestry Publishing, 1987.

Rutman Darrett B. and Anita H. Rutman, "'Now-Wives and Sons-in-Law': Parental Death in a Seventeenth-Century Virginia County," *The Chesapeake in the Seventeenth Century*. Thad W. Tate and David L, Ammerman (eds.) Chapel Hill: University of North Carolina Press, 1979.

Savitt, Todd L. and James Harvey Young (ed) *Disease and Distinctiveness in the American South*. Knoxville: University of Tennessee Press, 1988.

Schaefer, Christina K. *Genealogical Encyclopedia of the Colonial Americas: A Complete Digest of All the Countries of the Western Hemisphere*. Baltimore: Genealogical Publishing Company, 1998.

Schlesinger, Arthur Jr. *The Almanac of American History*. New York: Barnes & Noble, 1993.

Schrader-Muggenthaler, Cornelia. *The Alsace Emigration Book*. Appolo, Pennsylvania: Closson Press, 1991.

Sewell, Samuel. The Diary of Samuel Sewell 1674-1729. vol. 1. M. Halsey Thomas (ed.) (New York: Farrar, Straus and Giroux, 1973.)

Shaw, Ronald E. *Erie Water West: A history of the Erie Canal 1792-1854*. Lexington, Kentucky: University Press of Kentucky, 1990.

Smith, Clifford Neal. "Missing Young Men of Wuertemberg, German, 1807: Some Possible Immigrants to America." *German-American Genealogical Research Monograph Number 18*. McNeal, Arizona: Westland Publications, 1983.

Smith, John Owen (ed. and webmaster) "Useful Dates in British History "<www,johnowensmith.co.uk/histdate> Printout dated 08/14/2006. Contacted webmaster 08/16/2006. 19 Kay Crescent, Headley Down, Bordon, Hampshire, UK, GU 35 8AH.

Smith Marian. *Immigration and Naturalization Records at National Archives (NARA)*. USCIS History Office and Library. (January 2008). <www.rootsweb.ancestry.com/~orjgs/Smith2.pdf> Printout dated 12/17/ 2002.

Snodgrass, Mary Ellen. *World Epidemics: A Cultural Chronology of Disease from Prehistory to the Era of SARS*. London: McFarland and Company, 2003.

Swierenga, Robert P. "Dutch Migration to the United States." *A Century of European Migrations, 1830-1930*. Rudolph J. Vecoli and Suzanne M. Sinke (eds). Urbana: University of Illinois Press, 1991.

"Symbols: History Timeline, 50 States" *State Handbook & Guide*. SHG Resources <www.statehousegirls.net/resources/symbols/timelines> Printout dated 02/09/2003.

Teeple, John B. *Timelines World of History*. New York: DK Publishing, 2002.

"Timeline of Immigration to U.S. 1815-1950. Ellis Island Immigrants." MyFamily.com Network. <www.ellisislandimmigrants.org/ellis_island_ immigrants.htm> Printout dated 05/08/2006.

Timetables of History. 2nd revised ed. New York: Random House, 1996.

"Top Colleges Flunk American History." September 16, 2002 Press Release. American Council of Trustees and Alumni. <www.goacta. org/Predss%20Releases/9-16-02PR.htm> Printout dated 12/17/2002.

Tuchman, Barbara W. *Practicing History*. New York: Alfred A. Knopf, 1981.

Urdang, Laurence (ed) *The World Almanac Dictionary of Dates*. New York: Longman, 1982.

"USA History: Wars". United States History. <www.usahistory.com/wars> Printout dated 02/08/2003.

Vigne, Randolph and Charles Littleton (ed) *From Strangers to Citizens: The Integration of Immigrant Communities in Britain, Ireland and Colonial America, 1550-1750.* Brighton, England: Sussex Academic Press, 2001.

Volo, Dorothy Denneen and James M. Volo. *Daily Life in Civil War America*. Westport, Connecticut: Greenwood, 1998.

Wacker, Peter O. "Patterns and Problems in the Historical Geography of the Afro-American Population of New Jersey, 1726-1860." *Pattern and Process: Research in Historical Geography.* Ralph E. Ehrenberg (ed.) Washington, D.C: Howard University Press, 1975.

Websters Ninth New Collegiate Dictionary. Springfield, Massachusetts: Merriam-Webster Inc., 1983.

Whitaker, Beverly. "Dominant Church Denominations in the Thirteen Colonies." *Early American Church Denominations* <freepages.genealogy.rootsweb.com/~gentutor/churches.html> 1998. Printout dated 05/19/2006.

Widdis, Randy William. *With Scarcely a Ripple: Anglo-Canadian Migration into the United States and Western Canada 1880-1920.* Montreal: McGill-Queen's University Press, 1998.

Index of People and Places, Wars and Battles

B

C

D

E

F

H

L

N

O

Q

R

S

X

Y

Z

CPSIA information can be obtained at www.ICGtesting.com
Printed in the USA
LVOW041028250412

278979LV00006B/36/P

9 780806 354392